A CULTURAL HISTORY OF MONEY

VOLUME 6

A Cultural History of Money
General Editor: Bill Maurer

Volume 1
A Cultural History of Money in Antiquity
Edited by Stefan Krmnicek

Volume 2
A Cultural History of Money in the Medieval Age
Edited by Rory Naismith

Volume 3
A Cultural History of Money in the Renaissance
Edited by Stephen Deng

Volume 4
A Cultural History of Money in the Age of Enlightenment
Edited by Christine Desan

Volume 5
A Cultural History of Money in the Age of Empire
Edited by Federico Neiburg and Nigel Dodd

Volume 6
A Cultural History of Money in the Modern Age
Edited by Taylor C. Nelms and David Pedersen

A CULTURAL HISTORY
OF MONEY

IN THE
MODERN AGE

Edited by Taylor C. Nelms and
David Pedersen

BLOOMSBURY ACADEMIC
LONDON • NEW YORK • OXFORD • NEW DELHI • SYDNEY

BLOOMSBURY ACADEMIC
Bloomsbury Publishing Plc
50 Bedford Square, London, WC1B 3DP, UK
1385 Broadway, New York, NY 10018, USA
29 Earlsfort Terrace, Dublin 2, Ireland

BLOOMSBURY, BLOOMSBURY ACADEMIC and the Diana logo are trademarks of
Bloomsbury Publishing Plc

First published in Great Britain 2019
Paperback edition published in 2023

Copyright © Bloomsbury Publishing, 2019

Taylor C. Nelms and David Pedersen have asserted their right under the Copyright, Designs and Patents Act, 1988, to be identified as Editors of this work.

Series design: Raven Design
Cover image © RubberBall Productions/Getty Images

All rights reserved. No part of this publication may be reproduced or transmitted in any form or by any means, electronic or mechanical, including photocopying, recording, or any information storage or retrieval system, without prior permission in writing from the publishers.

Bloomsbury Publishing Plc does not have any control over, or responsibility for, any third-party websites referred to or in this book. All internet addresses given in this book were correct at the time of going to press. The author and publisher regret any inconvenience caused if addresses have changed or sites have ceased to exist, but can accept no responsibility for any such changes.

A catalogue record for this book is available from the British Library.

A catalog record for this book is available from Library of Congress.

ISBN: PB Set: 978-1-3503-6718-0
HB: 978-1-4742-3711-6
PB: 978-1-3503-6649-7
ePDF: 978-1-3502-5356-8
eBook: 978-1-3502-5355-1

Series: The Cultural Histories Series

Typeset by RefineCatch Limited, Bungay, Suffolk
Printed and bound in Great Britain

To find out more about our authors and books visit www.bloomsbury.com and sign up for our newsletters.

CONTENTS

LIST OF ILLUSTRATIONS — vii
NOTES ON CONTRIBUTORS — xii
SERIES PREFACE — xv

Introduction: Money—Cultural, Historical, Modern — 1
Taylor C. Nelms and David Pedersen

1 Money and its Technologies: Making Money Move in the Modern Era — 27
Lana Swartz and David L. Stearns

2 Money and its Ideas: Between Technocracy and Democracy — 53
Michael Beggs

3 Money, Ritual, and Religion: The Horror of It (the Prosperity Gospel and the Myth of Deterritorialization) — 83
Jon Bialecki

4 Money and the Everyday: Instability and Inventiveness in the Modern Age — 105
Taylor C. Nelms and Jane I. Guyer

5 Money, Art, and Representation: Six Artists, Two Crises (1973, 2008) — 135
Max Haiven

6 Money and its Interpretation: The Future of Money in
   Speculative Fiction   165
   Sherryl Vint

7 Money and the Issues of the Age: The Nature of Money and
   Post-Crisis Proposals for Reform   191
   Yeva Nersisyan and L. Randall Wray

NOTES   217
BIBLIOGRAPHY   225
INDEX   255

LIST OF ILLUSTRATIONS

CHAPTER 1

1.1 The Wells Fargo Express Company travels with $250,000 gold bullion, Deadwood, South Dakota, 1890.   31

1.2 Private express companies like American Express and Wells Fargo shipped by train over the New York Central Railroad. Painting, *c.* 1884.   32

1.3 Map showing the lines of the American Express Company, *c.* 1874.   34

1.4 Clerk preparing a money order, early twentieth-century United States.   36

1.5 Early check demonstrating the use of MICR (magnetic ink character recognition).   39

1.6 Bank of America's Electronic Recording Machine-Accounting (ERMA) System.   41

1.7 Comedian Marty Allen, 1960.   42

1.8 BankAmericard from 1974.   46

1.9 Rebranded VISA card from 1983.   46

1.10 Bitcoin ATMs in Hong Kong, Helsinki, and Seattle.   50–1

CHAPTER 2

2.1 Piles of paper: banknotes fill a German bank basement during hyperinflation, 1923. — 58

2.2 US Treasury Secretary Henry Morgenthau, Jr. and British economist John Maynard Keynes at Bretton Woods, July 1944. — 63

2.3 Hospital workers on strike in New York, November 1973: a 7.5 percent wage increase, agreed-to between the union and management, was held back by the Federal Cost of Living Council for being "inflationary." — 68

2.4 The gold anchor becomes a curiosity: Irina Posner, CBS News producer, in the US Federal Reserve Bank in New York, December 1965, with bullion reclaimed by France. — 69

2.5 Crowd outside a Bronx, New York branch of the Bank of the United States during a bank run, December 1930. — 73

2.6 Margaret Thatcher, holding up a one-pound note, campaigns on inflation in London, April 1979. — 77

2.7 Economists testify on anti-inflation policy before the US Senate Banking Committee on anti-inflation policies, March 1980. Left to right: Walter Heller, Alan Greenspan, Herbert Stein, Paul McCracken. — 79

2.8 US Treasury Secretary Henry Paulson and Federal Reserve Chairman Ben Bernanke testify before the US House of Representatives Financial Services Committee on a proposed bank bailout plan, September 2008. — 80

CHAPTER 3

3.1 A Christian Gospel tract, disguised as a US ten dollar bill. Purchased online in 2018. — 84

3.2 The Bethel Bible School in Topeka, Kansas in the United States, c. 1900, one of the sites where modern Pentecostalism originated. — 86

3.3 On April 18, 1906, the *Los Angeles Daily Times* published an article headlined "Weird Babel of Tongues," which reported on the Azusa Street Revival led by Black Pentecostal preacher William J. Seymour. — 89

3.4 Pentecostal preacher Oral Roberts lays hands on the sick in his prayer line at evening service, July 1962. — 97

3.5	Joshua Magezi, a Ugandan Pentecostal pastor, touches a woman's forehead during a ceremony on April 5, 2010.	99
3.6	Pedestrians pass in front of a branch of the Meezan Bank in Karachi, Pakistan, June 2012. Meezan Bank is Pakistan's largest Islamic lender.	101
3.7	Delegates talk at the Global Islamic Finance Forum in Kuala Lumpur, Malaysia, September 2014.	101

CHAPTER 4

4.1	A little boy examines a display of newly decimalized currency at Harrods department store in London, in advance of the United Kingdom's Decimal Day, February 15, 1971.	106
4.2	A kina shell necklace from the highlands of Papua New Guinea alongside a cropped Papua New Guinea five kina note, picturing shell valuables.	111
4.3	People wait in line outside a currency exchange, January 2002, in Buenos Aires, Argentina.	112
4.4	A supermarket employee in Rio de Janeiro, Brazil puts up new price signs as Brazil changes its currency from the "cruzeiro" to the "real cruzeiro" in an effort to curb inflation, August 1993.	113
4.5	A woman burns "ghost," "spirit," or "hell money" in a fire in the street in Hanoi, Vietnam, June 2015.	114
4.6	In 1929, the United States stock markets crashed, triggering bank runs and sparking the Great Depression.	115
4.7	Coffee pickers gamble in a game after getting paid in Ciudad Bolivar, one of the most productive coffee towns in Colombia, at the peak of the coffee harvest season, October 2017.	122
4.8	Patrons of the MGM Grand Hotel & Casino in Las Vegas, Nevada, gamble on US college basketball games, March 2013.	122
4.9	Taylor Nelms's son plays with a functioning toy calculator and cash register, made by the Swedish company, Ikea, 2018.	124
4.10	Roadside signage advertises money transfers, check cashing, and short-term payday and title loans in Birmingham, Alabama, in the post-GFC (Global Financial Crisis) US, 2015.	126

4.11 An M-Pesa agent in Kenya checks a customer's identification, July 2013. 128

4.12 Red envelopes with money (known as hóngbāo in Mandarin) are given to friends, family, and others during Chinese New Year or for special occasions like births, weddings, and graduations. Below, a student uses WeChat Pay to send a digital red envelope to friends, 2018. 131

CHAPTER 5

5.1 Evening sales at Christie's London headquarters, June 2014. 136

5.2 Police officer stands guard outside the New York Stock Exchange, March 2003. 137

5.3 Father and son with a warning sign during the 1973 oil crisis. 138

5.4 Undated poster for the Wages for Housework campaign, deposited in the MayDay Rooms in London by feminist scholar, teacher, and activist Silvia Federici. 142

5.5 Joseph Beuys's "KUNST=KAPITAL" (1979). 144

5.6 British penny inscribed with the words "VOTES FOR WOMEN" by suffragettes in the early 1900s. 145

5.7 Installation view of Hans Haacke's "MoMA Poll" (1970). 148

5.8 Two pages from Lee Lozano's notebooks concerning her *Real Money Piece* (1969). 151

5.9 Geheimagentur's "Schwartzbank" (2012). 156

5.10 Zach Gough's "Bourdieu: A Social Currency" (2014). 159

5.11 Zach Gough's "Bourdieu: A Social Currency" (2014). 159

5.12 Núria Güell and Levi Orta's "Arte Político Degenerado" (2014). 162

CHAPTER 6

6.1 Interior of the Hong Kong Stock Exchange, *c.* 1990s. 167

6.2 Sacks of gold exchanged against currency are stocked in the vaults of a New Jersey bank, 1993. 168

6.3 Brixton pound notes featuring British musician David Bowie, a local currency introduced for use in the south London borough of Brixton. 170

LIST OF ILLUSTRATIONS xi

6.4 A stock ticker is introduced for the first time in
     New York, 1929.   172

6.5 The ATM is introduced in Paris, France, 1968.   173

6.6 The company floor of Interactive Brokers, a leading electronic
     and online trading firm, 2014.   173

6.7 A commuter pays her fare using a bank card and a
     chip-and-pin machine on the Moscow Underground, 2016.   178

6.8 A sign displaying "Bitcoins accepted" is seen on the front door of
     the Old Fitzroy Pub in Sydney, Australia, September 2013.   181

6.9 Inside a Bitcoin "mine" near Kongyuxiang, Sichuan, China.   182

CHAPTER 7

7.1 John Maynard Keynes, "unofficial economic adviser to Great
     Britain," in his study at Bloomsbury, London, 1940.   192

7.2 People rally in front of the New York Stock Exchange in New
     York City to protest the proposed government buyout of financial
     firms, September 25, 2008.   199

7.3 A sign at the entrance to the payments industry conference
     Money 20/20 in Las Vegas, Nevada exhorts attendees to
     "treat your badge like cash," October 2016.   203

7.4 Tally sticks from the British Exchequer, *c.* 1440.   208

7.5 The original design for the new Euro banknotes are displayed
     at the European Central Bank in Frankfurt, Germany in
     August 2001.   211

NOTES ON CONTRIBUTORS

Michael Beggs is Senior Lecturer in Political Economy at the University of Sydney, where he works on the history of monetary theory and policy. He is the author of *Inflation and the Making of Australian Macroeconomic Policy, 1945–85* (2015).

Jon Bialecki is a fellow in the School of Social and Political Science at the University of Edinburgh. His academic interests include the anthropology of religion, anthropology of the subject, ontology and temporality, religious language ideology, and religious transhumanist movements. He is the author of *A Diagram for Fire: Miracles in Variation in an American Charismatic Movement* (2017), which received the Sharon Stephens Prize from the American Ethnological Society.

Jane I. Guyer is Professor Emerita of Anthropology at Johns Hopkins University, having held previous positions at Harvard, Boston, and Northwestern Universities (where she directed the Program of African Studies for seven years). Her research has focused on economic life in West and Central Africa: on farming for urban food supply and on money management across time and space. Her works include *An African Niche Economy: Farming to Feed Ibadan* (Edinburgh University Press for the International African Institute, 1997); *Marginal Gains: Monetary Transactions in Atlantic Africa* (University of Chicago Press, 2004), and *Legacies, Logics, Logistics: Essays in the Anthropology of the Platform Economy* (2016), as well as a new translation of Marcel Mauss's *Essay on the Gift* (2016).

Max Haiven is Canada Research Chair in Culture, Media and Social Justice at Lakehead University in Northwest Ontario and director of the ReImagining

Value Action Lab (RiVAL). He writes articles for both academic and general audiences and is the author of the books *Crises of Imagination, Crises of Power: Capitalism, Creativity and the Commons* (Zed, 2014), *The Radical Imagination: Social Movement Research in the Age of Austerity* (with Alex Khasnabish; Zed, 2014), and *Cultures of Financialization: Fictitious Capital in Popular Culture and Everyday Life* (2014). His latest book is *Art after Money, Money after Art: Creative Strategies Against Financialization* (2018).

Taylor C. Nelms is Senior Director of Research at the Filene Research Institute, a non-profit consumer and cooperative finance think tank. He is an anthropologist and ethnographer of money, technology, and alternative economies, and he has written on topics ranging from Ecuador's solidarity economy to zombie banks, mobile money, and Bitcoin.

Yeva Nersisyan is Assistant Professor of Economics at Franklin and Marshall College in Lancaster, Pennsylvania. She is a macroeconomist working in the Modern Money Theory, Minskyan, and Institutionalist traditions. Her research interests include money, fiscal and monetary theory and policy, and financial instability. She has published a number of papers on topics related to the nature and origins of money, government deficits and debt, and shadow banking.

David Pedersen is Associate Professor of Anthropology at the University of California, San Diego. His research focuses on capitalism in the hemisphere of the Americas throughout the twentieth century and up to the present. He is the author of *American Value: Migrants, Money, and Meaning in El Salvador and the United States* (2014).

David Stearns is Senior Lecturer in the Information School at the University of Washington, where he teaches on the intellectual foundations of informatics as well as information systems development. He is the author of *Electronic Value Exchange: Origins of the VISA Electronic Payment System* (Springer, 2011) and a co-author of the *Enterprise & Society* article "How the Future Shaped the Past: The Case of the Cashless Society" (2014).

Lana Swartz is Assistant Professor of Media Studies at the University of Virginia. She is the co-editor of *Paid: Tales of Dongles, Checks, and Other Money Stuff* (MIT Press, 2017). She has written on topics such as the Diners' Club Card, Bitcoin, and Venmo and has been published in academic journals such as *Cultural Studies, Theory, Culture and Society*, and *Women's Studies Quarterly*. Her research has been featured by the BBC's *Newshour*, Netflix's *Explained*, *USA Today*, and the *Financial Times*. Her monograph on the cultural politics of money technologies is forthcoming.

Sherryl Vint is Professor of Media and Cultural Studies at the University of California, Riverside. She is an editor of the journal *Science Fiction Studies* and has published widely on the genre. Her most recent works include *Science Fiction and Cultural Theory: A Reader* (2015) and *Science Fiction: A Guide for the Perplexed* (Bloomsbury, 2014).

L. Randall Wray is Professor of Economics at Bard College and Senior Scholar at the Levy Economics Institute. His most recent book is *Why Minsky Matters: An Introduction to the Work of a Maverick Economist* (2016). Wray is also the author of *Money and Credit in Capitalist Economies: The Endogenous Money Approach* (1990), *Understanding Modern Money: The Key to Full Employment and Price Stability* (1998), *The Rise and Fall of Money Manager Capitalism: Minsky's Half Century from World War Two to the Great Recession* (with É. Tymoigne; 2013), and *Modern Money Theory: A Primer on Macroeconomics for Sovereign Monetary Systems* (2012; 2nd rev. ed., 2015). He is also coeditor (with Jan Kregel) of the *Journal of Post Keynesian Economics*.

SERIES PREFACE

When the British Museum decided in 2012 to redesign Room 68, the hall containing objects from its Department of Coins and Medals, its curators made a bold departure from how numismatic material had conventionally been displayed. Rather than cases filled with rows upon rows of gold, silver, and bronze coins of European antiquity, the new gallery design featured all manner of objects, not limited to coin or paper currency, capturing the history of transactional artifacts and infrastructures from shells to mobile phones. Each case had a theme: cases on one side of the gallery spotlighted money's institutional supports and issuing authorities, while cases on the other underscored all the myriad ways people use money, not just for exchange or payment but for ritual or religious observance, political contestation, adornment, and storytelling.

The intention in preparing these six volumes was to provide readers with a similar experience, inviting them into the wonder-cabinets of money in all its variegation, multiplicity, and complexity. What emerges is money's irreducible plurality, the multiple stories it tells. Money opens windows into plural economic and moral worlds, too, worlds of value and evaluation, wealth and worth. Never merely coin, cash, or credit rendered in strictly economic terms, money is so much more than the old couplet would have it: "Money is a matter of functions four: a medium, a measure, a standard, a store." Instead, money is always also a medium of communication, a set of instruments with which people exchange messages with one another—about price, to be sure, but also about political conviction and authority, fealty, desire, or disdain. And money is a method of memorializing the past so that relations established among people, institutions, the gods, and the ancestors can be carried forward through the present and into near, distant, and imaginary futures.

Money is in this sense both irredeemably "cultural" and "historical," and so it is apt that this six-volume *Cultural History of Money* should spotlight money's relation to religion, technology, the arts and literature, everyday life, metaphysical interpretation, and a wide variety of issues of the age. While many contributors to the first several volumes are numismatists and archaeologists, trucking in the material evidence of coin and bullion, the volumes also contain contributions from scholars of digital infrastructures, literary and legal historians and science fiction scholars, sociologists and anthropologists, economists and artists.

Archaeologists have long bemoaned the fact that the great majority of ancient coins in museums and private collections today were unearthed without any data having been collected on their surrounding context, rendering much of the ancient and even more recent past a mystery. Even where the context for a particular find is present, its interpretation is always ambiguous. In the contemporary period, money is surrounded by context—cables and wireless signals, data protocols and computer servers, lobbying groups' and legislators' voluminous writings, television soap operas and online social media. Yet just as with ancient hoards, we have difficulty escaping our own assumptions about what money is, what people do with it, and the style with which they do so.

Take a basic plastic credit card transaction at a physical till. How many users of this everyday payment device would be able to explain how it works? How would a museum curate this technological assemblage? Moving from the simple act of paying to more involved interactions with money, how might an archaeologist of the future deduce, for example, the practice in some central Asian Muslim immigrant communities known as the "Imam Zamin," which consists of wrapping a coin in a piece of cloth tied about the upper arm to protect a traveler? Or the practice from around 2005–2009 of what people called "doing tuning"(튜닝하다) to a transit card in Seoul, Korea—dissolving the plastic payment card with acetone so as to remove the radio-frequency identification (RFID) antenna and chip, and creatively stitching it into one's pocketbook, bracelet, or the elbow patches of one's blazer, so you can breeze through the turnstile, with style?

Trapped in our own "coin consciousness," we assume money has to be, or that its value should be found in, a tangible thing, despite the fact that our own interactions with it are increasingly dematerialized in digital networks. We hold on to bullionist conceptions of money's worth, despite our bearing continuous witness to its fluctuations based on prevailing political whims. We think of money as abstract, even as we use it in the most concrete and interpersonal relations. We believe money equilibrates values, rendering goods and services commensurable with one another measured on one scale of value, even as we use money to demarcate difference—national difference, religious difference, intergenerational difference, differences in class, race, and gender.

The periodization of these volumes is somewhat arbitrary, but still Eurocentric. The selection of authors and themes is intended to help disturb this Western-oriented history by globalizing it and insisting on bringing into the frame its political, imperial, and often racial dynamics.

The chapters in these volumes capture money's complexities in both substance and form. In substance, insofar as they attempt a cross-cultural, transhistorical survey of money technologies and cultures that will illuminate its variability and complexity. In form, in that each volume takes up the same thematic areas, but in reading across the volumes one will discover that these themes are themselves complicated by having different eras' understandings of said theme juxtaposed with other eras' often incompatible understandings. Like a ledger book, then—one of the most basic manifestations of money's recordkeeping devices—the volume can be read "down," reading the chapters within one historical period, and "across," reading the affiliated thematic chapters from volume to volume. What emerges is an affirmation that money itself is a cultural history.

Bill Maurer
University of California—Irvine

Introduction

Money—Cultural, Historical, Modern

TAYLOR C. NELMS AND DAVID PEDERSEN

"Money makes the world go 'round," caroled Liza Minnelli and Joel Grey in the refrain to their duet from the 1972 film adaptation of *Cabaret*. The movie, like the musical before it, showcased the devil-may-care sensibilities that flourished during the Weimar period in Germany, an era defined by the collapse of the national currency's relative worth and the country's parallel plunge into Nazism.

Karl Polanyi also famously turned to money to grapple with the implications of that fractured geohistorical moment. In *The Great Transformation*, Polanyi (2001: 75) explored the intellectual genealogy and political limits of free-market capitalism as a utopian project and identified money's commodification, alongside that of land and labor, as necessary for the creation and expansion of capitalist markets into new domains of life. The world market at the beginning of the twentieth century, structured by a British-led, gold-based system of international trade, embodied exactly the practice of treating money *as if* it were a commodity that could be freely bought and sold according to the abstract forces of supply and demand.

Polanyi pointed out that efforts to establish free markets in land, labor, and money were doomed to produce a social backlash, as people experienced their corrosive effects and moved to defend themselves and their communities. This "double movement" assumed many guises, both progressive and reactionary. "Fascism, like socialism, was rooted in a market society that refused to function," argued Polanyi (2001: 248). The rigidity with which governments sought to maintain the international gold standard in the early twentieth century appeared in the form of relentless "shortages and surfeits of money"

(76). As this system broke down, people became "currency-conscious"—riveted to daily fluctuations in money's value and influence, newly cognizant of its caprice and contingency and desirous of stability (26).

In a sixty-year echo of *Cabaret*, the US music group Wu-Tang Clan sang out in the 1990s, "cash rules everything around me." The song was performed during a moment of relative price stability in the United States—a period described as "monetary nirvana" by economist Anna Schwartz (2008)—but a deep financial crisis would soon ripple across the planet, triggered initially by US home mortgage defaults in 2007–08. Longstanding inequalities in wages and wealth were exposed anew amid financial instability, state-imposed austerity, and the worldwide resurgence of populist and nativist authoritarianism. Catalyzed by sluggish post-crisis economies and concomitant technological experimentation—and accompanied by new hopes and anxieties about what such changes might mean for the future of communities, national projects, and world society—money surfaced again as a topic of popular reflection, critical inquiry, and political and practical intervention.[1] In the early twenty-first century, we find ourselves in the midst of a new period of currency consciousness and, relatedly, a renaissance in the study of money. This "revisionist" resurgence in research on money crosses scholarly disciplines: anthropology and sociology, business, communication, history, law, literature, philosophy, political science, psychology, theology, and economics (Bandelj et al. 2017: 3).[2]

This volume of *The Cultural History of Money* considers the geohistorical span opened and closed by these two world-turning crises and the acute focus on money that marked each, nearly a century apart. The first of these crises, and the responses it occasioned, laid the political and intellectual groundwork for money management and experimentation during the century that followed. The second, as Brett Christophers, Andrew Leyshon, and Geoff Mann (2017: 5) have written, echoing Polanyi, may have again changed "how we understand modernity [itself], locating money and finance [. . .] much nearer the center of our conceptual consciousness." The century in between saw the consolidation of nation-state control over money, then the rise of global financial institutions and instruments that often fell outside the purview of central bank regulation. It saw the multiplication of national currencies in the wake of decolonization movements around the world and the creation of regional currency unions and blocs, including the Eurozone. This "modern" age of money opened with the denomination of international payments in currency convertible to precious metal; it later saw the centralization of the US dollar as international unit of account and reserve currency. Yet it was also an era during which money substitutes and money-like tokens and coupons proliferated, and it ends in the midst of a profound diversification of money's technologies. It witnessed the stabilization of central bankers' technocratic expertise and the standardization of monetary policy around inflation-avoidance, but it was also rocked by waves of popular and expert criticism, doubt, and discontent.

The contributors to this volume thus examine money and money relations across a variety of settings and from a variety of perspectives, from the beginning of the twentieth century up through the present. Organized according to themes shared across the volumes in this series, the following seven chapters address money in relation to technology, ideas, religion, everyday life, arts, literature, and politics. The chapters in this volume tend toward US-Anglo-European contexts and draw primarily upon English-language sources and evidence; at the same time, they also endeavor to situate this North Atlantic emphasis within a larger world perspective.

Writing at the start of our period of consideration, John Maynard Keynes (1930: vi), admitted that he felt "like someone who has been forcing his way through a confused jungle" to confront "the theory and facts of representative money as it exists in the modern world." Our volume follows the modern premise that this jungle is constantly changing: clearing in some places, regrowing in others. Yet money has not always been positioned historically in this way. As Geoffrey Ingham (2000: 17) and others have noted, money has often been treated by experts as unchanging across time and space, a neutral "veil," "lubricant," or "vehicle" facilitating one-off transactions between unencumbered economic actors. It made no difference what form it took, who wielded it, nor to what ends they did so. Such flat, synchronic approaches to money are products of a period of relative stability in the North Atlantic in the thick middle of the twentieth century; technical, functional, and impersonal understandings of money appeared alongside a sense of stasis and continuity in money's history. Such understandings dampened and redirected critical reflection by refusing to recognize money's contested pluralism across space and time, its dynamic diversity of form, content, meaning, and practice. Yet this dynamism and diversity makes itself known in times of crisis; debates resurface about what money is, what form it should take, how it should be valued, what should be the limits of its exchangeability, and who has the right to create it and control its circulation. Our pragmatic approach arises—unsurprisingly—in such a moment of instability and flux. Our volume is as much a product of the contemporary conjuncture as a contributor to it.[3]

Still, "money"—the thing and the category, the token and the institution—is only ever an effect of such debates. Even in its most settled form, money is the outcome of mediations and negotiations: between the local and global, material and abstract, surface and essence, momentary and enduring, liquid and illiquid, authentic and counterfeit, state and market, autonomy and solidarity. This is one of the central lessons we learn looking back on the modern age from the perspective of our twenty-first-century currency consciousness. The process of figuring and contesting what "counts as" money is nothing less than the process of making and remaking money itself. "Money is a creature of network effects," Lana Swartz (2018: 623), one of the contributors to this volume, writes elsewhere:

it requires a community of shared belief to "work," to exist as something recognizable as money. These beliefs are reflexively produced in the technologies of money, which are instantiations of these shared expectations. A theory of money, then, is [. . .] a theory of the larger social order (or a challenge to it) and a way of materially enacting that theory.

Money, we might say, mediates itself. The chapters in this book consider the looping, multiplex practices and processes through which this mediation happens. We begin by asking: What does it mean to write a cultural history of money in the modern age? What makes money cultural? What makes it historical? What makes it *money* at all?

Thinking about money in the modern age, in sum, invites a reflexive mode of dialectical thinking that we want to harness rather than dismiss. In what follows, we identify several key lessons about modern money: that far from being asocial or anti-social, money is a medium of cultural imagination and practical inventiveness that animates processes of re-socialization. That change in money's forms and functions does not progress evenly—towards, for example, financial abstraction—but is instead additive, layered, and at once contingent and durable. That ideas and ideologies of money as a store of value run parallel to other approaches treating money as a balance-sheet operation of circulating credits and debts. That an apparent depoliticization of monetary policy and expertise has given way to renewed public debates about the micro-politics of money creation and conversion—money as a form of liquidity—and money's macro-political distributional effects—money as a claim on wealth. That money can never be "given" in advance, even if it appears gifted to us, by God or government. That it is, in short and at once, a technological, political, and above all social and cultural accomplishment.

Thus, even as we interrogate the cultural and historical processes through which money becomes "modern," we keep in mind Marshall Berman's (1983: 21) characterization of one of modernist thinking's "distinctive virtues," "that it leaves its questions echoing in the air long after the questioners themselves, and their answers, have left the scene."

THE CULTURAL

Our temporal remit is the "modern age," loosely demarcated as 1920–present. "Modernity" is not a twentieth-century invention, yet it remains powerfully periodizing. We have evidence of some five hundred years of becoming and unbecoming modern, yet the modern still signifies the disruption or erosion of "tradition" in all its forms and the inauguration of a new epoch. Modernity's historiography is one of origins and crises, roots and ruptures. Money figures importantly in this historiography, mediating the modernist visions of a range of actors in the long twentieth century, from socialist planners to neoliberal free marketeers. As Jon Bialecki (in Chapter 3, "Money and Religion") and Taylor C. Nelms and Jane I. Guyer (in Chapter 4, "Money and the Everyday") suggest, money throughout the modern era was often seen as "a microcosm through which modern culture could be explored" (Dodd 2014: 276). Facilitating impersonal transactions and abstract accounting, money was thought to weaken traditional (especially indigenous or feudal) corporate forms of social status and attachment and promote individual freedom, alienating people from things and from one another. It was thought to propel shifts from *Gemeinschaft* to *Gesellschaft*, mechanistic to organic solidarity, local to global society.

Yet modernity also works through the moral and political organization of spatiotemporal difference. The properties of the modern—liberal law and government, bureaucratic administration, free-market capitalism and wage labor, secularism and scientific reason—are defined in explicitly racial or civilizational terms, juxtaposed with those who have been colonized, enslaved, anachronized, and marginalized in modernity's name. Liberal economic and political thought were predicated on the exclusion of New World indigenous peoples from money, property, and government (Cattelino 2018), and this thinking, Nelms and Guyer show, continued to inform colonial and postcolonial encounters as Western currencies confronted and seemed to overcome local, socially embedded forms of value and exchange. As Bill Maurer (2006: 17) has pointed out, the story told about money returns again and again to this modern "morality tale": a Polanyian "great transformation" that positions money at the start and heart of the division of "economy" from "society" and thus invites lamentation about "the world that 'we' have lost."

At the beginning of the modern age, then, under conditions of industrial capitalist transformation, money marked the difference between "economy" and "society" and was often accused of threatening to transform social and cultural relations into crudely economic ones. From this perspective, money transcended society; it had no culture. As Nelms and Guyer point out, this way of thinking remained prevalent throughout the next century, becoming evident, for example, in arguments about the dangers of mixing markets and morality. Modern accounts of money thus often portrayed it as the epitome of all that is "cool, rational, base, and worldly," Max Haiven writes (in Chapter 5, "Money, Art and Representation"), from which social and cultural domains were said to offer romantic escape. Art, for example, represented that which could not be captured by money, offering privileged access to the passions that threw money's "otherwise rational clockwork into disarray." Yet it was precisely money, especially in its high-financial guise, that shored up these distinctions in the modern era—by transforming artwork into a speculative asset and investment vehicle with real returns and by exerting control over artistic institutions and ideologies that shape real livelihoods. Art is paradigmatic of money's sociocultural alters, Haiven shows, yet "money and art share a strange and fateful symmetry."

In Chapter 3, Jon Bialecki describes similar parallels between money and religion and the "horror of mixing" that both provoke. Bialecki's primary example is twentieth-century Pentecostalism, which brought vastly different people into often-intimate contact with one another in ways that elicited comparisons to money and markets. Like money, "Pentecostalism smashed both metaphorical and sometimes quite real social barriers"—mingling bodies, languages, races, genders, rich and poor—and spoke to widespread anxieties about the transgression and dissolution of cultural differences and social hierarchies in the modern era. In fact, however, Bialecki shows that both money and religion held out the promise of new social forms—a promise that, as with art, became especially charged when the two came together. "Money, expressed through religion, as well as religion, expressed through money, turns out in the end to be not merely erosive, but socially and culturally productive at the same moment," in ways that fly in the face of modernist narratives of social fragmentation and disintegration.

This contradiction opens both Bialecki's and Haiven's chapters, but as they and the other contributors to this volume show again and again, such category distinctions are red herrings. To introduce another: even as money and its management appear increasingly technical—the object of specialized and institutionalized expertise—money lives a double life: in academic journals and central bank policy papers, but also, as Nelms and Guyer show, in people's pockets and popular cultures, under their mattresses and on their phones, in household budgets and personal savings accounts. Here again, money is not simply an instrument for the attenuation or dissolution of the social and cultural. It is, instead, embedded in and often a vector for processes of re-socialization, culturalization, moralization, even sacralization—whether, to echo Haiven, "as the earthly representative of capitalist circulation" or "as a medium of daily life." Indeed, it is these very dualities, Bialecki argues, that best capture the cultural modernity of money.

Culture is a capacious term, as Raymond Williams (1983) famously suggested, and contributors deploy several different cultural approaches to money, even as they also surface money's historical commonalities and structural continuities in the modern age. As Williams would have predicted, these perspectives are not mutually exclusive. The roots of "culture"—like modernity—lie in parochially European understandings of universalist intellectual, spiritual, artistic, and ultimately civilizational development. In the twentieth century, however, "culture" has come to indicate more pluralist and relativist visions of social difference, as a term for a particular community's way of life. Used as a modifier for money, culture can be understood in this first instance to indicate the link between a particular monetary token or form of value and the "people" who use it, ringed about by a relatively coherent and durable set of habits, norms, and meaningful worldviews. This approach to the "cultures" of money is most clearly referenced in anthropological and sociological studies of money, described by Nelms and Guyer in Chapter 4. One benefit of this approach is that it emphasizes the diversity of money across time and space. Nelms and Guyer catalog some of this diversity, and in Chapter 2 ("Money and its Ideas"), Michael Beggs provides a complementary perspective from the world of monetary experts and policymakers, whose theories, models, and policies reflect differences in elite social networks and bureaucratic cultures, as well as geopolitical inequalities.

Second, money is also cultural in the obvious sense suggested by our references to *Cabaret* and the Wu-Tang Clan—as an object of reflection or commentary in novels on Broadway, in Hollywood, in pop music. Culture, from this perspective, belongs to particular domains: the visual and performing arts, poetry, fiction, cinema, television, music, games, and media more generally, from "high" to "low" and including its "mass" and digital variants. To participate in these realms is to produce "culture," and to study such production and its products is to analyze culture, even so much "the culture industry." Money here offers aesthetic and artistic inspiration, and both Haiven and Sherryl Vint begin their explorations of money in radical artwork (in Chapter 5) and money in science fiction literature (in Chapter 6, "Money and Its Interpretation") by lining up the cultural dimensions of money in this way.

We are faced, in these two approaches to culture, with two kinds of borders or oppositions. One is a boundary between distinct money cultures. Another is the boundary separating culture or society from its others: the political, the economic, or the material. These approaches share an assumption that there are other domains and conditions of social life that are non- or other-than-cultural. The actions of governmental and financial institutions might be seen primarily as political and economic, rather than cultural; similarly, there are underlying mechanisms or material conditions that might be assumed to operate "behind the backs" of social actors, and these are also often seen as beyond or at the limits of culture. The polymers that infuse paper banknotes to help them withstand exposure to moisture might not, for example, appear in a cultural study of money as a chemist might synthesize or measure them.

These understandings of culture nonetheless open a window onto a third approach, which positions money as the object of creative practice more broadly. Money is "a medium of the imagination," to use Haiven's phrasing, and as such, it becomes the target of everyday invention, to echo Nelms and Guyer. Culture in this sense is the effect of individual and collective capacity to make things happen, evident in the sheer diversity of ways to organize social life. To inquire into the cultural aspects of money from this perspective means to examine the plurality of ways of doing things with money and, accordingly, how our relations with money are socially embedded and context-specific. Nelms and Guyer thus argue in favor of "foregrounding not only *what* people do with money, in its many material forms, but also *how* they do it" in order to "highlight, in particular, people's inventiveness."

Reading synthetically across this volume's contributions, it is possible to discern a final but related approach, which puts these boundaries at the center of inquiry and sees culture as at once process and effect. If culture is the process through which behavior and belief take on shared meaning and through which those meanings are consolidated, circulated, and contested, the question is not whether culture is transformed by money or money transformed by culture, but in what ways money is made and remade by particular people, in particular places, towards particular ends, always with particular—but never entirely predictable—effects. This approach results in, as Haiven writes, "an accounting of culture not as a secondary, residual, or contingent element of economics, but as an integral, dialectical force." Money does not simply reconcile differences; money makes a difference.

How, for example, does money stuff come to be systematically bound up in relations of meaning, so that it might come to signal something about something else? Money in this way might resemble something else, gesture to something else or even come to fully stand for it. Money talks! Second, how might money become the *object* of something else—a sermon, say, or a central bank circular—which seeks to communicate something about it? "Show me the money," an announcer from the golden era of competitive boxing might say, and—like a prize-winning punch—it is the money-ish quality of the communication that has an impact. Finally, how might money also be the emergent effect of something referring to something else? Like an algebra equation, or a deduction in a murder mystery—say, the discovery of a life-insurance policy taken out on the victim by a suspect—money precipitates out of other relationships: "Of course! The money!" When the relations described above appear stable, consistent, and coherent, so too does money itself. Any apparent coherence, however, is achieved, and our attention must shift to the routes through which such coherence comes into being, is sustained, and also changes, sometimes dramatically. Any money culture expresses distinct and enduring qualities; at the same time, this durability provides lived material through which people put money to use and creatively sustain, inflect, rework, or even radically alter its patterns.

Haiven and Vint offer compelling examples. For both Haiven and Vint, the very boundary between money and culture provides a resource for social and cultural, as well as political and economic, production and reproduction. Both authors focus on the modern "financialization" of money—that is, its capture by private actors and institutions as a vehicle for the accumulation of profit through the transaction and speculation of capital assets and instruments, "the management of money's ebbs and flows" (Martin 2002: 3; see also Krippner 2005, 2011; Van der Zwan 2014; Pitluck et al. 2018).

Haiven writes about six artists working with money as both material and theme, three from the middle of the modern era, around the year 1973 and three from the period after the global financial crisis (GFC). Haiven suggests that these two moments should be read as turning points in the production and reproduction of modern money and its financialization. 1973 and 2008 are two moments of political economic upheaval, which opened money up to contestation by revealing its contradictions. They are also two moments when, in response to that upheaval, institutional patterns and political dynamics were further entrenched: first, through the systemic reproduction of global capital flows, especially as financial actors sought to secure pathways for these flows; second, through the institutional reproduction of class and identity, especially as workers' capacity for cultural consumption expanded and contracted with their wages; and third, through the social reproduction of labor and life itself, especially as reproductive and other forms of affective or care labor became increasingly commodified through service work.

Against assumptions about the opposition of money and culture, Haiven and Vint show how modern money is made and remade through the labor—both material and meaningful—of cultural reproduction, whether art or literature. Vint focuses on the place of money in twentieth- and twenty-first-century science fiction (SF). Vint's focus on SF is resonant in large part because, as she writes (echoing Haiven), modern finance makes wealth appear speculative and value a fiction. Many have described finance in this way: fictional in its opaque abstractions and chancy windfalls. But for Haiven and Vint, the idea that money is a kind of "speculative fiction" is more thoroughgoing. Money is "made up" in the sense that it is only ever an effect of future-facing meaning-making practices. As William Davies (2018: 12) writes, money practices "facilitate trust, not only in individual moments of market exchange but in terms of future expectations and guarantees." Yet they are not fixed. "Institutions such as money or contract cannot work if they're not accompanied by a normative sense that commitments and promises are binding into the future. Yet the nature of those commitments and promises is malleable" (12).

Both Haiven's money artists and Vint's SF authors are thus also concerned with critique and change. Haiven explains that it is the "special place" of art in the modern era that makes it uniquely available and powerful as a site for the cultural—critical and reflexive—interrogation of money. "Art is a form of labor and a commodity that, to maintain institutional legitimacy and market value, must constantly and in new ways reject its own commodification," Haiven writes. This tension provides the ground from which to launch a political and ethical critique of money and finance. For Haiven, as for Vint, "'finance' is itself a technology of the imagination, a set of techniques by which capitalism as a whole and its privileged functionaries gain a sense of an increasingly complex world system." Art, literature, and other kinds of representation and interpretation offer moments of "reflexivity within financialization."

For SF authors, this is explicit, for in the speculative futures they describe, utopian or dystopian, they seek out alternatives. "Imagining how the world might be different," Vint writes, "SF gives voice to anxieties and preoccupations about money and its role in social organization" today. These anxieties and preoccupations are many and noisy, but they converge on the future. "The real issue," Vint writes, "is not what money will look like in the future, but rather what the future will look like because of how we theorize and use money." The goal, then, is not simply to document the economic fictions that fabricate our past and present, but, as Mark Fisher (2018: xiv) puts it, to compose new "fictions that not only anticipate the future but that can already start to bring it into being."

HISTORY

Modern money is both culturally and historically situated; as a material, representational, and practical ensemble draws its content and significance from across space and time. If by history we mean a record of continuity and change, then a history of money must not only describe money's shifting forms and functions. It must also take into account its own history and its own place within that history. Histories of money are typically bounded by periods like the one under consideration in this book. This approach transforms "the past" into history itself: The historian must leave behind her present and venture into the past to discover or unearth it; when she records what she finds, she produces "a history." But, writing a history of money in the modern age is complicated by our own temporal position "in" the era we are describing. The past here cannot be understood as a time separate and distinct from the present.

As Haiven and Vint remind us, neither can modern money be clearly disentangled from the future. A history of money in the modern age must also confront the in-process, speculative, and future-oriented character of money's transformations throughout that period. Change in money is "additive rather than substitutive," Nelms and Guyer write, and what results is, to echo Davies (2018: 12), a "patchwork of institutions and mechanisms" that are always "amenable to reimagining and recombining." As Lana Swartz and David L. Stearns argue, money—"like modernity (and whatever comes next)"—is "palimpsest."

In Chapter 1 ("Money and Its Technologies"), Swartz and Stearns offer an overview of communications technologies that fundamentally undergird this palimpsest of modern money: money orders and travelers' checks moving through state mail and express shipping, telecommunications-based clearinghouses and card networks, digital and mobile payment systems, cryptographic protocols. Swartz and Stearns argue that the history of this infrastructure, of "how it would be structured, funded, operated, and governed," is a crucial part of the modernity of money in the long twentieth century. Swartz and Stearns thus expand the temporal purview of this book by beginning in the nineteenth-century United States—the "'prehistory' of the modern era," they call it. During this period, both US state institutions and private companies worked to lay down the foundations of today's payments system and lay claim to money itself.

The story Swartz and Stearns tell is one of communications networks that spread, scaled, sped up, and automated—qualities typically associated with modernity. Yet theirs is not a story "of evolutionary progress, with one technology displacing the next," in a race towards national consolidation, global integration, and money's eventual de-materialization. They describe how late twentieth-century efforts to speed money through digital networks reaching around the world paralleled the earliest efforts (by, for example, American Express) to create consumer-facing systems of value transfer that could bypass institutional and political borders. Swartz and Stearns thus take care to place their history: The technologies of modern money, they argue, were often "pioneered" on the frontier—specifically, the American West—and shaped by an ideology of digital frontierism that contrasted with the high financial cultures of New York, London, and other more traditional—that is, colonial and postcolonial—metropoles.

Bialecki similarly counters arguments about modern money's "de-territorialization"—through the anonymity of cash or the globality of finance—by routing those arguments through two examples of money in modern religion: the Prosperity Gospel in Christian Pentecostalism and Islamic banking in reformist Islam. Payments and pledges that in other contexts might be seen as secularizing are used by Pentecostals to secure a transmission channel for divine blessings. Islamic bankers, meanwhile, compose financial contracts that carefully write out interest through profit- and risk-sharing agreements to conform to sharia prohibitions of usury. In both cases, Bialecki writes, money does not collapse space and time, but is instead enrolled in particular "chains of material entanglement" and cultural negotiation that provide the creative and material resources for social "invention."

The authors in this book thus write about money's many social and material layers rather than a supposed drive towards, as Swartz and Stearns write, "abstraction and minimalism." They describe the diversification and diversion of money's forms alongside its consolidation. They emphasize not only the quicksilver threads of high finance, but the mundane paper of consumer finance. And they point out money's persistent fragmentations—in the earmarking of everyday savings, the gaps that interrupt cross-border remittances, the distinctions between users of different payment instruments—as well as efforts to create interconnection and interoperability. What emerges is a piecemeal and uneven process that nonetheless produces results with staying power: history that is contingent yet durable.

Beggs presents a complementary account of the links between monetary ideology and monetary policy across the twentieth century. Beggs's intellectual history traces "a succession of orthodoxies," but like the infrastructural settling of payment technologies in Swartz and Stearns's chapter, these orthodoxies are durable without being divorced from social and political context. Ideas and ideologies of money, value, and governance emerge from particular contexts and feed back into them. Increasingly during the modern era, this feedback happens through the policies, models, and strategic decision-making of an emergent class of monetary technocrats.

One example of such feedback can be found in the transition away from the gold standard at the beginning of the modern age, which set the stage for the consolidation and institutional entrenchment of monetary expertise in the states and central banks of the global North. Commodity anchors like the gold standard, Beggs suggests, did not so much guarantee the value of money itself as impose "a constraint on states" in their authority over money's issuance. Yet gold also bolstered confidence in "paper whose market value [would be] shored up by its own demand" and carved out a domestic space within which discretionary policies of such "managed money" might be tested. It thus provided the conditions within which state and bank-backed credit money could be "incubated." In this context, a "late twentieth-century consensus" emerged in monetary policy circles "around flexible exchange rates and inflation targets." That consensus meant the ideological elevation of price control over other possible policy objectives and, with it, the embrace of the idea that money's value could be controlled through its supply.

These are the basic tenets of monetarism, with its quantity theory of money. Beggs argues that academic monetarist models represented a more "sophisticated" challenge to prevailing, essentially Keynesian understandings about how interest rates shape banks' portfolio decisions and thus the demand for money. But the entrance of monetarist ideas into public political debate promised a more fundamental and thoroughgoing transformation: a way to fix the value of money by providing "a technical solution" to the problems of wage and price inflation. This brand of "political monetarism" shaped expert and popular understandings of money around the world, animating a sustained desire and search for "sound money"—that is, money whose value remains stable over time by removing it from the corruptible influence of human beings and institutions. It would, in short, create the conditions for money's apparent "depoliticization." As Beggs demonstrates, however, and as we discuss below, these decisions were in fact thoroughly political, in their origins and their distributional effects.

In the United States, the implementation of monetarist principles—most famously through the sudden raising of federal interest rates under newly appointed Federal Reserve Chairman Paul Volcker in 1979—was motivated and justified by arguments that framed inflation as a kind of theft. Inflation was, as Volcker himself put it, "a moral issue" (quoted in Cooper 2017: 29). As Melinda Cooper (2017) documents, inflationary tendencies in the 1970s US primarily affected owners of capital and credit, not those dependent on wages (which typically rose alongside prices) nor those who held debt (the cost of which was eroded by rising prices). Volcker's decision to crack down on inflation thus privileged the former over the latter; it was an attempt to safeguard savings and financial assets at the expense of workers and debtors.

The resulting recession pushed up unemployment and undermined the bargaining power of organized labor. "Restoring price stability," Beggs writes, "required smashing organized labor with chronic unemployment." These decisions laid the groundwork for a vertiginous rise of bond, stock, and asset prices, multi-decade wage stagnation, and, ultimately, the upward redistribution of wealth. As Cooper (2017: 132–133) writes, this moment "heralded a paradigm shift in American fiscal and monetary policy. [. . .] Henceforth the central bank would demonstrate its independence from potentially profligate governments by steadfastly disciplining wage and consumer price inflation, whatever the social costs."

Such monetary theorizing was centered mostly in the North Atlantic, but Beggs shows that the history of the production and distribution of monetary policy and ideology is an unequal and postcolonial one. The cultural politics of sound money were exported around the world and became a central pillar of monetary policy and neoliberal state transformation in the global South, with dramatic, often detrimental effects. "Sound money" ideas played a key role in the international emergence of neoconservative movements and the installation of violent authoritarian governments, most famously by the so-called "Chicago Boys" in Chile (Valdés 1995; see also Fourçade and Babb 2002). It shaped international institutions' embrace of austerity and conditional loan-making, which produced national debt crises around the world. Finally, it fed into growing expert pressure on governments in the global South to float their currencies, which led to speculation-fueled exchange crises in East Asia and elsewhere.

Sound money aspirations remained strong even as experts and central bankers shifted and changed their monetary theories and practices. As early as the Great Depression, Beggs writes, policymakers and economists recognized that control over the supply of money "ran through bank balance sheets." One of Keynes's central points, in fact, was that money's value was, at least in part, a function of demand, as banks circulated money in the form of loans in response to interest rate shifts. But during the twentieth century, banks and non-bank financial institutions increasingly innovated new financial liabilities and instruments, "improvising" markets in money substitutes, which then became part of "part of the financial web of life." "Strange beasts began to appear," Beggs writes.

This proliferation of new forms of money through the expansion, intensification, and diversification of finance is pivotal to the modern cultural history of money. Contributors to this volume, like many political economists, locate the turning point in the transition from "national capitalism" to this kind of "financial capitalism" in early 1970s, with the collapse of the Bretton Woods system centered on the gold–convertible US dollar (Hart 2009). As Haiven suggests in Chapter 5, the end of dollar–gold convertibility represented for many observers the end of any "representational" link between money's material form and its abstract value. While international trade in the first part of the twentieth century was centered on the exchange of raw and manufactured goods, by the end of the century, it was dominated by trade in financial instruments—that is, the exchange of (some categories of) money for (different categories of) money. Money, under these conditions, is not primarily a medium of exchange facilitating the trade of goods and services; it is a sign of value *per se*: a unit of measurement and wealth and a vector of savings, investment, or speculation.[4]

As the modern era advanced, Beggs writes, "much of what circulated as 'money itself' was not state-issued currency, but privately-issued bank deposits, acceptable because of confidence in their rapid convertibility into currency at par." The rise of monetarism in the second half of the twentieth century thus also poses a puzzle. Alongside the popularization of sound money fantasies and the concomitant institutionalization of a singularly inflation-focused monetary policy, the definitional boundaries around "money" itself were being increasingly muddied by the proliferation of new financial instruments that could, to greater and lesser degrees, be converted into other money forms.

As a result, central bankers increasingly accepted that theirs was, as Beggs puts it and as others like Benjamin Braun (2016), Douglas Holmes (2013), and Simone Polillo (2011) have also written, "a creative, strategic, and communicative enterprise." That enterprise could only indirectly shape the quantity of money and money-like value in circulation and, as a result, the consolidation of technical monetary expertise was accompanied by a consolidation of the idea of a "public" to which experts were, at least in theory, accountable. Prior to the GFC, this public was often figured in terms of "the markets"—that is, investors, bond owners, and other owners of financial capital who were to be recruited to collaborate with policymakers in achieving goals like price stability and market confidence.

Still, the very idea of a "discretionary" policymaking that corresponds to some kind of monetary public also made it possible for other interests and constituencies to assert pressure, especially in the midst and wake of crisis. Policymakers could be forced to take into account popular demands—by individual consumers and organized labor, for example—on state resources and state interests. Money, Beggs writes, does not exist in isolation but is "tied to many other aspects of economic life: wages and the labor market; trade and international capital flows; public spending and taxation; the banking system and financial markets." While the gold standard furnished useful "ideological and practical" justifications for any "ill consequences" of monetary policymaking, the system of central bank management that emerged over the course of the twentieth century opened money's managers up to public pressure in all these areas.

The accountability of monetary policymakers was once standardized in the dual mandate of central bankers around the world: not just to maintain low inflation, but also to pursue full employment. While the former overtook the latter in practice and in ideology, as we write this introduction, new questions and demands are being posed about the ability and responsibility of monetary policymakers to shape the economic lives of citizens by confronting the increasing control of private interests over the issuance of forms of value substitutable for state-issued denominations. Such demands might, Beggs suggests, in a limited way, "admit democracy into the monetary realm."

OF MONEY(NESS)

During the latter part of the modern age, commercial bank and non-bank liabilities, stamped with the authority of the state, increasingly circulated not just as debt but as means of payment and sources of liquidity. The authors in this volume draw attention to the growing importance of such private money creation, highlighting the push-and-pull of private and public interests in money. We argue that money is a public good, but that throughout the modern era, private players stepped into the gaps public actors failed to bridge, with sometimes ambiguous, sometimes disastrous results.

Money is authorized by and identified with governments, but in the modern era, it must increasingly pass through the portals and gateways of privately owned and operated institutions. Modern philosophy from Kant on has focused on the distinction and relation—figured as contract, bargain, obligation, belonging, alliance—between people and government. Yet this modern binary arguably did not reach its peak until the global replication of the nation-state form through mid-twentieth-century decolonization movements and nation-building efforts. It is a profound irony that just as hundreds of new national currencies were established, state monetary sovereignty was zipped away through processes of financialization and the privatization of payment. Thus, as Swartz and Stearns explain, efforts to facilitate "the unfettered flow of monetary value" were always both economic enterprise and "political project." This is as true of private shipping companies in the nineteenth century as it is for Diner's Club in the twentieth and PayPal in the twenty-first, and it is just as true in finance as it is in payment. Businesses sought and seek to make money with money by controlling its movement through fees, interest, and speculative investment—all forms of enclosure, capture, gating, or differential (non-par) access and acceptance, which at once surface and attenuate the hyphen linking people and states.

It is in the wake of such late twentieth-century processes—and the Polanyian-like, post-GFC counter-struggles to limit them—that money has again been made public. If Swartz and Stearns begin the story of modern money in the nineteenth century, Yeva Nersisyan and L. Randall Wray (in Chapter 7, "Money and the Issues of the Age") end the story in the twenty-first, confronting vehement debates that emerged after the GFC about how best to reform the global financial system. Like Depression-era debates that led to New Deal reforms in the United States, a series of popular and populist proposals for post-crisis financial reform circulated in the 2010s. Some initiatives (like the 2010 Dodd–Frank Wall Street Reform and Consumer Protection Act in the United States) sought "to tinker around the edges of the system," as Nersisyan and Wray put it. Others aimed for more "radical" change. One plan—known as "narrow" or "full-reserve" banking—proposed an alternative to traditional fractional reserve banking by requiring banks to maintain on hand the full amount of reserves deposited in the institution, thus limiting or even eliminating bank lending in an effort to restrict private money creation. A second proposal called for government "to finance its spending by directly issuing currency," thus allowing governments greater freedom to use "fiscal power to encourage growth and employment" and creating what proponents termed "debt-free" money.[5]

Animated by "popular reaction against banking excesses" leading up to and during the GFC, Nersisyan and Wray point out that like Volcker's monetarism, these were ultimately "moral" proposals targeting the expanded power of private financial institutions over money. In their search for money that does not devalue or produce speculative bubbles, reformers reiterated longstanding anxieties that banks "get something [. . .] for nothing" and demanded a return of control over money "to the public sphere." Even as we write this introduction, a variant of such proposals, known as the "Vollgeld" ("sovereign money"), has gained some momentum in Switzerland. (Although a popular vote in June 2018 rejected the initiative.) "It was a surprise—we were simply not aware," one Swiss banker and Vollgeld supporter said about the role that private financial institutions play in creating and circulating money. But "our view is that money is a public good" (Atkins 2018).

Nersisyan and Wray, like all the contributors to this volume, agree that there is a public interest in money. They argue, however, that reform proposals often misconstrue the nature of money's publicness by "lamenting the ills of 'ex nihilo' money creation, its production 'out of thin air.'" They instead propose an understanding of money that focuses on the historically specific way that money is made by and moves through both governmental and financial institutions. Money is always, as Nelms and Guyer write, "caught between the sovereign who bestows and maintains the unit of account and the people who then use it, taking it up to settle their debts with one another, make individual and collective investments, and much more." It is thus "backed" by these vertical and horizontal relationships. "Even if not explicitly stated," Nersisyan and Wray write, "thinking of bank money creation as happening 'out of thin air' seems to imply the possibility of a different form of money, a proper one, perhaps money that is made of something with intrinsic value."

Nersisyan and Wray show that these ideas have deep roots. They are resonant of debates at the beginning of the modern era, when crisis and depression sparked similar proposals—by, for example, the economist Irving Fisher (1935), who argued that a 100 percent reserve system would eliminate bank runs and recessions while reducing indebtedness. They also echo the sound money paradigms traced by Beggs. These include Milton Friedman's midcentury proposals to finance government spending through new money creation and impose a 100 percent reserve requirement on banks, such that "there would be no 'net' money creation by private banks—they would expand the supply of bank money only as they accumulated reserves of government-issued money."

Nersisyan and Wray argue that these recurrent debates circle between two approaches to money, one that sees money as a commodity and medium of exchange and another that understands it "as a credit-debt relationship." "These two radically different perspectives on the nature of money," Nersisyan and Wray write, "have crystallized during the modern era." The commodity money view suggests that money arises to solve the problems of barter and that its primary function is to smooth exchange. Money's value, according to this perspective, ought to derive from something fixed, as it supposedly did when it was tied to a commodity like gold; lacking such a material anchor, its supply ought to be strictly controlled to avoid devaluation. In the US, this argument has been presented again and again, from nineteenth-century goldbugs who resisted the creation of paper "greenbacks," to the midcentury monetarists like Friedman, to twenty-first-century crypto-libertarian supporters of digital currencies like Bitcoin, which Vint describes in Chapter 6. From these perspectives, Duncan Foley (2004: 44) writes, modern credit money is a kind of "bubble, a worthless token whose value is sustained by belief in its future acceptability."

Discussions about the financialization of money in the modern era often partake of similar broadsides. This volume, however, draws on heterodox approaches to money and finance—from cultural and political economy, anthropology and sociology, communication, science and technology studies, and other fields—to show that transformations grouped under the umbrella of financialization unfolded across particular sites through particular social forms, ideological arguments, and institutional attachments. Nersisyan and Wray draw, for example, on the work of a range of twentieth-century thinkers, from Keynes and Polanyi to A. Mitchell Innes, Georg Friedrich Knapp, Abba Lerner, and Hyman Minsky. These thinkers, among others, have inspired a trajectory of thought that, in the early twenty-first century, was grouped under the banner of "Modern Monetary Theory" (MMT). MMT's dual empirical focus on the modern institutions of states and banks was elaborated explicitly for the first time by thinkers at the beginning of the modern age, especially through so-called "chartalist" and "credit" theories of money (associated with writers like Knapp and Innes). But it has been taken up and popularized again in the wake of the GFC (see, e.g., Nersisyan and Wray 2016).[6]

What is it that makes MMT "modern"? MMT reflects a prolonged grappling with the tension between private and public money management, the currents of financialization, and the creation and control of crisis. Arguably the central pillar of MMT is the realization that money is neither "neutral" nor supplied directly and "exogenously" by a monetary policy authority like a central bank. It is instead, modern monetary theorists like Nersisyan and Wray argue, an effect of demand for credit and debt. That is, money is supplied primarily through the decisions of financial institutions in response to broader economic conditions shaping that demand. As Nersisyan and Wray point out, this "endogenous" view of money echoes Keynes's "monetary theory of production," which insisted that "not only is money not neutral, it is fundamental to the production process. All capitalist production begins with money in the expectation of ending up with more money later." At the same time, this understanding of money creation became increasingly widely accepted even in mainstream monetary policy circles in the early twenty-first century (see, e.g., McLeay et al. 2014).

This leads to an expansive view of money, even at the heart of the mainstream financial system. "Money" encompasses not only cash, nor only what economists call "the monetary base" (which also includes bank deposits), but the liabilities issued by all manner of nonbank financial institutions. The number, variety, and influence of such institutions—"not banks," Beggs writes, but also "not outside the banking system"—grew dramatically over the past half-century and, in the process, surfaced money's internal diversity of form and function. As Nelms and Guyer argue, the digitization and seeming dematerialization of money—the decreasing dependence on any physical token and concomitant increasing reliance on units of account and the database infrastructures that facilitate record-keeping—ran alongside these processes of financialization. These were by no means new developments. But the proliferation of new financial instruments and new digital and mobile technologies reopened debate about the nature of money and value, even as they were heralded as harbingers of a coming "cashless" or "cash-lite" world. The result was an increasingly explicit recognition of monetary pluralism: M0, M1, and M2, dollars and pesos, gold and airline miles and Starbucks points.

Practices of and discourses around financialization, digitization, and the privatization of money shifted ideas about money in expert and popular domains away from the strictly definitional (Bryan and Rafferty 2013; Cooper and Konings 2016; O'Dwyer 2018). As Nersisyan and Wray explain,

> While we may want to draw lines between assets for analytical purposes, where we draw them depends on what we are trying to accomplish (and who the "we" are in a particular political context). There is no single definition of money that is appropriate for all purposes.

In the spirit of Nersisyan and Wray's contribution, we join a range of observers to emphasize different categories of monetary liquidity—what in anthropology might end up being called "spheres of exchange," and in sociology, "circuits of commerce"—and the points of conversion between them. If all monies are forms of liability, a central empirical question is to identify the limits of their exchangeability. At the same time, then, we also highlight that which, at another level, ties money's diversity together: the relative capacity to exchange one form of money for another, often through recourse to a unifying unit of account. This capacity for circulation is what we call *"moneyness."* The defining feature of moneyness (a term used by Beggs and by Nersisyan and Wray) is the variable capacity of different forms or denominations of value to trade against one another and the resulting degrees of liquidity, fungibility, or negotiability that obtain between them.[7]

As Swartz and Stearns show, the social and material systems facilitating money's movements became explicit "sites of modern and modernist innovation and aspiration"—and thus "infrastructures" of modernity itself. Movement was long identified with the modern experience, and part of the dream of those who sought and still seek to realize it has long been to smooth and speed the circulation of value and information across time and space. One key avatar of this dream was, Swartz and Stearns and Nelms and Guyer show, the so-called "cashless society"; another, as we see throughout this book, was the proliferation and intensification of financial "innovation," as bankers and traders responded to demands for increasingly liquid returns on investment by searching out flexibility and fluidity in the financial system (Ho 2009: 183–188; Bourgeron 2018). Both the cashless society fantasy and the search for liquidity were shaped by "expectation[s] that any kind of money should be instantly transferable, anytime, anywhere." "[A] monetary artifact," Swartz and Stearns write, "isn't really 'money' until it moves," but the apparent "seamless[ness]" of that movement is the effect of "a vast technical and industrial apparatus." These systems provided the paths, plumbing, and wiring through which payment happens and value circulates—and it is the circulation of value, Swartz and Stearns suggest, that makes money modern.

Focusing on moneyness also complicates understandings of monetary policy and authority by orienting us to the multi-tiered "hierarchy" of modern money and to the pathways and practices of conversion and circulation between levels in that hierarchy (Bell 2001; Mehrling 2013). "Modern money," Beggs writes, "has a hierarchical structure: the 'base' of state-issued currency supports a much larger volume of private bank-issued money." The moneyness of liabilities at each level is a function, in turn, of "its convertibility to the money of the higher level." Moneyness, that is, is an effect of convertibility. That convertibility, in turn, "depends upon the issuing institution's ability to 'make the market' in its own liability: to keep its promise to exchange it for the higher-level money at par." The institutions historically most capable of meeting these expectations are, of course, those of the state. Hence the most common definitions of money in terms of legal tender: "it is," Nersisyan and Wray write (citing Pozsar 2014: 9), "'proximity to the government' that defines the moneyness of various financial instruments, rather than their function as a means of payment."

Yet the position of the state "at the top of the national monetary pyramid cannot be taken for granted: it is a historical outcome" (Beggs 2017: 464). Indeed, in the latter part of the modern age, the increasingly diverse "black box" of financial instruments constituted, as Beggs put it, "a new layer in the monetary pyramid"—a whole "shadow" system of money creation and circulation that challenged easy distinctions between monetary and non-monetary assets and necessitated new forms of expertise (Bryan and Rafferty 2006; Mehrling 2011; Gabor and Vestergaard 2016). The creation of innovative forms of risk management and the imperative to find new sources of liquidity—or to transform traditionally illiquid assets (mortgages, pensions, municipal bonds, student debt) into tradable instruments—not only multiplied the forms of value crisscrossing the interstices between states' units of account and the circulating debts that materialized that unit. They also widened the gap between the money supply and changes in price, "undermining monetary restraint by providing money-substitutes and techniques for economizing on money holdings," Beggs argues. As a result, as we described above, monetary authorities could not act unilaterally but instead had to navigate through "a complex, mostly private financial system" that became regularly subject to crisis. This, Beggs (2017: 474) writes elsewhere, "is more a question of strategy than of fiat."

Nersisyan and Wray argue that, whether money is circulated through state or non-state channels, the goal should be careful risk assessment of the strength of the claim behind any promise of future liquidity. They explain that what determines whether money is "sound" is not the quantity of monetary assets or its relation to a quantity of another asset, such as reserves. Instead, *what matters is the quality of the debt*, or the IOUs that back the creation of liquid money-like liabilities."

—emphasis added

In other words, what lies behind money is not some fixed form of value, but a social and political promise: "the promise to pay is not ex nihilo—it is a social relation" (Ingham 2002: 141). The problem with private money creation, then—in contradistinction to the complaints of some twenty-first-century reformers—is *not* that there is "nothing" behind the money circulated in this way, that it is "only" debt and thus "backed only by trust." The problem is the instability and inequality that such institutions create in the absence of transparency and accountability.

The twenty-first-century GFC was simply the latest in a recurring series of cyclical crises: moments of intensified financial innovation, followed by the expansion of banks' balance sheets, a bubble (in asset prices, dot-com start-ups, subprime mortgages), its bursting, and the incorporation of new forms of money into, as Beggs puts it, the "ever-shifting network of flows and promises" that constitute the wider financial landscape (see also Tooze 2018). The growth, in the early twenty-first century, of a non bank and mostly unregulated shadow banking sector, as Nersisyan and Wray argue, is yet another example. Indeed, Nersisyan and Wray show that "eliminating banks' ability to create demand deposits out of 'thin air' will not eliminate private money creation." Instead, "restrictions on banks will simply move more of the money creation into the 'shadow' and 'parallel' banking universe, as other institutions step in to fill the void left by banks"—further swinging the pendulum of money towards the private sector.

CONCLUSION: IN THE MODERN AGE

The rise of modern money management and its confrontation with finance entangled experts and policymakers in a series of negotiations that reopened money to political contestation. However limited these negotiations, their outcome was far from assured in advance. States and banks have constituencies, so to speak, even if states and banks are differentially responsive to the needs of the public or the force of popular pressure. States have citizens who make demands; financial institutions and instruments depend in a very real way on people, households, and communities: their labor, their wages, their assets, their debt. Money, in short, is directly implicated in real economic activity—simply put, "a method of representing and moving resources within a group" (Desan 2016: 21)—and debates about money are powerfully shaped by conflicts over how to parcel out that activity's effects. Such debates are, as Beggs writes, "distributional struggles" that mobilize different groups to define and defend "their monetary claims over real income and wealth."

Focusing on money's moneyness allows us to foreground money's *politics* by virtue of surfacing its *pragmatics* (as Nelms and Guyer put it): everyday and elite practices of issuing liabilities, circulating and converting them, and redeeming or settling them. Money's politics is twofold, at once a micro- and macro-politics. It encompasses money's creation and regulation by institutions—governmental and financial, bank and non bank—and the uses to which it is put by people. Modern money's micro-politics trucks in the channels and thresholds of its circulations and conversions; its macro-politics centers on the distributional struggles that crisis often brings (back) to the surface. Liquidity and distribution: to focus on one to the exclusion of the other risks missing a crucial part of modern money's history—and risks misunderstanding its possible futures.

Interventions in money's micro- and macro-politics seek to remake the pathways and patterns of value conversion and distributional struggle. Take, for example, the artists Haiven discusses in Chapter 5, who inventively mobilized "techniques at the cusp of art and activism" to appropriate forms and functions of money and finance in order to critique them. These artists confronted a heightened version of a paradox faced by many throughout the modern age: to make sense of—and challenge—hegemonic forms of money and finance, they have only those forms on which to rely. As Haiven explains, drawing on the work of Randy Martin (2015), the financialization and privatization of money was, in part, a response to global social movements seeking to resist oppressive and exclusionary economic structures. "Financialization," Haiven writes, "offered a way to respond to the 'decolonial' demands of youth and marginalized people," especially in the postcolonial world, by furnishing many with "a more flexible, even personalized economic system, tolerant of various modalities of reproduction."

The result was the emergence of "a palate" of forms of consumer and household indebtedness—mortgage, medical, credit card, student, auto—which then fueled the securitized finance boom that followed (La Berge 2018; see also Langley 2008; Cooper 2015). As Nelms and Guyer also point out, efforts to expand the reach of finance were often motivated by democratic ideals combined with everyday aspiration. Yet in this way, those best positioned to see the limits and inequalities of money were drawn into its circuits, only to be turned into scapegoats when those circuits turned illiquid. The austerity programs that followed were efforts to discipline the hopes and desires of those deemed risky or subprime, by sanctioning excess and re-inscribing normative forms of family and economy (Cooper and Mitropoulos 2009).

Many people have nonetheless uncovered ways to confront the paradox of financialization, however compromised and complicit they found themselves in the systems they sought to critique. The artists discussed by Haiven, for example, "set ideological trap[s]" to reveal money's social and institutional foundations; others "attempt[ed] to appropriate and expropriate a globally integrated financial system in the name of other, non- or anti-capitalist values." Their politics were thus of an unusual kind. Haiven describes a series of performative interventions in global finance by Nuria Güell and Levi Orta, who actively adopted elite financial practices and institutions—setting up a tax haven in Panama to embezzle public arts funding, funneling corporate sponsorships to explicitly anti-capitalist cooperative initiatives—"to kick open holes in the capillaries of global capital and redirect energies and funds to living anti-capitalist alternatives." Like the activists of the GFC-era Occupy movement or the diverse community iniatives to create complementary currencies described by Nelms and Guyer, Güell and Orta learned the techniques of modern money and finance in order to subvert them. At the same time, these artists used art's "strange semi-autonomy and institutional liquidity," its "residual prestige and ideological immunity," to insulate themselves legally and culturally.

This kind of "post-cynical pragmatism [. . .] does not stake its success on a moment of revelation" that sparks a revolution. A radical vision of transformation is paired with more immediate, practical goals. In the hands of artist-activists like Güell and Orta, modern money becomes, as Haiven puts it, "a platform for other projects of grassroots creativity, militant imagination, and anti-capitalist economic cooperation." That such efforts target the technical infrastructures, social networks, and institutional pathways through which money circulates is no accident. In this, Güell and Orta join theorists of modern finance like Robert Meister (2016), who argues that what we call moneyness may become the target of collective political organization and intervention, to interrupt the flow of value and redirect it to other ends. Such efforts do not dwell on scholastic questions of money's value or purpose so much as they wield such questions like a hammer—or maybe, a wrench—to fit the micro-politics of moneyness into the macro-politics of its uneven distributional outcomes.

The reformers discussed by Nersisyan and Wray propose a complementary intervention—not so much tinkering with the plumbing of money's financialization and privatization as hunting out an end-around, through full-reserve banking or the disintermediation of banks. Nersisyan and Wray, however, insist that such an end-around does not exist. Money is debt—and trust—all the way down. The crucial difference is who makes the promise and what form of value is accepted in return, to pay it off.

> When a non-sovereign entity (firm, household, state or local government) issues debt, it promises to service the debt by paying interest and eventually to retire the debt. Payment is made using liabilities of a third party [. . .]. A sovereign government, on the other hand, usually only promises to make

payments in its own debts, including currency, but mostly central bank reserves—in other words, swapping one liability for another.

When a state pledges to accept its own debt for payments due, this is simply another variety—although perhaps the "highest" variety—of conversion. Typical framings of taxation suggest that taxes are due in advance of government spending, to raise revenue in support of public expenditure. Nersisyan and Wray argue the inverse: spending—and thus the creation of money itself—happens before taxation (conceptually and sometimes chronologically). A tax is in fact a "return," a "revenue" (to reference the Latin and French etymology): "the taxpayer 'returns' the sovereign's liability in payment." Taxation offers an important tool in the policymaker's and regulator's toolbox—to address financial crisis, redistribute collective wealth or reallocate the costs of public spending, and discourage publicly detrimental behavior. But its "more fundamental" purpose is to drive demand for currency by redeeming it. Indeed, this is a crucial way colonial governments often sought to exert political control, by setting new standards for the payment of tax (Gregory 1996; Roitman 2005). Yet also for this reason, Nersisyan and Wray insist, states—at least states like the United States with their own sovereign currencies—are "not financially constrained under modern monetary arrangements." That is, a sovereign government can always "afford" to respond to the distributional demands of its citizens; "it cannot become insolvent in its own currency; it can always make all payments as they come due in its own currency."

The modern monetary system, therefore, especially in the North Atlantic context, in which commercial banks act with the implicit and explicit backing of the state, "should really be viewed as [a] private-public partnership," Nersisyan and Wray argue. Theirs is a call for regulatory action—to supervise and limit the circulation of money through private financial institutions and infrastructures. But it is also a call to recognize and wield the full fiscal power of the state in the service of the public. "We need to ensure that banks serve a public purpose," they write. In the aftermath of the GFC, one key lesson—implicit but insistent—is that to grapple with money's politics, we need not just new theories of money, but *new monetary theories of the state*. The issuance and control of modern money are outcomes of ongoing conflicts of governance, caught (as Beggs puts it) "between technocracy and democracy." It is not enough to suggest that money is a creature of the state. Instead, Beggs argues, "money in the modern era has [itself] created (and recreated) states, by throwing up problems of management with ramifications reaching the heart of modern politics."

Taxation *redeems* a debt. At the beginning of Chapter 3, Bialecki offers up the unusual image of a faux dollar bill—just similar enough to the real thing to catch the eye, but in fact a vehicle for Christian proselytizing, inscribed with Gospel verse and a message about the debt of sin and the divine gift of everlasting life. The note asks its reader to consider if they will be worthy of that gift. For Bialecki, the missive grasps a contradictory truth of modern money, the need for it to "continue to circulate" and the simultaneous desire—achingly and perpetually unfulfilled—for "a moment of redemption and final settlement, when the debt is paid off." Such redemption suggests, as Nersisyan and Wray write of the state's acceptance of tax in return for its own promises, that it is possible "to 'wipe the slate clean' and emerge debt-free by returning to the creditor—whether public or private—the creditor's own IOU." Yet the value of that IOU only ever exists as a function of its future exchangeability and thus convertibility. All modern money is marked by this duality: its liquidity, its moneyness, and the necessary fiction of its final conversion, its ultimate redemption.

The cultural history of modern money, however it is written, is necessarily implicated in money itself. It is implicated in debates around money's definition and in conflicts around its use and distribution. These debates and conflicts are not resolved; redemption remains out of sight, over the horizon. Yet neither are those debates and conflicts neutral. They directly shape the politics and pragmatics, micro- and macro-, of moneyness—delineating what actions are politically feasible in a given moment and hinting at those that can be *made* politically reasonable, showing us the lines of contestation of future struggle. This is one of the challenges of our assignment. Money is in fact far from settled. The modern era remains our own!

CHAPTER ONE

Money and its Technologies

Making Money Move in the Modern Era

LANA SWARTZ AND DAVID L. STEARNS

INTRODUCTION

In 2015, most US Americans found the everyday ritual of payment unsettled by what seemed to be a minor change in its technologies. Instead of swiping a card with a magnetic stripe, they were suddenly required to insert one with an embedded chip. Perhaps for the first time in decades, many in the United States had reason to pay close attention to the act of payment—and to the technologies of money generally—and on the whole, they didn't like it.

For months exchanges were accompanied by variations on the same back-and-forth: *Do I swipe or. . .? Oh, sorry you have to insert. Yeah sorry it takes a minute to go through. Do I sign? Oh you took it out too soon.* At Walmarts and Targets, Home Depots and Dollar Trees, chain restaurants and small businesses alike, there were countless moments of confusion and complaint.

Merchants complained about costs. Unwilling to fully migrate to the new chip-and-signature system, many covered the new slots with branded inserts or pieces of tape. Consumers were annoyed, with some wondering if the new system even made a difference in terms of fraud. Plenty suspected conspiracy theories. Some were relatively quotidian: Which company is harvesting our data for profit this time? Others were all-encompassing: Surely (then-President) Obama could now shut down payment cards and usher in the New World

Order; first chips in our card, next chips in our flesh. Mundane changes to our idioms of practice are rarely welcome.

The transition to chip-and-signature in the United States was particularly rocky because, for a long time, most of the systems and processes that undergird the everyday transfer of money appeared seamless. Every payment depends on a vast technical and industrial apparatus, but if everything is in normal working order, the only difficulty the card holder or cashier might experience is a few seconds of waiting. There is a lot happening behind the scenes to produce this moment. Few people who use payment systems every day understand them as complex technical achievements.

Payment, like all infrastructures, has a history that shaped how it would be structured, funded, operated, and governed. Susan Leigh Star (1999) makes a case for the importance of studying infrastructures. "Study a city and neglect its sewers and power supplies (as many have), and you miss essential aspects of distributional justice and planning power," Star writes. "Study an information systems and neglect its standards, wires, and settings, and you miss equally essential aspects of aesthetics, justice, and change" (1999: 379). What can we learn about our world by looking at how we pay, and how the systems that allow us to pay came to be?

As Paul Edwards has noted, "To be modern means to live within and by means of infrastructures" (2010: 8). We flip on lights, turn on faucets, throw things "away," check "the time," send messages around the world in a blink of an eye, and indeed, we swipe (or insert) cards. If being modern means anything, it means to depend on massive systems and simultaneously learn not to see them. The practice of money changed quite a bit during the long twentieth century. It became "modern"— that is, infrastructural, and normally invisible.

In this chapter, we show how innovations in money and payments during the modern era have tracked alongside changes in the underlying communications infrastructure: from paper mail and express shipping, to telecommunications, to digital computers and internetworking, to mobile telephony, to cryptographic protocols. As we soar over this busy and tumultuous time period, we touch down to examine four key innovations in our payments infrastructure that were enabled by changes in the underlying communication networks: money orders and travelers' checks; automated clearinghouses; payment card networks; and the more recent internet-based payment networks. We show how the historical context surrounding these innovations influenced their resulting structure, economics, and politics.

We offer a rough chronology of changes in everyday financial technology from the late nineteenth century to the late twentieth century. These include important developments from the "prehistory" of the modern era, which (whether the work of private shipping companies or the consolidation of the

US Federal Reserve system) we suggest laid the technological and infrastructural foundations of modern money. This is not, however, intended to be a narrative of evolutionary progress, with one technology displacing the next. Indeed, the periods covered, like the actual practices described, are not discrete; rather, they are often messy and overlapping. We also focus on the United States, mostly because that is the area of our academic expertise, but this is not intended to overlook or dismiss important developments in other parts of the world during this time (Rona-Tas and Guseva 2014; Bátiz-Lazo and Efthymiou 2016; Nelms and Guyer, this volume).

Our focus on payments—that is, the mechanisms of monetary exchange—is purposeful. Many histories of money focus exclusively on monetary artifacts, or the physical forms that money takes, but these histories overlook an important aspect of monetary systems: a monetary artifact isn't really "money" until it *moves*. Monetary artifacts, like all assets, are representations of *potential* exchange value. It's only in the moment of exchange, when another person treats them as valuable, that this value is realized and reified. These mechanisms of exchange are what allow monetary artifacts to become money, currency to become current, and thus their histories and configurations are fundamental to understanding how money changed during the modern era.

Scholars across fields have defined modernity in terms of movement.[1] As Tim Creswell puts it, "mobility seems self-evidently central to Western modernity" (2006: 15). Indeed, the infrastructures of movement—trains, highways, and, we will demonstrate, payment—are central to what is meant by modernity. Beyond the actual uses of these technologies, though, Creswell continues, modernity "suggests a way of thinking in terms of mobility—a metaphysics of mobility that is distinct from what came before it" (2006: 16). Cultural geographer Doreen Massey describes how modernity has entailed both the "speeding up and spreading out" of geographic experience (1991: 24). Our story of payment technology is one of expansion: across the American continent, not just from coast to coast, but more thoroughly penetrating into its rural mountaintops and valleys. It is a story of automation, of money transfer becoming faster and more efficient as it is reduced to more abstract, standardized informational forms. It is a story of people moving faster and further within that geography, of money that keeps pace with travel along highways and in commercial jets. It is about open loops and opened borders.

If this story maps to existing metanarratives of modernity—of speed, of mobility, of infrastructure—that is because many of the actors we describe more or less self-consciously saw themselves as part of the project of modernity and whatever comes next: building the nation-state, building the information age, building the global market society. The technologies and infrastructures of money, as they are designed and experienced, become sites of modern and modernist innovation and aspiration.

PAPER AND RAILS
Sending money through the mail

Paper money, like other forms of print culture, was tied to the emergence of the nation as an "imagined community" (Anderson 1983). State currency delineated the nation as an economic territory, providing citizens with a "common economic language with which to communicate" (Helleiner 1998: 1414). However, establishing a single national currency was not a naturally occurring development. It was an achievement of governments that required significant effort over decades. In the United States, national currency was not fully consolidated until after the Civil War (Henkin 1998). Prior to that, foreign currencies, private bank notes, and scrip produced by railroads, insurance companies, and other private businesses circulated alongside currency issued by the US Treasury (Mihm 2007). Once enacted, however, the exchange of a single paper money provided a "daily affirmation of the nation state," both as a vector of iconography and as an assent to the continued value of these notes and the legitimacy of the government that issued and backed them (Gilbert 1999: 42).

Debates over monetary policy are widely recognized as an important characteristic of the late nineteenth century, but this era was also a time of tension over not just the authority, backing, and production of money, but also its transport and transmission (Lawrence 1978; Ritter 1997). These conflicts laid the groundwork for the technologies of money in the twentieth century, although they centered on another key infrastructure of the state: the postal service.

The postal system has been widely praised for its contribution to modern American public life. It brought newspapers and messages from afar, binding the country together and forging a national imaginary from a loose confederation of states (John 1998). Like the exchange of paper currency itself, the functioning of the US mail service provided an everyday affirmation of the power of the nation-state. In rural areas, postmasters were likely the most familiar representatives of the federal government.

The mail also functioned as an infrastructure for the movement of monetary value. It was used by banks and merchants to ship large sums of money and other financial instruments, but it was also used by ordinary people to send money across the country. Before the twentieth century, checking accounts were common only among the wealthy, so when most people wished to send a payment long distance, they "put their money into an envelope, sewed the envelope shut, and sealed it with wax," then mailed it (Grossman 1987: 80).

The flow of money across the United States, and thus the imagined community which it traced, was determined by the material organization of the postal infrastructure. But the post office lacked the resources, and the infrastructure, to provide universal service to the entire nation. As the country expanded, the federal Post Office Department (in operation from 1792 to 1971, the predecessor of the US Postal Service) made decisions about subsidized routes that promoted settlement but did not generate enough revenue to cover their costs. At times, the department delivered mail using new, experimental relay techniques along routes that were still being actively forged. In general, the federal system prioritized slowly developing, reliable infrastructure over speedy delivery (United States Postal Service 2007).

Numerous regional private express mail companies rushed to compete with the federal postal service by targeting areas where public service was poor. While private mail companies principally sought the business of banks and other bulk shippers, they also transported small payments for individuals. Private shipping companies made swift profit transporting bullion, banknotes, and all kinds of freight from coast to coast via stagecoach, courier, canal, and rail. In the American West, private expresses were more ubiquitous than the federal government. The industry "went everywhere, did almost anything for anybody, and was the nearest thing to a universal service company ever invented"; indeed, private express shipping was often "the first thing established in every new camp

FIGURE 1.1: The Wells Fargo Express Company travels with $250,000 gold bullion, Deadwood, South Dakota, 1890. Library of Congress Washington DC.

FIGURE 1.2: Private express companies like American Express and Wells Fargo shipped by train over the New York Central Railroad. Painting, *c*. 1884. Library of Congress Washington DC.

or diggin's" (quoted in Fradkin 2002: 27). By 1900, the express industry had consolidated into four main companies: Adams Express Company, Southern Express Company, American Express Company, and Wells Fargo.

The US Post Office Department was widely criticized as overpriced, inefficient, insufficient, and weighed down by political patronage (John 1998). But the benefits of the private expresses came at a price. Although it fought against government regulation, condemning the "monopoly" held by the US mail, the express industry itself was not actually competitive. Instead, the expresses divided up territory regionally and agreed not to compete on prices within those regions. They also kept unions out, banding together against organized labor to fire unionized employees and hire scab workers. This cartel setup thus allowed the express companies to engage in price fixing and discrimination (Grossman 1987). This was in sharp contrast to the federal system, which offered stable employment and standardized, subsidized pricing.

Various pieces of legislation throughout the nineteenth century sought to fight competition from the private expresses, expand routes, keep fees down, and provide universal service to customers, no matter where they lived in the country and territories (United States Postal Service 2007). While the public mail attempted to build infrastructure for long-term universal service, the private express industry was able to provide targeted service in the meantime. Competition between public and private financial infrastructure—to move money across the country and bring the American continent together as an economic territory—was found not in direct challenge to the state's monopoly on the issuance of money, but to its efforts to deliver the mail.

Private money for immigrants and wealthy travelers

The United States postal service came into its own at the turn of the century. In 1898, it instituted universal Rural Free Delivery, which delivered mail directly to farms and households, whose residents were previously forced to travel to centralized post offices or pay private expresses to deliver their mail, including deliveries of money. In 1913, it began to offer improved parcel post services. In 1917, as part of the war effort, the United States nationalized its railroad and private express mail services. These three developments effectively ended the era of competition between the private expresses and the public post. By that point, however, American Express, then by far the largest private shipping company, had already moved on to new, lucrative, and unregulated ways to move value: first money orders, then travelers' checks. Once again, American Express imitated what the Post Office was already doing, but focused on filling in gaps in service—more efficiently, but at a cost.

The federal postal system had, following the British system, long offered postal money orders. Even in its nascent period, the postal service was a retail financial institution capable of moving value all over the country, from post office to post office, at a low cost. In this way, postal money orders functioned as a *de facto* state currency, a medium of exchange and store of value, especially for travelers and itinerant workers. In 1893, one supporter wrote that "cases have been known, and, it is believed, are not rare, in which persons permanently abiding in locations where there are no reliable banks, have, for security, invested their savings in money orders issued upon application made by themselves in their own favor" (Cushing 1893: 207). In a way, the postal money order system offered an important financial public good.

In 1888, American Express began to issue its own money orders. American Express identified a key weakness in the postal money order system: only post offices that did a sufficient amount of business to have cash on hand to pay out on money orders were allowed to administer them. Just as it did with mail delivery, American Express targeted those areas where the infrastructure of the federal government was limited (Hines and Velk 2009). At the same time, American Express created a more efficient but less secure system. The US postal money order system was a frustratingly complicated one, involving not only the transfer of the money order itself between buyer and payee, but extra documentation, the "Advice of US Postal Money Order," which was prepared by the issuing postmaster, mailed to the payee's local post office, and then kept for up to four years. The main reason for this bureaucratic complexity was security. If a postmaster had not received the advice form, a money order could

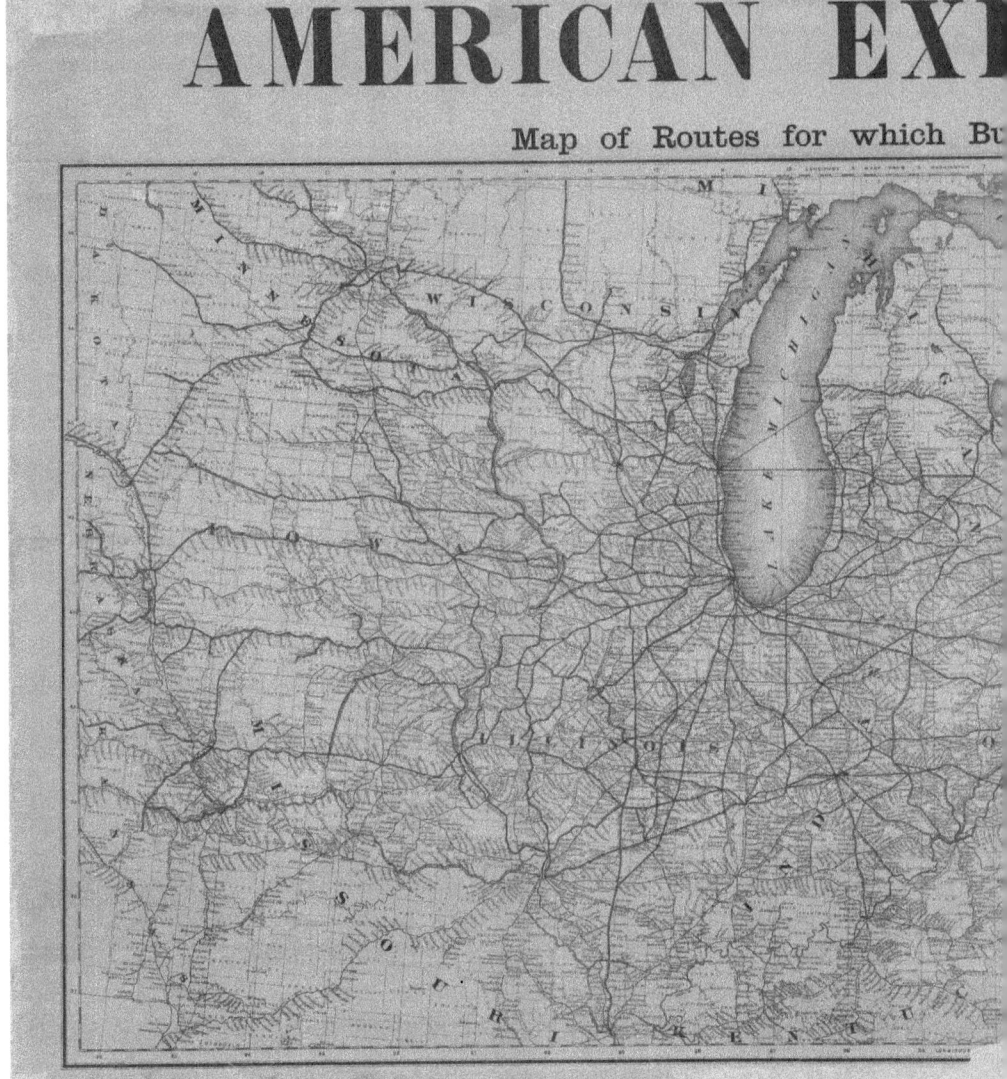

FIGURE 1.3: Map showing the lines of the American Express Company, *c.* 1874. The New York Public Library Digital Collections.

not be cashed (Hines and Velk 2009). But this system was confusing for immigrant and illiterate customers; even those proficient in the language often found it difficult to collect on lost orders (Grossman 1987).

American Express developed and later patented a paper engineering solution to these problems (Massengill 1999). When an American Express money order was purchased, the clerk wrote the name of the payee and the amount on two stubs, gave one to the buyer, and kept the other for the company's records.

RESS COMPANY.

ss is Received and Forwarded.

Map
SHOWING THE LINES OF THE
AMERICAN EXPRESS COMPANY

Then, instead of writing the amount on the money order, the clerk cut the "protective margin," a column of nine figures on the money order that depicted 5 cent denominations, to the proper sum. This basic design concept lasted into the twentieth century.

American Express explicitly competed with the federal postal system by catering to non-English speakers, and its immigrant customer base grew. In addition to sending money domestically, customers with international ties began to use American Express to send money orders abroad. Unfortunately for

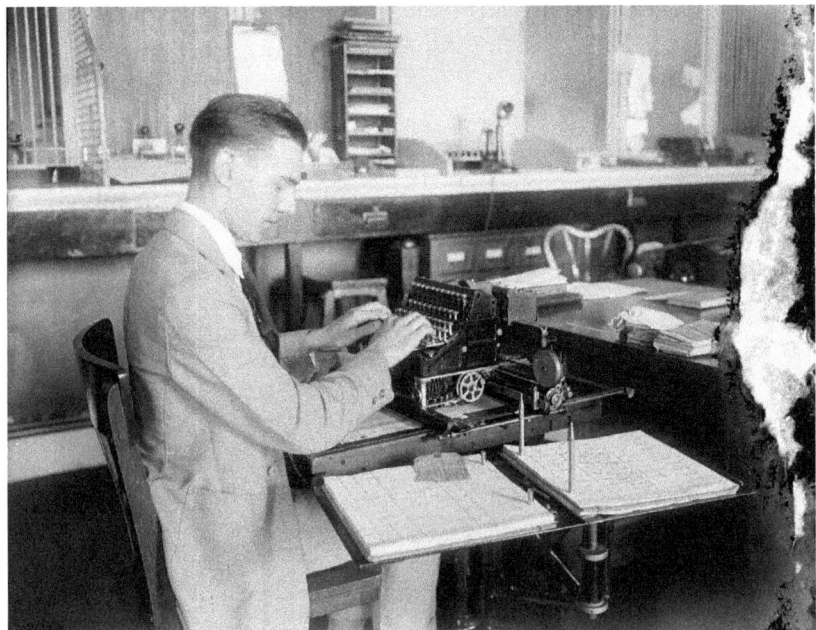

FIGURE 1.4: Clerk preparing a money order, early twentieth-century United States. Library of Congress Washington DC.

these early customers, American Express money orders could not, in the early years they were offered, be cashed abroad. American Express was aware that many money orders purchased by immigrants went uncashed, but it did not establish the necessary correspondent banking relationship until 1886, when it announced that Baring Brothers of London would handle payment of money orders in Europe. Because of the large number of immigrants to the United States from Ireland and Italy, American Express eventually developed an especially large network of correspondent banks in those countries. By the late 1880s, American Express was transacting millions of dollars in foreign money orders per month to both (Grossman 1987). Dollars mapped the territory of the United States, but American Express money orders were an early form of remittances and mapped a transnational territory of kinship and community.

In addition to money orders, which were marketed to the poor, the immigrant, and the illiterate, American Express soon offered a private payment technology for the elite. By the end of the 1880s, American Express developed a new form of paper value transfer: the traveler's check. According to company lore, company president J.C. Fargo took a long leave of absence to make the grand tour of Europe. At the time, international travelers, usually wealthy, carried a letter of credit from a leading bank in their home country. Letters of credit had existed since the Renaissance: they represented an amount of cash on deposit at the home bank that the carrier could draw upon at corresponding banks abroad. The identity of the carrier was verified by the signature on the letter. When Fargo returned from his trip, he complained that his letter of credit had been a huge inconvenience. It took a long time to be verified at each bank, it provided no guarantee on exchange rates, and, once he left major cities, it was of "no more use to me than so much wet wrapping paper" (in Grossman 1987: 89).

The new American Express Travelers Cheque—as the company originally styled the item, using the European spelling perhaps to promote a sense of old-world prestige—preserved one of the essential features of the letter of credit: the double signature. But unlike the letters of credit, which were a guarantee of a store of value to be drawn upon, the Travelers Cheques were more like money orders, issued in small denominations. Typically, travelers would purchase a book of them in varying amounts. Because exchange rates were fairly stable at the time, American Express listed rates it guaranteed to honor on the Travelers Cheque itself. Although Travelers Cheques were intended by the company to be used only by elite travelers, their success rested on the extensive network of European corresponding banks that American Express had developed through their trade in foreign remittances made by immigrants (Grossman 1987). Travelers Cheques, widely referred to as "blue paper money," had the additional benefit over cash of being replaceable if lost or stolen (Massengill 1999).

Although American Express charged fees for both its money order and Travelers Cheques products, these fees were not its primary source of revenue. Soon after beginning to offer money orders, in part because of the large number purchased by immigrants that went uncashed in the early years, American Express executives began to notice that the company always had a large surplus of cash on hand waiting to be redeemed. As long as that surplus (or "float," as it would come to be called) could be tracked and predicted, American Express could use it to fund investments. This combination of fees and float remains the fundamental business model of payment companies today.

By the time its express business came under federal regulation during World War I, American Express was a payments firm as much as a competitor to the Post Office, well on its way to becoming a modern financial powerhouse. Indeed, when World War I broke out, the company was stable enough in terms of finances, infrastructure, and reputation to be able to pay out money to customers in Europe. More so than traditional banks, more so than governments, it was able to provide at a time of crisis—or so the story went. Of course, its responsibilities were much smaller, and its mission clearer than banks' or governments', but American Express was widely lauded in the press, which portrayed it as a savior to wealthy Americans otherwise stranded abroad. At the same time, its technical innovations and business model presaged many changes in the technologies of money to come later in the twentieth century, when the systems that facilitated the movement of money were outcomes of an ongoing negotiation between public and private interests.

AUTOMATION AND COMPUTERIZATION

Automated check clearing

Another common way that businesses and other trusted account holders moved money during the twentieth century was the bank-issued paper check.[2] Like postal orders, paper checks are simply written instructions to debit the payer's account and credit the bearer's account for some specific amount. But unlike the postal system, the banking system in most countries is made up of many separate, independent, and often competing financial institutions. In countries like the United States, that system was also purposely fragmented so that no one bank could amass too much power. Thus it was possible for the payer's and bearer's accounts to be managed by different banks, which naturally required some cooperation: the banks had to agree on a set of rules by which checks were verified and processed, as well as a method for safely transferring funds between the institutions.

The process by which checks are routed between institutions so they can be verified and paid is known as "clearing." In theory, this should be a relatively simple process, but clearing checks in the early twentieth century was a complicated affair due to the patchwork of commercial laws in effect at the time. In order for a check to be cleared "at par," meaning the depositor received the full value of the check, the physical piece of paper had to be presented to the issuing bank by an agent of the depositing bank. If the check was simply mailed or delivered by third-party courier, the issuing bank could "discount" the check, meaning it would pay to the depositing bank the check's face value, less a "discount fee" that the issuing bank kept for its troubles.

Banks avoided these discounts by forming cooperative organizations within a given geographic area (known as "clearinghouses") or establishing relationships with large banks in other cities (known as "correspondent relationships"). The combination created a complex communication and transaction network through which checks could be cleared at par, even if they had to make several hops to get back to the issuing bank. Since competing banks in the same area often did not want to cooperate through a common clearinghouse, they would have to clear each other's checks by sending the checks through their correspondent network until the checks reached some common hub. Several sources recount extreme cases, such as a check traveling 4,500 miles over two weeks to get to an issuing bank that was only four miles away from the depositing bank, only to be returned along the same route due to insufficient funds (Klebaner 1974; Fernelius and Fettig 1992)!

MONEY AND ITS TECHNOLOGIES

These cases were no doubt atypical, but they became part of the justifications for major reforms of the US banking industry, which culminated in 1913 with the creation of the Federal Reserve System (typically shortened to "the Fed"). The Fed effectively created a new national correspondent network between all its member banks, with the regional Fed banks as hubs. All Fed members were required to maintain accounts with their regional Fed bank, so moving funds between banks was now as easy as debiting one institution's account and crediting another's.

But a significant part of the Fed's mandate was also to fix the way checks were cleared between institutions. Their solution was to create a new centralized clearinghouse for the entire nation, which started operations in 1915. This clearinghouse was free to all Fed members, and all checks were cleared at par, regardless of how the checks got to the clearinghouse. This created an expectation of universal par clearing, which would become a thorn in the side of debit card acceptance later in the century. Participation was low at first, but usage of the Fed's clearinghouse grew over the next few decades, creating a need for automation.

A clearinghouse must do four primary tasks: sum the checks submitted by a depositing bank; separate and group the checks by the issuing bank; sum the checks being sent to each issuing bank; and calculate how much each bank is owed or owes the clearinghouse. While volumes remain low, these tasks can be done manually with an army of clerks, but as volumes rise, some kind of automation becomes necessary to keep up. From 1945 to 1955, the volume of checks processed by the Fed each day rose from thirty-eight to sixty million,

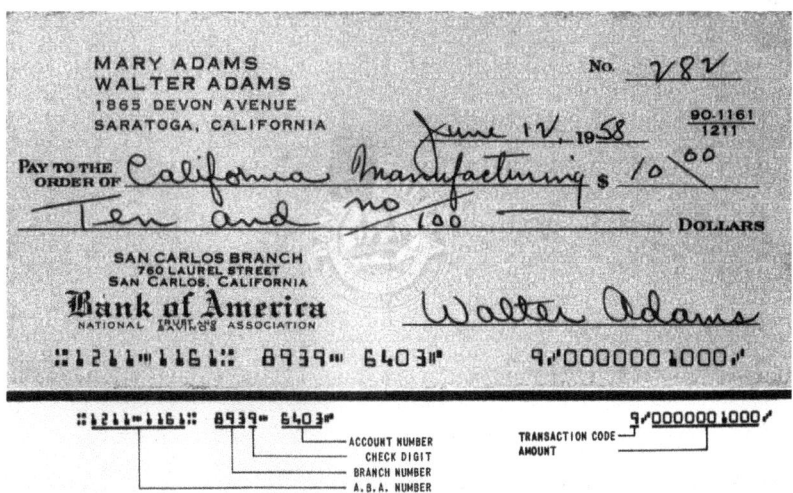

FIGURE 1.5: Early check demonstrating the use of MICR (magnetic ink character recognition). SRI International, Wikimedia Commons.

and the projected growth rate for the following decade was even higher. By mid-century, the Fed was pushing the limits of manual processing and desperately needed to automate the summing and sorting process. But automating this process required a machine that could "read" information inscribed on checks, especially the issuing and depositing banking numbers and the check amount.

A few mechanical solutions were developed to do this reading, such as the "Top Tab Key Sorter," but the US banking industry eventually settled on a much nimbler technique known as Magnetic Ink Character Recognition (MICR). Check issuers printed their bank routing and customer account numbers on the face of the check using magnetic ink. When the check was deposited, the depositing bank then added their routing number and the check amount. The clearinghouse could then use electro-mechanical sorters to read the magnetic ink, automatically summing and sorting the checks as they passed through. This enabled a far greater processing scale, which was necessary to keep up with the growing use of checks in the post-war era.

Computerized banking and dreams of a "cashless society"

Although the MICR standard supported the growing volume of paper checks, it was originally developed as part of a much more ambitious project to computerize banking operations and get rid of the paper entirely. In 1955, the Bank of America became the first bank in the United States to purchase a computer, and they hired SRI—the Stanford University-founded, Menlo Park-based research institute—to develop a software system to automate their demand deposit accounts, known affectionately as ERMA (an acronym for the more literal Electronic Recording Machine-Accounting).

Other banks quickly followed suit, provoking futurists to predict a "coming checkless/cashless society."[3] Once all of the banks adopted computers and connected them through telecommunications links, they reasoned, money could flow smoothly and safely around the nation via electronic transactions, eliminating the need for cumbersome paper instruments and mechanical sorting equipment. The Dynamic Analysis and Control Laboratory at MIT published a report in 1954 discussing the potential of such a system, and by the mid-1960s, several industry leaders, including Thomas J. Watson, Jr. of IBM, were predicting that, "In our lifetime we may see electronic transactions eliminate the need for cash" (Watson 1965: 13).

Although they might have been optimistic in their timelines, these proponents of the checkless/cashless society did spark a collective vision for a national, and eventually international, electronic funds transfer system (EFTS). In this vision, most (if not all) of the money supply would cease to have any physical representation in circulating tokens. "Money" would become numbers in computer-maintained accounts, and exchanging that money would be

FIGURE 1.6: Bank of America's Electronic Recording Machine-Accounting (ERMA) System. Courtesy of Bank of America Corporate Archives.

accomplished by transmitting standardized, secure electronic messages that instructed those computers to debit one account and credit another. With high-speed digital telecommunications connecting every home, business, and financial institution, money could flow almost instantly, anytime, anywhere.

CARDS, CLUBS, AND NETWORKS

Travel and entertainment

While bankers were automating deposit accounts and imagining a cashless society, a parallel effort was underway to promote the idea that paper currency and other older forms of everyday financial technology were becoming obsolete. Although commercial banks regularly extended credit to businesses, most consumers received their credit directly from the merchants selling them goods or services. As these merchants expanded their clientele and geographic reach, they began issuing their trusted customers cards or other tokens identifying their credit accounts. Western Union issued what is likely the first such card in 1914, and the major department store chains soon followed, eventually adopting the "Charga-Plate" system developed in 1928. These cards spread to the oil and airline industries in the 1920s and 1930s, providing a convenient payment mechanism for frequent travelers. Although these merchant-specific cards were handy, they were limited in scope, requiring consumers to open credit accounts with each business and carry a large stack of cards. In 1949, a new company formed that promised to unify all of these into one card that could be used at a wide array of merchants all over the nation. Its founders called it "The Diners' Club."

The nature of travel, especially in the United States and other Western countries, had changed since the end of the nineteenth century, when letters of credit were the coin of cross-border commerce. By the mid-twentieth century, rapid mobility became possible for more Americans as a result of innovations and infrastructural investments, both public and private, from personal automobile financing, rental cars, and motels to highway systems, commercial jet travel, and corporate business trips. For the first time, people moved faster and farther than their money could. From a consumer perspective, the US banking industry was still relatively fragmented. Banks were mostly small and local entities (Evans and Schmalensee 2005). Out-of-town checks were so slow

FIGURE 1.7: Comedian Marty Allen, 1960. Al Ravenna, New York World-Telegram & Sun Collection, United States Library of Congress.

to clear that many merchants refused to accept them, and it was difficult for a traveler to withdraw cash while away from home (Mann 2006). As one contemporary writer put it, "the traveler—the man who needed it the most—was creditless [. . .]. [U]nless he went around with pockets full of money, he was unlikely to find a friendly face in a strange town" (*Changing Times* 1952).

Diners Club, the first charge card company, sought to exploit this gap between the mobility of modern Americans and the relative stability of their money. Matty Simmons, the company's Executive Vice President, even wrote an "obituary" for cash in 1963: "Cash died [. . .] because it simply can't keep up with the fast-moving world. Cash simply hasn't become modern."[4] Cash, to Simmons, was insufficiently modern because it failed to efficiently interoperate with the networks of rapid physical and informational mobility that, at mid-century, were beginning to be assembled.

Most Diners Club cards were used for business entertainment and travel. Diners Club sought out corporate accounts in large part because they represented significantly less default liability than those of individuals. At the end of the pay period, Diners Club mailed a list of itemized receipts to the cardholder's office, effectively outsourcing the accounting of travel expense labor. This became particularly useful when, in the late 1950s, the IRS raised the standards of documentation for tax-deductible business entertainment expenses. The Diners Club statement was "in orderly contrast to the promiscuous scattering of bills" that other companies presented (Grutzner 1965). Such orderliness was the "perfect way to squelch the doubting Thomases at the Bureau of Internal Revenue" (Tucker 1951). The "cash-free and check-free society," along with the perfectly bureaucratized luxury it offered, had become as much a part of an idealized modern near-future as the jet pack (Bátiz-Lazo, Haigh and Stearns 2014). It was a novelty: There are reports of crowds gathering just to watch someone pay with a charge card (Nocera 2013). A book of traveler's checks had begun to seem as old-fashioned and cumbersome as a wad of dollar bills.

Although the terms are sometimes used interchangeably, the Diners Club card was not a "credit card" but a "charge card." Unlike later true credit cards, the Diners Club card was not tied to an account of revolving credit. It did not allow members to carry a balance and therefore carried no float to invest. Diners Club's revenue came from its annual membership fee, transaction fees charged to the merchants, and advertising in the magazine it sent to its members. These fees, borne by the merchant, reintroduced at scale the practice of non-par clearance of payments.

The Diners Club was, indeed, like a private club. The elimination of "vulgar cash" added a "pleasant, club-like feeling that comes from walking into a beanery and paying with a card instead of cash" (Sutton 1958). It marked its members as an elite group to whom "country club-style billing" was available for an expanding number of goods and services. Like Western Union, department stores and gas stations had offered regular, trusted customers lines of credit, which could be accessed using cards or metal Charga-Plates, but Diners Club allowed the same convenience everywhere the charge card was accepted. This feeling of regularity and trust was no longer limited to a particular building in a particular city, but spread out widely through the merchant network.[5] Once members became accustomed to using the card for business purposes, they often ordered additional accounts for personal use. In 1958, Diners Club started a "Women's Division" to cater to wives and the emergent class of professional women.[6] Although "putting it on the card" began for most as a business practice, soon it became a part of everyday life.

American Express and banks attempted to compete with Diners Club throughout the 1960s, but neither brought charge card products permanently to market until the end of the decade. American Express took over the high end of the market, using their nearly century-old reputation as a trusted purveyor of travelers' checks and other non bank financial services to offer universal charge cards to the elite (Grossman 1987).

It was not just market segmentation, however, that led to the decline of Diners Club. It was also the superior computing power of American Express, whose head of card operations had been in charge of data processing in the Air Force during World War II and understood that the computerization of accounts could make the company's card products more efficient and profitable (Grossman 1987). Similarly, the Bank of America had adapted its ERMA system to maintain cardholder accounts and process sales drafts. Although these systems were partial and slow, they were more sophisticated than Diners Club's system of old-fashioned paper accounting. Throughout most of the 1950s and 1960s, Diners Club relied on a system of paper accounting. Although the system was efficient, it would have been hard to scale. When Diners Club attempted to computerize in 1967, it was done, according to one executive, "in a state of confusion and ineptness of classical proportions," and this organizational chaos was blamed for their first year of net loss since 1951 (Simmons 1991: 103).

It seemed that Diners Club's management was not really interested in competing with bankers and private express companies to develop an efficient, computerized system of accounting. Instead, Alfred Bloomingdale, heir to the Bloomingdale department store fortune and then-president of Diners Club, preferred to take on flashier ventures, such as a chain of floating hotels, or "floatels," the most of ambitious of which was the *Queen Mary* cruise ship, which remains permanently docked in Long Beach, California (Unger 1968).

Bank-issued payment card networks

The "Travel and Entertainment" cards demonstrated that merchants were willing to accept a universal card with discounted transactions in exchange for more business and less credit risk. Several banks attempted to create similar programs in the late 1940s and early 1950s, but within a few years only a handful were still operating. Most banks were unable to build a critical mass of adopters because banking regulations at the time prohibited banks from operating across state lines, and many states restricted banks further to a small geographic area, or even to just one physical branch. Without a sufficient number of cardholders and merchants, the programs could not generate enough revenue to be profitable.

But there was one bank that had the resources, scale, and organizational culture to make it work: the Bank of America. The BofA (as it is typically abbreviated) operated in the populous and wealthy state of California, which allowed statewide branching, and it had a banking relationship with 60 percent of California's residents. With US$5 billion in assets, it was one of the largest banks in the world, so it could finance the development of large-scale infrastructure, as well as absorb the initial losses that nearly all payment card systems experienced. But it was also *culturally* predisposed to offer credit to middle-class consumers when other banks were not. The BofA was founded by the son of an Italian immigrant, who focused on serving everyday consumers, and it was the leader in consumer installment credit at the time. Automating the process using a card made perfect sense.[7]

As noted earlier, the BofA was an early adopter of computer and telecommunication technology, so they also had the technical expertise to create a computerized clearinghouse for their numerous branches. Payment card sales drafts are similar to checks and have to be cleared and processed in similar ways, but instead of encoding information using MICR, the BofA chose to create a multi-layer sales draft, with an IBM eighty-column punch card as the bottom layer. Transaction information was punched into the card when the draft was deposited, so processing could be done using computerized punch card readers and sorters.

The BofA launched their "BankAmericard" in 1958. Within a year, they put cards in the hands of two million account holders and enrolled more than 20,000 merchants to accept it. Fraud and credit losses were staggering at first, but the BofA eventually brought them under control, and by 1961 the system was generating a profit.

Other banks responded by creating their own credit card programs, and connecting them through a cooperative network known as "Interbank," which would eventually be rebranded as "Master Charge" and then "MasterCard." This prompted the BofA to license their BankAmericard to other banks across the nation, creating a parallel network that was still mostly controlled by the BofA. In 1970, the BankAmericard licensees wrested that control away from BofA, forming an independent cooperative network initially named "National BankAmericard Incorporated" and eventually rebranded as "VISA."

FIGURE 1.8: BankAmericard from 1974.

FIGURE 1.9: Rebranded VISA card from 1983. Author's personal collection.

Both of these cooperative credit card networks leveraged advances in computer and telecommunications technologies to build nationwide electronic authorization and clearing systems in the 1970s. By the 1980s, inexpensive point-of-sale terminals allowed merchants to "swipe" cards, capturing the card's information from the magnetic stripe, and submit transaction information over their existing telephone lines. Payment card transactions became entirely electronic: accounts were maintained digitally, and standardized electronic messages zipped between the various institutions.[8]

Although these credit card networks built electronic transaction systems that approximated the "cashless society" vision formulated in the 1960s, the banks did not consider them to be the proper infrastructure upon which to build a nationwide electronic funds transfer service (EFTS). Some of their reasons were technical: card transactions in the United States did not require a PIN and could originate in offline situations. But the more significant reasons were strategic and cultural. EFTS was a significant competitive weapon at a time when banks were highly regulated, so the large, technically savvy banks wanted to develop their own private systems and charge their competitors for access. The bank's EFTS plans were also controlled by those in charge of the bank's deposit accounts, and many of these bankers did not consider the unsecured consumer lending of the credit card programs to be "real banking." Thus, most banks formed separate, parallel cooperative networks to process ATM transactions, which they eventually extended to the merchant point-of-sale.[9]

In the 1990s, the ATM and payment card networks began to interconnect, and in some cases merge. As the technologies and practices of monetary policy and investment finance changed (see Beggs, this volume; Nersisyan and Wray, this volume), banks began issuing debit cards to consumers that could be used with either the online PIN-based ATM networks or the major payment card networks. By the turn of the century, the seamless flow of electronic transactions between networks in the United States, and similar contexts, made the distinctions between those networks murky at best in the minds of most consumers. This created an expectation that any kind of money should be instantly transferable, anytime, anywhere.

Elsewhere, the infrastructures for moving money remained comparatively fragmented. Cross-border payment remained a special challenge, addressed by banks through traditional correspondent-banking relationships or tackled by the contemporary descendants of private shipping companies like Western Union, now targeting growing remittance markets. Just as before, the tensions between private and public payment infrastructures reappeared in the spaces where people wanted their money to move faster and easier than the banking systems currently allowed.

THE VIRTUAL AND THE GLOBAL

Digital cash

With increasing immigration and the explosive growth of the Internet in the 1990s came a new spatialized market—not only global, but translocal—and new imaginations for how to move money within it. Utopian visions for a fully decentralized, peer-to-peer world were reflected in the dreams and business models of many entrepreneurs, before and since. Many of these businesspeople saw themselves as new pioneers endeavoring to, as Howard Rheingold put it, "homestead on the electronic frontier" (1993)—an ideology that was concentrated and became associated with California's Silicon Valley. But whereas American Express and other private express outposts had been a fixture at any new settlement on the frontier of the American West one hundred years before, no such simple system of value transfer was yet available for the wild new frontier of the Internet.

At a time when ownership of personal computers was rapidly increasing, it was costly and onerous for small businesses to accept card payments, and virtually impossible for individuals to do so in person—let alone over the Internet. In order to conduct commerce online, individuals and small businesses usually did what mail-order businesses long had: ask buyers to handwrite checks, mail them, and then wait several days for them to clear before the seller could ship the merchandise. In an age of email, this process seemed especially antiquated. A 1996 special section on "Electric Money" in the home computing magazine *Byte* described a variety of experimental approaches to digital payments, such as E-cash, digital checks, digital bank cards, stored-value smart cards, and electronic coupons and tokens. It concluded, however, by suggesting that the best strategy for understanding the future of money would be to "check back at the millennium" (Flohr 1996). Money, for ordinary people, did not scale to World Wide Web.

But for early Internet subcultures, money was an important social and political building block of a radical future they hoped technology would bring about. Some believed that financial privacy would be the most powerful form of self-determination in the coming information age. Others took it a step further and argued that "digital cash" not only enabled privacy but—untethered from governments and traditional banks—would be essential for a truly free global market society. In his "Crypto Anarchist Manifesto," co-founder of the Cypherpunk email list Tim May (1992) wrote that "crypto anarchy" was a "specter" "haunting the modern world." May predicted that, "Just as the technology of printing altered and reduced the power of medieval guilds and the social power structure, so too will cryptologic methods fundamentally alter the nature of corporations and of government interference in economic transactions."

Over the last decades of the twentieth century and the first decades of the twenty-first, cryptographers attempted to design and implement systems that would accomplish some of these goals. In 1985, cryptographer David Chaum (1985) wrote an influential paper describing an electronic cash system that promised to "make big brother obsolete" and later formed the basis for his company, DigiCash. Founded in 1990, DigiCash was an innovative payment system that could be incorporated into existing infrastructures and still protect privacy, but it was a commercial failure and filed for bankruptcy in 1998 (McCullagh 2001). Other attempts were more thought experiments than implementable technologies. In 1996, May described a cryptographic black market called BlackNet powered by a form of digital cash he called CryptoCredits. In 1998, computer scientist Wei Dai published a description of an anonymous, distributed electronic cash system which he called "bmoney." And in the late 1990s and early 2000s, Nick Szabo (2005) proposed "bit gold," a system in which computers "mined" for "scarce" digital commodity tokens. While none of these proposals achieved practical success, they animated the techno-economic imaginary of the Internet.

"World domination" or world liberation?

In 1999, Peter Thiel and Max Levichin founded PayPal, a technology company that allowed users to "beam" money between Palm Pilots (early "personal digital assistants" and forerunners of the smartphone). Their company would eventually be acquired by eBay in 2002, but initially they had nothing as mundane as online auctions in mind. What they imagined was nothing short of "world domination," according to *PayPal Wars*, a laudatory history of the company's founding by early employee Eric M. Jackson (2004). The PayPal vision included not just the tremendous wealth that came with "world domination," but also vast political and economic change. Like the crypto anarchists, PayPal's political project entailed the unfettered flow of monetary value.

Unlike the cypherpunks and crypto anarchists, however, who mostly aspired to social as well as economic libertarianism, Thiel was an extreme social conservative, if an idiosyncratic one.[10] He would go on to question the enfranchisement of women, write that he did not believe that "freedom and democracy are compatible," and become a major donor to first the Ron Paul and then Donald Trump presidential campaigns (Thiel 2009). The cypherpunks and crypto anarchists were largely technological counter-culturalists, but Thiel would argue that scientific "progress ended" when "the hippies took over the country" (2014).

And unlike the digital cash systems envisioned by the cypherpunks and crypto anarchists, PayPal was widely adopted. Today, it is one of the most ubiquitous peer-to-peer electronic payment systems and arguably one of the most successful technology companies to survive the "dot-com" boom of the late 1990s and early 2000s. Of course, PayPal alone has not achieved Thiel's political vision, but it has provided him with a tremendous amount of money with which to do so. Ironically, however, PayPal's success was only possible because it bypassed the card networks and fees associated with them by running settlement and clearance through the Automated Clearing House (ACH), a low-cost interbank network established in the 1970s and partially operated by the Federal Reserve. In its attempt to create a post-national economic imaginary, PayPal effectively created a private on-ramp to a semi-public infrastructure.

PayPal represents only the tip of the iceberg in today's rapidly diversifying payments industry. Following closely on the heels of the changes wrought by personal computing and e-commerce, the widespread adoption of mobile phones has led to a similar "revolution" in peer-to-peer payment and personal banking, especially in the global South, but increasingly in the United States and Europe, too (Nelms et al. 2017; see also Nelms and Guyer, this volume). Such experiments in new mobile applications, point-of-sale devices, and new back-end settlement and data-management systems recall the longer history of modern money's infrastructural dreams: for spatial ubiquity, temporal instantaneity, and digital disintermediation and dematerialization. These dreams have only intensified in the present moment.

CONCLUSION

The technologies of money linger. Though they may compete viciously for dominance of a particular market at a particular time, payment forms rarely disappear entirely. Nearly every mode of payment described in this chapter still exists, in one form or another. Cash, declared dead in 1963, continues to be the most widely used form of payment worldwide. People still send checks through the United States Postal Service. Private, high-security express firms still transport commodities and large amounts of cash. Money orders, gifts certificates, and other prepaid instruments have their purpose. Western Union still sends remittances all over the world, albeit using more recent communications technology than telegraphy. Similarly, Diners Club, now owned by Discover, is widely used in parts of the world where its brand still has cachet. VISA and the card networks are still the dominant payments processing system, and the ACH remains a crucial—and exceedingly reliable—part of the payments landscape, even as new government-led "faster payments" projects are pursued around the

FIGURE 1.10: Bitcoin ATMs in Hong Kong, Helsinki, and Seattle. Courtesy of *bertconcepts, Andrés Gómez García, and Charlene Mcbride* (Flikr.com).

FIGURE 1.10: *Continued*

world. PayPal is still the leader in peer-to-peer payments, both on eBay and off. The digital cash dream lives on in Bitcoin—at least for now (see Vint, this volume). It is currently common both to pay a friend for a round of drinks with the mobile phone app Venmo and to hear the once-familiar, now-uncanny sound of a modem dialing up and communicating with a network coming from an ATM at the back of a dive bar.

Attempts at dematerialization always wind up newly materialized. The "cashless society," long dreamed of but still not achieved, has left us with plastic cards, fragile cell phones, and industrialized server farms mining cryptographic tokens. If modernists dream of abstraction and minimalism in the service of speed and scale, in practice, modern money is marked only by material and spatiotemporal complexity. The technologies of money, like modernity (and whatever comes next), are palimpsest.

CHAPTER TWO

Money and its Ideas

Between Technocracy and Democracy

MICHAEL BEGGS

Money, John Maynard Keynes wrote at the beginning of his *Treatise on Money* (1930: 3–4), has two basic aspects. There is "money-of-account," in which prices and debts are expressed. Then there is "money itself"—what people use to pay the prices and settle the debts. For Keynes, money "is peculiarly a creation of the State" in the sense that the state manages the bridge between the two aspects, nominating the money-itself that settles payments denominated in money-of-account and thereby monopolizing the creation of legal tender.

But it is just as true to say that money in the modern era has created (and recreated) states, by throwing up problems of management with ramifications reaching the heart of modern politics. First, the *value* of a "money-of-account"—in terms of the currencies of other states and in terms of goods and services—could not be simply declared. That was determined on markets, by those who wrote the price lists and drew up the contracts. To the extent that policymakers wanted to influence these values, they had to act strategically within evolving economic systems and shifting political contexts that they did not design or control. At the beginning of our period, the once-stable anchor of the gold standard broke down. It left policymakers with no choice but to take responsibility for stability of the "money-of-account," but with no guarantee of success, pulled as they were in different directions by the rise of the labor movement and the extension of democracy, both at home and abroad. Second, much of what circulated as "money itself" was not state-issued currency, but privately issued bank deposits, acceptable because of confidence in their rapid convertibility into currency at par. Managing "money itself" entangled state agencies in a broader private financial system, which adapted in response to regulation.

In this chapter, I track both these problems as they played out over the century following World War I. In the process, I describe the emergence and evolution of ideas about money as they become embedded in institutionalized forms of expertise, even as that expertise becomes, at different points and in different ways, subjected to and channeled through the pressures of policy, politics, and social conflict. With the space available, it is inevitably a sketch, or a linked set of sketches. But there is something useful about a survey from a distance, which picks out points of interest that others have developed in detail, while linking them together so they put one another in a much wider context. Drawing on both primary and secondary source material, the chapter is divided into two parts, each discussing one of the two problems.

The first, "Standards," tracks the evolution of policy concern with the value of money—in terms of commodities and in terms of other currencies. The value of money turned out to be tied to many other aspects of economic life: wages and the labor market; trade and international capital flows; public spending and taxation; the banking system and financial markets. The quest for monetary stability therefore entangled the state in all these areas. The gold standard committed states to manage the value of their currencies with respect to one particular commodity. Any ill consequences could be treated as necessary conditions of "sound money." The ideological and practical breakdown of the gold standard left governments in something of a monetary void, discussed in the first section. In the second, I discuss Bretton Woods and the international monetary order it established: an attempt to combine the stability of the high gold standard with more flexibility. In the third section, I focus on the tension at the heart of post-World War II political economy between full employment and price stability. Finally, I trace the emergence of the late twentieth-century consensus around flexible exchange rates and inflation targets.

In the second half of the chapter, "Moneys," I turn to the management of "money itself." Modern money has a hierarchical structure: the "base" of state-issued currency supports a much larger volume of private bank-issued money. The central bank acts strategically within a complex, mostly private financial system. In the first section, I discuss how Keynes and Milton Friedman understood this in different ways, interpreting the problem of monetary management in the 1920s and 1930s differently. In the second section, I deal with the growth of a further layer in the monetary system after World War II, as financial institutions developed near-monies and money substitutes that challenged policy control. Third, I tackle the irony that a version of the quantity theory of money resurged even as money seemed harder than ever to pin down for purposes of quantification. Finally, I argue that the back-and-forth between financial regulation and innovation continues, as a fixture of contemporary capitalism.

Economics usually presents a confident face, presenting orthodoxies as laws of nature. But taking the perspective of a century, we see a succession of orthodoxies. The inflation-targeting central bankers of the 2000s have the status the "sound money" men of the gold standard once enjoyed, as the upright guardians of stability. But their version of "managed money" would have sounded dangerously radical in the 1920s, well beyond what reformers like Keynes were advocating. This chapter aims to explain that transition—not as one of ideas alone, but ideas in a context of social conflict. Monetary policy has been a focal point for monetary ideas, but policy is implemented by agents acting strategically within society, not laying down the law from above. Policymakers have been informed by the economic rationalities of their time, but they are also pushed and pulled by political forces from outside that frame. Politics too shaped the strategic environment of policy, and this fed back into the economic models at a fundamental level, determining what was a parameter to be taken as given and what a variable subject to policy control. The evolution of modern money is thus also the evolution of the modern state.

STANDARDS

Breaking away from the gold anchor

A footnote in Keynes' (1919) *Economic Consequences of the War* remarks on a blunder of the Belgian government. In the hopes of arriving at the Paris Peace Conference with a strong claim on German assets, it had undertaken to buy German marks from Belgians at the rate of 1.2 francs per mark. This was a very good offer, and getting better by the day. An estimated six thousand million smuggled mark-notes flooded into the Kingdom. At 1913 exchange rates, that would have amounted to around a quarter of the value of Belgium's total pre-war wealth. By 1918, the mark had lost almost half its pre-war value, but this was still an enormously valuable pile of paper. But the conference determined otherwise: Belgium's position in the creditor queue was behind that of the only one that mattered, the Reparation Commission itself. Reparations were reckoned in *gold*marks, shipping, territory, and coal, while Belgium was left holding paper whose market value had been shored up by its own demand. Within a few years, all the paper marks in Belgium would not buy a hot dinner in Berlin.

The value of currencies had long been secured by commodity anchors. To be "on the gold standard" meant two basic commitments (McKinnon 1993: 4). First, the state guaranteed convertibility between gold (or some foreign currency itself backed by gold) and the domestic currency at a fixed official rate. Second, residents should be able to import and export gold freely, whether for purposes of trade or capital movement. Meeting these promises meant that some branch of the state served as market-maker for its own currency, ready to exchange it for gold or foreign currency at the fixed rate. That depended on having reserves of gold or foreign exchange or being able to obtain them from abroad in a pinch. This kept a check on its issuance of domestic currency, while the fixed exchange rate anchored the prices of tradable goods directly.

In retrospect, the gold standard appears as a constraint on states: policy was subordinated to the need to maintain world money reserves, and this could demand high interest rates and budgetary restraint. Taking a longer view, commodity standards had incubated national currencies, helped organize the regulation of private bank-issued money, and made strategic monetary policy possible in the first place (Knafo 2006, 2013). Metallic backing had been necessary to sustain confidence in state-issued currency and bank money. In most countries of Europe and North America, the last half of the nineteenth century had seen an enormous expansion in both currency and bank money (Knafo 2006: 84–86; Friedman and Schwartz 1963: 684–685). Confidence in convertibility helped a mass of paper to grow relative to the metal base, even as international flows of value—ultimately settled in metal—also expanded. The institutions of the gold standard allowed for a relative autonomy of domestic circulation from international circulation, carving out domestic monetary spaces and eventually enabling domestic policy discretion (Knafo 2006: 90–91).

Expert opinion had been drifting away from the gold standard for years before the war. The standard's classic period, between 1870 and 1914, has also been called the "golden age of the quantity theory" of money (Laidler 1991). But the quantity theory was not at all the natural ideology of the gold standard. The quantity theory suggested that the institutions of the gold standard could have consequences for the money supply that would destabilize the price level and the economic system. It was a natural step from that conclusion to the idea that a rational monetary policy would and could be based on the quantity theory itself. Abandoning gold need not be a nihilistic embrace of monetary chaos, the reasoning went, but could mean a superior system of "managed money."

Political economists of the nineteenth century had been willing to admit that inconvertible paper currency could *in theory* be managed to be as stable, or even more stable, than metal-backed currency. As William Stanley Jevons put it, "there is plenty of evidence to prove that an inconvertible paper money, if carefully limited in quantity, can retain its full value." The problem in practice was "the great temptations which it offers to over issue and consequent depreciation" (Jevons 1898: 229–230). While the leading monetary economists of the early twentieth century—Marshall, Fisher, Wicksell, Hawtrey—saw the gold standard as theoretically inferior to a competently managed money supply, it was better than *in*competent or misguided management. It was *politically*, rather than economically, rational. So long as the gold standard was more or less stable, pressures for reform were weak. But all the while, reformers were making the case for managing the value of money in terms of a representative basket of commodities—such as the collection of goods and services purchased by the typical household. The pursuit of stability in terms of gold—a single, atypical commodity—could mean instability in the prices that mattered to households and firms. Whether this should be done by managing the money supply (Fisher) or the interest rate (Wicksell, later Keynes) was a secondary question.

But the old broke down long before the new was politically ready. War showed once again that the sacrosanct institutions of the gold standard could easily be tampered with given enough necessity. In most countries, the basic legal framework of the gold peg largely survived during the war itself (Moggridge 1989: 251). Governments hedged around it here and there with restrictions on imports or exports of gold, mandatory gold purchases, temporary suspensions of specie payments, and so on, and they arranged official lines of credit (especially flowing east across the Atlantic) to shore up reserves. Temporary suspensions in times of war were nothing new, but this time "temporary" dragged on. The Great War had decisively knocked out the patterns of trade and capital movement that had made the gold standard so stable before 1914: disrupting European trade, building the massive inter-Allied debt owed ultimately to the United States, and leaving uncertainty around the reparations that would be squeezed out of Germany. Emergency measures could not hold forever, and currencies fell decisively away from gold. Only the United States was in a strong enough external position to restore its dollar to full convertibility in 1919; other currencies broke into blocs that floated against one another.

Inflation was the domestic counterpart to depreciation. Keynes (1919: 220–221) attributed to Lenin the idea that "there is no subtler, no surer means of overturning the existing basis of society than to debauch the currency."[1] By the end of the war, "all the belligerent governments practised, from necessity or incompetence, what a Bolshevist might have done from design," and "even now, when the war is over, most of them continue out of weakness the same malpractices" (221). (As for the Bolsheviks themselves, the Soviet government reintroduced a gold-backed currency in 1922, and its State Bank and People's Commissariat of Finance became "the cautious conservative guardians of financial orthodoxy" (Nove 1976: 92).)

"Necessity or incompetence"?—that is the milliard mark question. Economic and political rationality often pulled policymakers in different directions and called for quite different kinds of "competence." For the technocrat, where political rationality diverged from the economic, it was regrettable irrationality.

But political rationality also had to navigate between the political expression of conflicting social forces. Economic strains fed political projects, movements, sometimes refusals or displaced cries of pain. Policymakers (and the experts who advised them) were caught at the intersection of the economic and the political, both real and constraining. Sometimes this involved managing political expectations to see the perceived limits of economic feasibility; other times projects of economic restructuring and institution-building aimed at changing those limits. Sometimes the economists adapted or replaced their models, as blind spots became evident and as the terrain itself changed. And from time to time, the economic and political smashed into one another like the proverbial irresistible force and immoveable object: nothing could budge and something would have to break.

The 1922–23 hyperinflations in central Europe dealt a blow to monetary reform by standing as an object lesson of how badly things could get out of hand. But it is hard to see them as cases of incompetence. The German inflation "did not happen because the Reichsbank's printing press had a faulty tachometer" (Webb 1989: v). It was a symptom of a ferocious distributional struggle in which all parties fought to defend their monetary claims over real income and wealth. It took place against the background of the French occupation of the Ruhr, food riots, strike waves, a communist uprising in Hamburg, and a fascist putsch in Munich (Tooze 2014: 441–452). Nobody wanted to lend to the German government, but pressures on the public purse were intense: reparations, reconstruction, and support for strikers in the Ruhr, even as the occupation hit the tax base (Kindleberger 1984: 318). Reparations obligations forced the government to purchase foreign currency on a grand

FIGURE 2.1: Piles of paper: banknotes fill a German bank basement during hyperinflation, 1923. Photo by Albert Harlingue/Roger Viollet/Getty Images.

scale, forcing down the mark and raising the cost of imports. Workers pushed to index their wages and firms raised prices to keep up their margins. Both public and private deficits were monetized, the latter through banking system accommodation of commercial bills (Burdekin and Burkett 1996: 82–85).

An inflationary spiral could be dampened either by persuading at least some of the combatants to moderate their claims—or by undermining their power to make them. After total exhaustion, the re-establishment of a stable German monetary system took more than an ingenious technical device: it depended on a massive international loan under the Dawes Plan. The ingenious device itself—the Rentenmark, backed by land mortgages rather than gold—involved a charge on landholders that "was not very different from a capital levy which the Reichstag had continuously rejected" (Kindleberger 1984: 327).

The hyperinflations and stabilizations of the early 1920s were only the most dramatic, concentrated episodes of monetary tensions developing everywhere. The general rule of the early 1920s was deflation rather than inflation, as governments sought to stabilize their monetary systems and return to the gold standard. According to Tooze,

> the deflationary wave driven forward by America from the spring of 1920 was the true key to the "world-wide Thermidor" of the 1920s, the main driver of the restoration of order, both domestically and internationally [. . .] to this day probably the most underrated event in twentieth century history.
> —Tooze 2014: 354

Calling for wage restraint and budgetary austerity, it pitted governments against rising labor movements and popular demands on government budgets, already stretched taut by the network of wartime credit.

The discipline of the gold anchor on both the claims of labor and the public finances was a large part of its attraction to conservatives and liberals alike. The gold standard was not so much an external imposition on national governments as a constraint chosen by some domestic forces to bolster their economic defenses against others. The hyperinflations stood as a warning of what could happen if money were cut loose, and so the return to gold could still win widespread support.

In the *Tract on Monetary Reform*, Keynes (1923) argued that policy should aim to stabilize the internal price level rather than the exchange rate. The prewar gold standard had not involved any great tension between the two goals mainly because of a fortunate balance of international flows, which the war had permanently knocked away. Keynes' position was by no means radical. He did not advocate floating exchange rates but only more flexibility, and he thought that if governments kept the price level steady, exchange rate stability would look after itself. Skidelsky (1992: 206) suggests that Keynes really wanted the gold standard to remain as a kind of "constitutional monarch." But the reaction to the book showed widespread worry about admitting democracy into the monetary realm. A review defended a gold anchor on the basis that "it prevents politicians from resorting easily to the manufacture of money" (quoted in Skidelsky 1992: 161), and others made similar points. Behind all this were deeper concerns around just what *kind* of human agency would be exercising their judgment, and who they answered to. The *Tract* had appeared days after the United Kingdom's hung election in December 1923, and days before the Labour Party formed its first government. Keynes' friend Bob Brand wrote, "Almost thou persuadest me [. . .] But I don't know what things will look like after a year or two [of Labour government]" (quoted in Skidelsky 1992: 161). Whatever the flaws of the gold standard, at least it seemed "knave-proof" (Tooze 2014: 465).

Countries stabilized their prices and international balances and returned to the gold standard one by one across the 1920s—but by the time the stragglers returned, "the reconstructed system had started to disintegrate" (Moggridge 1989: 258). The countries with the worst inflation were some of the first to return, using the anchor to restore confidence. France had great trouble stabilizing but eventually returned at a much lower exchange rate than it had before the war and subsequently boomed. Britain's sterling, on the other hand, was restored at its pre-war par. This demanded a deeply painful deflation beforehand, and the pound's subsequent overvaluation kept the screws tight. Ultimately, sterling, erstwhile global currency, would be the pivot point of the system's collapse.

In 1929, economist Henry Clay surveyed the transformation that had taken place in wage-setting since 1910. Trade unions had grown spectacularly—though declined from a 1920 peak—and along with them the proportion of workers covered by collective agreements. At least as important was the expansion since the war of wage regulation and official centralized bargaining between representatives of the workers, the employers, and the "general public." Clay reckoned that more than half of employees were covered by some form of collective bargaining, and since such bargains tended to set norms which spread more widely, "there are few important gaps left in the provision for the settlement of wages by collective bargaining in Great Britain" (Clay 1929: 323–324). The effect of market forces on wages had always been channeled and moderated by custom, but now the whole process of wage-setting had been "constitutionalized," further insulated from market forces.

This system was now grinding up against gold. Years of deflation had been required to reach and sustain the restoration of sterling to pre-war gold parity. Prices continued to decline, while money wages for the most part held up, supported by the bargaining system. For Clay, the message was clear: people's ideas about "'fair' and 'living' wages" and "pseudo-principles such as the sanctity of pre-war *real* wages" had little to do with the wages at which industry could profitably employ the workforce. Something had to give.

The politicization and bureaucratization of the labor market was not limited to Britain but was a general trend across the global North (Bayoumi and Eichengreen 1996). Gordon (1982: 40) argues that money-wages were more rigid in the United States than in Britain in this period, despite being less unionized, due to more legalistic labor relations. At the same time, rising unemployment put greater pressure on government budgets and made tight money more uncomfortable. After the Great War, governments were "rendered more susceptible" to political pressures against the gold anchor "by the extension of the franchise, the development of parliamentary parties, and the growth of social spending" (Eichengreen 2008: 44). Once Britain succumbed and left gold in 1931, it fed a chain reaction that completely ended the system by 1937. There were many factors at play, but it was the fact that it was now harder to place the burden of adjustment on wages and maintain consent for austerity that made the system unsustainable. Once investors lost confidence in the absolute solidity of a government's commitment to gold, capital ebbed abroad, making the commitment impossible to sustain.

Nowhere in the world was left untouched. Governments at the center of the world monetary system could negotiate with one another; smaller and poorer countries had to ride out the storm, defensively. Commodity exporters were hit hard before the onset of the Depression: most of the big countries of Latin America saw the dollar value of their exports fall by around two-thirds between 1928 and 1932; Chile's fell by seven-eighths. "Money doctors" flocked from Northern central banks and public services, bringing prescriptions for the hard medicine of austerity. Southern countries desperately needed international loans to tide them over, while the United Kingdom and the United States jockeyed to secure members in the rival currency blocs now developing. As the center itself began to crumble, the promised loans went with them, and Latin America turned away from the money doctors, to devaluation, foreign exchange controls, and debt defaults (de Abreu 2006: 105–109).

"A balance of hopes and desires"

In 1955, John Hicks looked back at Henry Clay's paper. It had been, thought Hicks, "a substantially correct analysis." But "a tide of events, which set in almost as he spoke, was to bring about a great transformation" (Hicks 1955: 389). Clay, Hicks, and many other economists had believed that "the 'social' wage-structure could stand up to a certain amount of unemployment," but "there must [. . .] be a limit beyond which it must give" (Hicks 1955: 390).

> That is what Clay expected to happen; but, as we know, it is not what did happen. Unemployment did increase, as he expected; but though the

wage-structure yielded a little, on the whole it did not give way. What did give was another link in the chain—the Gold Standard.

—Hicks 1955: 391

Now, Hicks declared, "it is hardly an exaggeration to say that instead of being on a Gold Standard, we are on a Labour Standard" (391).

Hicks' vision of a "labour standard," with exchange rates adjusting to national wage and price levels rather than the other way around, now looks out of historical place. In the mid-1950s, the sterling and European devaluations of 1949 were a recent memory, and it may have seemed that the exchange rate adjustment allowed for in the Bretton Woods Agreement would not be uncommon. In fact, exchange rates were remarkably rigid (McKinnon 1993: 15), at least among developed countries. France devalued in 1957, 1958, and 1969; Britain devalued in 1967; West Germany revalued in 1961 and 1969. Each adjustment was small. The devaluations were not treated as alternatives to domestic disinflation but were accompanied by stern restraint intended to fend off further devaluation. In other episodes, policy pursued domestic disinflation to defend the exchange rate: for example, in Japan from the mid-1950s to early 1960s, Australia in the 1950s, and the United Kingdom in the early 1960s (de Vries 1987: 27–53; Beggs 2015: 31–71).

The norm from 1945 to the 1970s was to anchor currencies to the US dollar (perhaps via an intermediary currency like sterling), itself officially pegged to gold at US$35 per ounce. Bretton Woods was, it seemed to some, a restoration of the gold standard. In 1946, an Australian Labor cabinet minister campaigned against signing up to the Agreement as worse than the gold standard, since it constrained governments from unilaterally devaluing:

the Agreement [. . .] quite blatantly sets up controls which will reduce the smaller nations to vassal States [. . .] will undermine and destroy the democratic institutions of this country—in fact as effectually as ever the Fascist forces could have done—pervert and paganise our Christian ideals; and will undoubtedly present a new menace, endangering world peace [. . .].

—Eddie Ward, radio address, March 27, 1946,
quoted in Crisp 1961: 19

Hyperbole aside, the labor movement was right to fear that the fixed exchange rate would clash with the ambition of full employment. The British plan for a postwar international monetary regime, drafted by Keynes, had called for "the least possible interference with internal national policies" (Keynes 1969 [1943]: 19)—but what did that mean? In an interdependent world, one government's decisions affected conditions elsewhere. A devaluation meant revaluation for others. The point of an international monetary agreement was to establish new

FIGURE 2.2: US Treasury Secretary Henry Morgenthau, Jr. and British economist John Maynard Keynes at Bretton Woods, July 1944. Photo by Alfred Eisenstaedt/Time/Getty Images.

"rules of the game" that would make it positive sum again. Governments had to be constrained in some ways to open up other possibilities. But the pursuit of positive freedom required some agreement about what it was for.

The two agenda-setters at Bretton Woods came with different expectations. Britain anticipated balance-of-payments deficits, the United States surpluses. "The British wanted a scheme which would enable them to borrow without strings; the American one which would lend with strings" (Skidelsky 2000: 182). In both countries, public opinion ran heavily in favor of "full employment," but this was embedded more strongly in a political consensus in Britain. In 1944, the Conservative-dominated government released a White Paper charting a basically Keynesian plan for "the maintenance of a high and stable level of employment after the war," which all parties backed in 1945. In the United States, fiscal conservatism was stronger, and the Full Employment Bill of 1944 met a suspicious House of Representatives and was watered down into the Employment Act of 1945, which made no specific promise for any measure promoting employment (Bleaney 1985: 84–90).

The gold standard had placed the burden of adjustment on deficit countries: they faced a depletion of reserves, while there was nothing to stop surplus countries from piling them up. Keynes' original plan for the postwar international monetary regime involved penalties for countries with persistent balance-of-payments surpluses. That would give their governments further incentive to bolster demand, some of which would spill out into imports from the rest of the world. In the United States, such devices were seen as unacceptable interference with national policy. The Keynesian argument was that the national policy of deficit countries was *economically* constrained, and encouraging surplus countries to expand would loosen that constraint.

The penalty on surpluses did not survive negotiations, but the Bretton Woods compromise still mitigated the balance-of-payments constraint in three ways. It set up the International Monetary Fund to provide a backup reservoir or reserves, which members could draw upon to tide themselves over through a temporary international payments shortfall. It allowed governments to maintain capital controls indefinitely, isolating the balance of payments from unpredictable short-term capital flows. Finally, it allowed for exchange rate adjustment in conditions of "fundamental disequilibrium"—rarely used in practice and accompanied by International Monetary Fund supervision, which meant it was no alternative to disinflationary policy.

As with the gold standard, an exchange rate peg could last only as long as official reserves. A persistent international payments deficit meant that foreign reserves were flowing out of the country, pushing a government to restrain demand to staunch the flow in the short term, and restrain wages and prices to restore balance over the longer term. Policymakers had to include "external balance" among their policy objectives, and this could come into conflict with a commitment to full employment. The balance of payments that mattered was a "balance of hopes and desires," as Fritz Machlup put it in 1950: there was no absolute "dollar shortage," but only a shortage relative to "the extent to which [domestic] hopes are fulfilled and targets attained" (Machlup 1950: 46, 60). After the war, "hopes and desires" ran high.

The value of money was thus a nexus of tensions between the various goals of policy. Or rather, the *values* of money, because what mattered was the relationship between the value of a country's money in terms of other currencies—the exchange rate—and its value in terms of commodities—the price level. Domestic wages and prices had some independence from those abroad—but only some. Economists developed analyses of a potential conflict between "external balance" and "internal balance" (Meade 1951; Swan 1960, 1963). Given (1) the state of demand abroad, (2) world market prices for a country's imports and exports, and (3) domestic wages and other costs, the level of domestic demand consistent with full employment might be different than the level consistent with international payments balance. A persistent balance-of-payments deficit could force a government into macroeconomic restraint, and disturbances in commodities prices could undermine "internal balance."[2]

It might seem that more exchange rate flexibility could have fixed the problems: at a stroke, a currency adjustment could bring domestic cost structures in line with tradeables prices. Certainly, a number of economists argued the case, as did labor. But it was not so easy. If trade was relatively insensitive to a change in relative prices, depreciation would make a deficit worse in the short term: residents would spend more on foreign goods despite their higher prices. Adjustment would take time, but in the meantime higher import prices and a shift of demand towards domestic goods could feed inflation. That would raise domestic costs relative to tradeables prices all over again and undermine the aim of the devaluation.[3] This is why devaluations, when they happened, were not an alternative to austerity: governments still had to keep policy tight to ensure stability at the lower exchange rate.

Full employment and price stability: "manifestly unsound"?

In a famous 1943 paper on "the political aspects of full employment," Polish economist Michal Kalecki predicted that full employment would prove unstable in a capitalist economy. The problems (again) would be political. High demand would be good for profits on the face of it, and if it boosted wages, most firms had the pricing power to deal with that. The problem was that full employment would mean

> "the sack" would cease to play its role as a disciplinary measure. The social position of the boss would be undermined and the self-assurance and class consciousness of the working class would grow [. . .].
> —Kalecki 1943: 326

So captains of industry would make common cause with rentiers threatened by inflation, "and they would probably find more than one economist to declare that the situation was manifestly unsound" (Kalecki 1943: 330). This has often been seen as a prophecy of Milton Friedman and the monetarist turn of the 1970s—but in fact there were already many such economists around at the time Kalecki wrote. Their main argument was that full employment was bound to lead to an erosion of the value of money. For example, Henry Simons—a mentor to Friedman—made the argument in his testimony opposing the Full Employment Bill in 1945 (Stein 1969: 199).

It would take at least thirty years for this view to win—and it took economic crisis to transform the politics of price stability and employment: the stagflation (combined high inflation and unemployment) of the 1970s. Much mythology has grown up around the relationship between policy and stagflation. It later became common to see stagflation as a deep anomaly for Keynesian economics and the inevitable outcome of Keynesian policy. The story goes that Keynesians believed in a stable trade-off between unemployment and inflation—the "Phillips curve," after A.W. Phillips' 1958 paper tracing an inverse relationship between wage inflation and unemployment over a century of British data. Treating the empirical regularity as a policy choice menu, policymakers decided they could accept a higher rate of inflation as the price of fuller employment. They allowed monetary policy to become loose and ultimately lost control of an inflationary process. Friedman (1968) spotted a flaw in the reasoning: once people learned to anticipate inflation, they would adjust their behavior. There was a "natural" rate of unemployment reflecting the intersection of supply and demand for labor if all market participants correctly assess "real" wages and relative prices. Lower rates could be achieved only temporarily, while people underestimated inflation.

In fact, as Forder (2014) has shown in an exhaustive review of the literature of the 1950s and 1960s, it is not the case that policymakers tried to exploit a stable "trade-off" between unemployment and inflation. The notion that, *other things being equal*, lower unemployment would probably put upward pressure on money-wages, and therefore prices, was not new. But other things would rarely be equal: labor market institutions, union organization and militancy, employer strategies, the state of competition—all these things would affect the relationship, they would change over time, and they might be the object of policy. Far from adding "the missing equation" to Keynesian economics, Phillips' (1958) research suggesting the relationship between unemployment and money-wage change had been stable in Britain since 1861 was met with general suspicion, since it suggested that "from the invention of the bicycle to the flight of the Sputnik, wage bargaining remained unchanged" (Forder 2014: 22). In the 1950s, economists already saw inflation as susceptible to momentum, as workers sought to recover living standards eroded by past inflation and firms sought to maintain their profit margins. This was important in explaining the novel so-called "creeping inflation" of the 1950s, whereby prices kept rising even through recessions (Beggs 2015: 87).

That meant policymakers were wary of "exploiting a trade-off," since they knew well before the late 1960s that inflation could feed on itself. There was a tension between full employment and price stability, to be sure. For conservatives like Simons, that was reason enough not to pursue full employment. For social democrats, it was not a reason to sacrifice price stability—which would sooner or later lead to balance-of-payments problems—but to supplement demand management with other measures to manage wage and price growth. Dutch theorist of economic policy Jan Tinbergen (1966: 84) argued that "wage rates have to be a deliberate instrument of economic policy if employment targets and monetary equilibrium are to be pursued at the same time."

No government really did control wage setting. Even in Australia, with an official system of centralized wage bargaining, policymakers were unable to wield it as an instrument. It was judicial in nature, and while macroeconomic arguments increasingly made their way into the arguments of those represented—unions, firms, and government—they were often trumped by other principles. Even when the tribunals were persuaded to restrain wages in the name of price stability, the pressure of demand out on the market pulled actual wages above court-set minima. Official awards were forced to catch up or risk further loss of control (Beggs 2015: 94–101).[4]

Nevertheless, a number of countries enjoyed genuine full employment (unemployment at 2–3 percent or lower) until the 1970s, without runaway inflation: Australia, Britain, France, Japan, Sweden, West Germany. This gives the lie to the idea that policy foolishly held the unemployment rate below the "natural rate." Indeed, early estimates of the "natural rate" in the 1970s put it at around the rates that had been sustained in the previous two decades—for example, in Australia between 1.7 and 2.3 percent (Beggs 2015: 192–97). Only later in the 1970s did estimates of the natural rate (or, as it came to be known more literally but awkwardly, the "non-accelerating inflation rate of unemployment," or NAIRU) rise, along with actual unemployment.[5]

Friedman himself did not consider the "natural rate of unemployment" to be truly *natural*: "many of the market characteristics that determine its level are man-made and policy-made" (Friedman 1968: 9). He suggested minimum wages, various labor laws, and the strength of unions as factors that would raise the "natural rate." But those countries with very low unemployment during the post-war long boom often had highly regulated labor markets and strong unions, and they had worse outcomes under "deregulated" labor markets in later decades. That labor productivity growth was relatively rapid in the 1950s and 1960s meant that real wage growth could satisfy the aspirations of labor without eating into profitability. This golden weather came to an end with declining productivity growth and the oil (and broader commodity price) shocks of the 1970s. A rise in labor militancy in Europe pre-dated stagflation and elsewhere followed it, as workers defended their incomes. In either case, restoring price stability required smashing organized labor with chronic unemployment. Gordon's (1997: 30) analysis of the "time-varying NAIRU" notes that it fell back in the 1990s, "a time of labour peace, relatively weak unions, a relatively low minimum wage and a slight decline in labour's income share."

The turn to sustained monetary restraint in the late 1970s was not responsible for the end of the long boom or the rise in unemployment—both came before the policy shift. But the concept of the "non-accelerating inflation rate of unemployment" did serve to lower expectations about what macroeconomic policy could do. The goal of "full employment" was rolled back, seen as incompatible with price stability. The labor movement and extension of

FIGURE 2.3: Hospital workers on strike in New York, November 1973: a 7.5 percent wage increase, agreed to between the union and management, was held back by the Federal Cost of Living Council for being "inflationary." Photo by Bettmann/Getty Images.

democracy had broken the gold standard and forced a revision of aims with respect to price stability, which was now firmly understood as "low and stable inflation," rather than *no* inflation. But eventually the defense of this reduced sense of price stability clashed with the forces of labor—and won.

Managed money

Keynes had argued that the gold standard was not natural but already "managed money," involving an ensemble of policy practices to anchor the value of circulating money to the value of gold (Keynes 1930: 8). "Managed money" had evolved without its architects being entirely conscious of it—but by the 1920s it was clear that the anchor was a choice. Keynes discussed alternative pegs for the value of money: other exchange rates, other commodities, and even "some composite representative commodity" (Keynes 1930: 22). The value of money could, in other words, be pegged to a representative basket of commodities. But Keynes had no premonition of a moving target—that policy would come to target a rate of inflation rather than a price level.

There was no indication of this in the formal design of Bretton Woods. Governments still pegged their currencies to the American dollar (directly or via another currency like sterling), which the United States committed to convert into gold at a fixed rate. In retrospect, though, Bretton Woods was the turning point. For at least a century and a half, price levels had fluctuated around a stable point. Inflations had been followed by deflations. After World War II, prices kept rising, sometimes rapidly, sometimes slowly (Shaikh 2016: 244–245). Fixed exchange rates meant balance-of-payments problems for a country whose prices were rising faster than those abroad. But dollar prices themselves were slowly inflating, and as the United States itself shifted into international deficit, it expanded the world's stock of reserves. If it had not, the external discipline on other countries would have been tighter. The dollar's gold anchor was fictional well before Nixon suspended convertibility in 1971. It depended on the cooperation of foreign governments in not testing their right to convert dollars to gold—cooperation France repeatedly threatened to end.

FIGURE 2.4: The gold anchor becomes a curiosity: Irina Posner, CBS News producer, in the US Federal Reserve Bank in New York, December 1965, with bullion reclaimed by France. Photo by CBS via Getty Images.

The break-up of Bretton Woods and the shift to flexible and floating exchange rates did not free governments to go their own way. Hicks' "labour standard" never eventuated. By the 1970s, capital was mobile again on a grand scale. Policy was under continual market judgment. It proved difficult to maintain a middle ground between a fixed exchange rate and a float: flexible pegs were easily defeated once speculators decided that the current rate was unsustainable. Governments feared an inflationary spiral, with inflation sparking currency depreciation, and depreciation feeding further inflation (Beggs 2015: 165–174).

Some countries still committed to a fixed exchange rate. Within Europe, stabilization under fixed rates was a prerequisite for the creation of the euro. In much of the developing world, currency pegs remained common. Devaluations had not been uncommon in the South under Bretton Woods—sometimes under International Monetary Fund supervision, sometimes not. Some countries, especially in Latin America, had repeatedly devalued in the midst of chronic domestic inflationary spirals—Argentina, Chile, and Uruguay had inflation rates well into double digits in the 1960s, flaring into triple digits in the 1970s without quite going over the edge into hyperinflation. Now, as the major currencies began to float, most developing countries recommitted to currency pegs—85 percent as of 1979 (Edwards and Santaella 1992).

There were two reasons. These countries depended on foreign investment. A fixed exchange rate reassured investors that their placements would not lose value through currency depreciation. When borrowing took place in foreign currency, devaluation would not relieve the debt burden in real terms anyway. In the 1970s, developing countries had easy access to international finance. The oil price shocks meant enormous windfalls for the governments of oil-producing companies. Not only did "petrodollars" finance domestic investment, but they were recycled through Western banks and borrowed in great quantity by firms and governments in other developing countries. Investment continued to boom in Latin America and Southeast Asia even as it fell back in the North. Between 1975 and 1982, the total debt of less developed countries jumped from US$160 billion to US$540 billion (Armstrong, Glyn, and Harrison 1991: 284–294).

Secondly, the discipline of a currency peg was often welcomed by technocrats and conservative forces. Currency pegs were critical to the stabilization programs with which various Latin American governments tried to hold back inflation between the 1970s and 1990s. An overvalued exchange rate held import prices down and set hard limits on macroeconomic policy. But these programs repeatedly failed as intractable distributional conflict collided with international monetary disorder. The real income squeeze was intensified from the end of the 1970s, when tight monetary policy in the global North drove interest rates sharply upward and it suddenly became much tougher to service the debt. Recession in the North and a reversal of commodity prices savaged export earnings. Governments bailed out financial capital even as unemployment climbed. Price and wage freezes were desperate attempts to repress the inflationary consequences of attempts to defend real claims over a shrinking pie (Burkett and Burdekin 1996: 175–201).

In such circumstances, exchange rate pegs were unstable, dependent on the continued confidence of mobile capital to bridge the gap in the balance of payments. As soon as that confidence was shaken, capital took flight, and governments could no longer hold the exchange rate. That would intensify inflationary pressures and increase the debt burden in terms of domestic currency. Where stabilization was relatively successful, as in Chile, it was at the hands of a repressive military government, and at deep costs to workers: real wages were almost a fifth lower in 1983 than in 1969, and unemployment was above 20 percent. Burkett and Burdekin (1996: 193–194) conclude that "exchange-rate pegging—in an environment of conflicting domestic and external claims—must eventually lead to crisis."

By 1990, the proportion of developing countries maintaining a fixed exchange rate had fallen to 69 percent (Edwards and Santaella 1992: 1), and this figure continued to decline. By the 2000s, only a handful of countries maintained strictly fixed exchange rates. More, though, managed their exchange rate in more or less flexible ways. In the rapidly growing countries of East Asia especially, central banks intervened to keep their currencies from rising too high in pursuit of export-led growth strategies. The region was much less affected by the commodity price reversal in the 1980s and pulled away from Latin America. A financial crisis in the late 1990s showed the same vulnerability to mobile capital and currency speculation. The setback proved temporary and led to a shift in strategies to defend the currencies with capital controls and by accumulating enormous foreign currency reserves.

In the 2000s, some spoke of a "revived Bretton Woods system," with different parts of the world pursuing complementary strategies, even without a formal agreement (Dooley, Folkert-Landau, and Garber 2003). The United States, Europe, and Latin America mostly floated their currencies, while East Asian countries intervened to hold theirs down. The latter ran large payments balances with the United States especially, exporting much more than they imported and building up dollar stockpiles. The floaters took the view that if policy kept domestic prices stable, exchange rates would look after themselves. The others focused on export competitiveness—but this depended on domestic discipline to keep the desired exchange rates credible and to build up the reserves to defend them when necessary. *Both* strategies involved a commitment to stern monetary management and domestic price stability.

MONEYS

The hierarchy of money

If, after the collapse of Bretton Woods, a nation's currency was no longer anchored to gold or a foreign currency, that made it fiat money, issued by the state and backed by trust. But most of what actually circulated as money was not officially issued currency, but the privately issued liabilities of commercial banks. State-issued currency had long occupied a middle level in a monetary hierarchy, and it was a small (and shrinking) proportion of circulating money.

Even in the early twentieth century, many economists had not considered bank deposits to be fully fledged money (Laidler 1991: 124). Rather, they were devices for economizing on money-proper. Marshall and Wicksell, both at the forefront of early neoclassical monetary theory, had reserved the term "money" for coins and notes. But this became awkward. Irving Fisher's version of the quantity theory treated bank deposits unambiguously as part of the money supply, rather than as a determinant of its velocity in circulation. By the 1920s, this was the norm.

A nation's money supply had a hierarchical structure (Mehrling 2013). At the beginning of our period, at the top was gold itself or another currency. The next level was the currency issued by the state: cash and the reserves banks held with the central bank. The third level was made up of the deposit liabilities of commercial banks. The "moneyness" of money at each level depended on its convertibility to the money of the higher level. That depended upon the issuing institution's ability to "make the market" in its own liability: to keep its promise to exchange it for the higher–level money at par. The twentieth century saw national currencies finally develop as unambiguous top-tier money in their own right. The promise of convertibility into gold or foreign exchange at a fixed rate was no longer essential to a currency's acceptability.

That left the relationship between bank money and currency. From most people's perspective, a dollar was a dollar, or a pound a pound, whether it was held in the wallet or the bank. For some transactions, cash was more acceptable or convenient, for others bank-money—and the line would shift with the advent of debit and credit cards. These forms of money were unified by being denominated in the same unit of account and by being mutually convertible: you could deposit and withdraw cash, and you could make payments between deposits at different banks. That convertibility depended on banks' ability to meet their promises. Banks needed to hold only enough reserves of the higher-level money to meet net outflows within the bounds of reasonable possibility—so a much larger quantity of bank-money could be supported on a given base of "high-powered money." States shored up its convertibility, often by forcing banks to keep above a certain reserve–deposit ratio and by stepping in to lend banks reserves as a "last resort."

MONEY AND ITS IDEAS 73

This complicated any stabilization policy built on the quantity theory. Even if the central bank controlled the supply of base money, transmission to the broader money supply ran through bank balance sheets. In the *Treatise*, Keynes (1930: II, 53) pointed to 1920s data suggesting that banks' reserve–deposit ratio was usually fairly stable "at any given time," though it would shift over longer periods. The ratio was steady around 9–9.5 percent in both the United States, where there was a regulatory reserve minimum, and in the United Kingdom, where this was convention. In retrospect, though, Keynes spoke too soon. In the United States, hundreds of bank closures in the early 1930s depleted the country's stock of deposits and left banks cautious. The reserve–deposit ratio had risen to more than 30 percent by 1940 (Friedman and Schwartz 1963: 685). The situation in the United Kingdom was much less dramatic, but the ratio rose there too (Capie and Wood 2012: 92).

Looking back on the 1930s from the 1960s, Friedman and Schwartz (1963) blamed "inept" monetary policy for the depth and length of the US Depression. The Federal Reserve system should have used its lender-of-last-resort position and open market operations to prevent the banking crises and maintain the money supply. Their monetarist analysis starkly highlights the difference between the quantity theory and the remnant gold standard ideology that restrained central bankers at the time.[6]

For them, the lesson of the Depression was that the financial system was "susceptible to crises resolvable only with [. . .] leadership" from the central bank (Friedman and Schwartz 1963: 418). The Federal Reserve Board's mistake

FIGURE 2.5: Crowd outside a Bronx, New York branch of the Bank of the United States during a bank run, December 1930. Photo by Ossie Leviness/NY Daily News Archive via Getty Images.

was to see "economic decline and banking failures as occurring despite its own actions and as the product of forces over which it had no control" (1963: 419). Of course, the Board never set out to drastically cut the money supply, but it had the power to prevent such a cut through extraordinary measures to shore up the private banks whose liabilities made up most of the money supply. It was culpable for sins of omission. The experience showed that a central bank in a capitalist financial system could not simply *set* the money supply, but only *target* it, and this depended on the cultivation and regulation of the banking system. Central banking was not technocratic lever-pulling, but a creative, strategic, and communicative enterprise.

For Keynes, to suggest that policy was about controlling the base in order to control bank deposits was to get things the wrong way around. In practice, central banking worked through interest rates. But from this perspective too, policy had to be channeled through the private banking system. Central banks controlled short-term money market rates, and what mattered for investment was the longer-term rates on securities. Private banking decisions mattered. Keynes (1930: II, 66–68) observed that banks actively managed their liquidity by shifting their portfolios between highly liquid bills, less liquid securities, and illiquid loans, according to their level of confidence. Banks' balance sheet management interacts with that of the public, and these together determine the longer-term interest rates that affect investment (Keynes 1930: I, 142–144). Again, the picture of policy is not a mechanical one: central bankers were involved in a complicated game in which they were not the only players.

Beyond the banks

The 1930s left a legacy of regulation reacting to the post-1929 panics. Most famously, in the United States, the 1933 Glass-Steagall Act transformed bank regulation: it put a ceiling on deposit interest rates (to prevent destabilizing bouts of inter-bank competition), established deposit insurance (to prevent bank runs), and prevented commercial banks from engaging "principally" in securities trading, setting up a legal and institutional distinction between commercial banks and investment banks (Sherman 2007: 3–4). World War II left an equally important legacy in the form of large stocks of outstanding government debt. Much of it settled on the balance sheets of commercial banks, where it could act as a buffer between reserves and loans—more remunerative than the former, safer and more liquid than the latter, especially where official intervention supported bond prices to keep interest rates low and stable. Banks were flush with liquidity, and monetary policy depended on balance sheet regulation such as reserve requirements to keep their lending in check.

In this environment, strange beasts began to appear. For example, 1950s Australia saw the rise of non bank finance companies in the cracks of a highly regulated banking system (Beggs 2015: 126–129). They raised funds by offering deposit-like instruments that they committed to redeeming for cash at short notice, and they lent to households and firms in the form of hire-purchase contracts for cars, white goods, and even industrial machinery. They were not bound by banking regulations: legally, they were leasing goods, not lending money (Schedvin 1992: 224). These institutions managed their liquidity in part through repurchase agreements with brokers—improvising a money market that had barely existed. By the end of the 1950s, they posed a problem for monetary policy, which had no easy way of restraining them as their flows of new lending came to rival the banks'. Only a severe credit squeeze brought them (temporarily) to heel, at the price of a recession: policy "fine-tuning" was impossible.

Meanwhile, in Britain, a Committee on the Working of the Monetary System reported in 1959 on a complex financial world. Financial institutions had invented practices and instruments that undermined monetary restraint by providing money-substitutes and techniques for economizing on money holdings. Money was now "only part of the wider structure of liquidity in the economy" (Radcliffe Committee 1959: 132). Policy must act "not upon the 'supply of money' (however that is defined), but on the liquidity position of the system as a whole" (Radcliffe Committee 1959: 42). Unfortunately, the "whole liquidity position" proved difficult to measure or understand as anything other than an ever-shifting network of flows and promises, which the report could only describe and not pin down by anything so simple as supply and demand schedules for money.[7]

Across the Atlantic, Minsky (1957) was divining long-term consequences from two developments in the American money market. The first was the development of the interbank market in federal funds (i.e., bank reserves held with the Federal Reserve). Surplus banks had long lent to deficit banks; what was new was scale and organization. Sharing between banks helped the system as a whole to economize on reserves and meant that no participating bank was truly constrained by its own reserve base: it did not need to wait for reserves to accumulate before expanding its lending.

The second development was more exotic, involving non bank institutions specializing in trading government bonds. These institutions borrowed and invested the money in public debt, profiting from the spread between the interest rates at which they borrowed short term and the yield on longer-term government debt. Borrowing short and lending long like banks, they ran the risk of being unable to roll over their borrowing at acceptable interest rates. In the mid-1950s, the rate at which banks lent to the bond houses rose above the yield on the bonds, and the houses had to adapt. They turned to a new source: repurchase agreements with nonfinancial corporations. In a "repo," the borrower sells an asset to the lender, with an agreement to buy it back on a later date for a slightly higher price—the price difference representing interest. The companies placing their money with the bond houses got a higher return than they did from bank deposits (demand deposits paid no interest), on an instrument that was still highly liquid, and with the security of being left holding the collateral if the borrower was unable to go through with the promised repurchase.

All these developments represented the emergence of a new layer in the monetary pyramid. Non bank financial institutions were issuing liabilities that were safe stores of value and easily convertible into bank deposits. They were not banks, but they were not outside the banking system. They still depended on banks for back-up finance, in the event that they could not roll over enough repos to finance their position. In 1955 and 1956, the Federal Reserve found itself drawn in to maintain the stability of the bond houses, entering into its own repurchase agreements with them. Otherwise, pressure on the bond houses would provoke a sell-off in government bonds and a rapid increase in interest against the aims of monetary policy.

Minsky remarked that because innovations in the financial system "often center around some technical detail of money-market behavior and as they usually start on a small scale, their significance for monetary policy is generally ignored at the time they first occur" (Minsky 1957: 172). Only once something goes wrong are the innovations noticed, and by that time they have become a part of the financial web of life, which has adapted around them. A collapse would not remain localized to the novel instruments and institutions, but risked dragging everything down. So the authorities would find themselves propping up the newcomers first, and regulating them second.

Thirty years later, Minsky could look back and see episode after episode of this story. As Treasury debt dwindled as a proportion of their assets, banks turned increasingly to managing their liquidity through borrowing. The federal funds market grew and became routinized. Still prevented from competing on deposit interest rates, commercial banks developed alternative sources of finance: certificates of deposit, repurchase agreements, borrowing from foreign banks on what came to be known as the Eurodollar market. The latter developed on a base of dollars accumulated abroad out of American payments deficits, beyond the reach of American regulation, which by the 1970s gave American banks a way to evade Federal Reserve tightening (Minsky 1986: 84–85; Stigum and Crescenzi 2007: 218–222).[8] Investment banking and a host of other institutions continued to grow alongside the commercial banks. One after another from the mid-1960s, new institutions and instruments went into crisis, only to be rescued by officially organized bailouts and then go on to become permanent parts of the landscape: certificates of deposit in 1966, commercial paper in 1970, real estate investment trusts in 1974–75. The savings and loan crisis of the 1980s could also be seen as part of the pattern: these institutions were not new, but they had been transformed by the changing financial landscape of the 1970s.

Monetarism and after

With the growing complexity of the monetary system, the rise of monetarism—a form of the quantity theory—seems perplexing. If it was harder to draw a line between "money" and "non-monetary" assets, what quantity was to be controlled? Was quantity even controllable in a system so adept at generating new forms of liquidity?

The monetarist response was to present econometric evidence that there did in fact seem to be a stable relationship between income and the demand for certain forms of money. The question "what is money?" was best answered empirically. Money was the collection of assets that made for the most stable demand-for-money function, and a more stable demand for money function was one "that required knowledge of fewer variables and their parameters in order to predict the demand for money with a given degree of accuracy" (Laidler 1969: 516).

Academic monetarism was more sophisticated than quantity theory of the old school. It was, as Friedman (1956) put it, "a restatement," specifically a restatement in the language of neoclassical-Keynesian macroeconomics. Keynes had departed from the quantity theory especially by emphasizing that the demand for money depended not only upon money-income, but also on the

FIGURE 2.6: Margaret Thatcher, holding up a one-pound note, campaigns on inflation in London, April 1979. Photo by Geoff Bruce/Central Press/Getty Images.

interest rate. Monetarism did not need to deny a role for the interest rate, but only show that it was relatively unimportant and that there was a strong direct relationship between money and income. The battle between monetarism and "Keynesianism" was over the specifics of the demand-for-money function—the estimation of parameters and their stability. It became "a struggle to occupy [the middle] ground" with each side "trying to put his opponent on the sidelines by displacing him to an extreme position" (Chick 1977: 28). The emergent consensus was that the truth was somewhere in the middle, with a small but significant effect of the interest rate on the demand for money, and stability in some periods but not in others (Goodhart 1989: 95).

Political monetarism was different. It promised a technical solution to the problem of the value of money. If only central banks would commit to keeping money supply growth low and stable, they could tame inflation. If people believed the central bank's promise, it might even be relatively painless: expectations would adjust without any need to hold unemployment above the "natural rate" for long. Friedman had long absolved labor of any independent responsibility for inflation.[9] His famous line that "inflation is always and everywhere a monetary phenomenon" (Friedman 1963) meant also that it was always and everywhere a *technical* problem. Political monetarism called for a depoliticization of money—like the gold standard, without its rigidity. Friedman straddled the divide between academic and political monetarism, making cautious arguments in one arena and grand promises in the other.[10]

Practical monetarism was thus far from apolitical. It was a critical ingredient in the political rise of the New Right. It had a bigger following among journalists and businesspeople than economists. Where monetary targeting was implemented it was generally a political imposition, with central bankers often skeptical. But many technocrats made their peace with monetarism not because they believed it was a route to painless monetary stabilization, but because it provided cover for a painful one. Charles Schultze, economic adviser to United States President Carter, later commented that the infamous "Volcker shock"—which raised interest rates to unprecedented levels and triggered a global debt crisis—was "a political move, not an economic move":

> In theory, the Fed could have kept on raising the bejesus out the interest rates, but that's what it couldn't do politically [. . .] [T]he Fed could say, "Hey, ain't nobody here but us chickens. We're not raising interest rates, we're only targeting the money supply."
> —Schultze, quoted in Greider 1987: 120

In the United Kingdom, Bank of England official J.S. Fforde noted that the Thatcher government's monetary and borrowing targets "enabled the authorities to stand back from output and employment as such and to stress the vital part to be played in respect of these by the trend of industrial costs" (quoted in Armstrong, Glyn and Harrison 1991: 308). It put labor on notice that money-wage rises could only worsen unemployment. In Australia, the Fraser government turned monetary targets into ultimatums at the Arbitration Commission: with monetary growth capped, the wage-setting decisions would determine how much nominal income growth would be used up by inflation and how much by real output growth (Beggs 2015: 205–206). A 1981 inquiry into the financial system defended monetary targeting not on theoretical monetarist grounds, but because "it provides an additional encouragement to the authorities to control the budget deficit" and signaled "the Government's resolve to pursue a disciplined monetary policy" (Campbell et al. 1981: 53).

In its own terms, the monetarist experiment failed. It could be hard to hit targets—authorities had imperfect control over the banking system, government deficits, and, where exchange rates were still pegged, the balance of payments. More importantly, predictability of the demand for money broke down. Early on, monetarists could dismiss this on the grounds that high and volatile inflation itself was responsible, which a return to money supply stability would fix. But this did not happen. Monetary tightness provoked further financial innovations that changed the relationships between income and the demand for money. Targets were no longer an anchor of stability or predictability (Goodhart 1989: 46, 95–103).

FIGURE 2.7: Economists testify on anti-inflation policy before the US Senate Banking Committee on anti-inflation policies, March 1980. Left to right: Walter Heller, Alan Greenspan, Herbert Stein, Paul McCracken. Photo by Bettmann/Getty Images.

FIGURE 2.8: US Treasury Secretary Henry Paulson and Federal Reserve Chairman Ben Bernanke testify before the US House of Representatives Financial Services Committee on a proposed bank bailout plan, September 2008. Photo by Alex Wong/Getty Images.

Monetary targeting was abandoned almost everywhere by the mid-1980s (Dalziel 2002). By the 2000s, most central banks no longer paid much attention to money supply targets (Goodhart 2007). Former Federal Reserve Governor Larry Meyer commented that "money plays no role in today's consensus macro model, and it plays virtually no role in the conduct of monetary policy" (quoted in Woodford 2008: 1561–1562). Deputy Governor of the Bank of England (later Governor) Mervyn King observed:

> [A]s central banks became more and more focused on achieving price stability, less and less attention was paid to movements in money. Indeed, the decline in interest in money appeared to go hand in hand with success in maintaining low and stable inflation.
>
> —King 2002: 162

Instead, central banks used interest rates. Whether through outright sales and purchases of government bonds or repurchase agreements, they had tight control over short-term rates in the money market. So tight, in fact, that merely announcing a target was often enough to guide the market there. Making the market for reserves at that rate, they let demand determine the quantity supplied.

But in another sense, monetarism had triumphed (de Long 2000). Other branches of policy were subordinated under the hegemony of central banking: disciplining fiscal policy, promoting flexible exchange rates to isolate the money supply from international flows, and demanding changes to financial regulation.[11] The idea of the "natural rate of unemployment" replaced "full employment." Central banks were isolated from the direct control of governments, monetary management treated as a purely technocratic pursuit. As Alan Blinder, Vice Chair of the Federal Reserve Board of Governors in the mid-1990s, put it, monetarism had been "a political heat shield" allowing the central bank to raise interest rates "to excruciating heights" (Blinder 1998: 29). From then on central bankers simply had to remain vigilant for the first sign of wage pressures and adjust rates incrementally. The "Great Moderation" (Bernanke 2012) was made possible by a harsh dose of immoderation.

Money evolves

By the 1990s, monetary policy was settled. Central banks managed interest rates to keep inflation low but positive, and seemed to have reliable strategies for doing so. With prices stable, exchange rates could look after themselves. Economists did not need to pay much attention to the details of policy transmission as long as it worked—though specialists expressed unease about treating the financial system as a black box (Laidler 2003; Goodhart 2007).

It was clear to anyone reading the financial pages that inside that black box, the workings had become increasingly complex and harder to understand as a whole. Derivatives had become fundamental to the financial strategies of all kinds of institutions, enabling them to slice, mix, and trade all kinds of risk, whether to mitigate it, take it on, or profit from mediating it (Bryan and Rafferty 2006; 2016; Lee and Martin 2016). Securitization transformed mortgages from illiquid assets that were stuck on bank balance sheets for decades, to sources of liquidity, and it seemed to provide a method for extracting safe assets out of pools of risky ones. A parallel banking universe developed around the money market, with non bank institutions (often in fact owned or supported by commercial and investment banks) borrowing short-term and lending longer, managing their liquidity with repurchase agreements or commercial paper. As yields on safe government bonds fell to very low levels, wealth managers sought returns in more exotic instruments. Though goods and services prices were under control, asset prices—equity and housing prices in particular—appreciated over a long period in many countries, supported by low interest rates and credit expansion.

In the 1980s, reformers portrayed the financial sphere as a system in chains, wrapped in a tangle of ad hoc regulations weighing down enterprise without any rational purpose. Later critics of this "deregulation" agenda often accepted the contrast with a post-war "regulated" financial system, and regretted the unleashing. In fact, the financial system of the 1950s and 1960s had never been fully tamed. It was never a machine designed by policymakers, but something organic and evolving. Policy was a force of artificial selection, but the garden was a tightly interconnected ecosystem, in which it could be difficult to distinguish noxious weeds from flowers, and pests from pollinators.

In such an environment, regulation could never simply follow the implementation of a blueprint. Regulation would block a banking practice or instrument; new ways of doing something similar would sprout. The banks would develop new instruments, or non bank institutions—falling outside the scope of banking regulation—would take over that business. It is misleading to think in terms of a single "regulated" system prevailing from the post-war period, straining in the 1970s, and finally being freed from its bounds in the 1980s and 1990s. The earlier system never stood still, and regulation and financial innovation responded to one another.

The "shadow banking" practices implicated in the crisis of 2007–08 cannot be blamed entirely on "deregulation." They involved things that would once have been prohibited, certainly, but they were also shaped by drives to route around things that were still (or newly) prohibited. Bank regulatory change had not been one-way. The international Basel Accord on bank regulation involved a program of new policy centered on capital requirements. Off-balance-sheet vehicles were a way for banks to increase activity beyond limits set by such requirements. The US shadow banking system found a ready market for its liquid liabilities among corporate cash pools: because of limits to the size of deposits covered by federal deposit insurance, large corporations looked to the money market, where their holdings could be secured in repurchase agreements (Poszar 2014: 25–26; see also Nersisyan and Wray, this volume).[12]

The basic form of the crisis that grew out of this financial garden, and the response that crisis provoked, would not have surprised Minsky: a liquidity crunch followed by an extension of central bank support to a wider range of instruments and institutions. As Mehrling (2011) put it, the Federal Reserve acted not only as lender, but also *market maker* of last resort, acting as an emergency buyer (or lender) in the money market and taking large quantities of mortgage-backed securities on its own balance sheet in the process. The "shadow banking" system is here to stay; money continues to evolve, as do its orthodoxies and heterodoxies.

CHAPTER THREE

Money, Ritual, and Religion

The Horror of It (the Prosperity Gospel and the Myth of Deterritorialization)

JON BIALECKI

Let's start with an object. Perhaps this is an object that you have actually come across, depending on where and when you are. You might have seen it purposefully left on the ground, set just off from a sidewalk that is known to be busy, sitting on a public table or bench, or intentionally tucked into a book in such a way that it wouldn't tumble out until the purchaser takes it home to read. Perhaps someone gave it directly to you, but that is the least likely scenario; it's something that is meant to be come by, not handed out like a flyer or a pamphlet (though it does have a flyer- or pamphlet-like quality in the pragmatic work it is intended to achieve). If you work or have worked in the service industry, perhaps you found it secreted away inside a gratuity or tip; and while it is hard to know, pawning it off disguised as a tip may be the chief means of this object's distribution.

The object has the color, shape, and design of US American paper currency, and you might even believe that it is a lost dollar bill of some sort. (There are also versions that take on the appearance of various non-US denominations, but they are harder to come across.) But you wouldn't believe it for very long, even if you are engaged in a cursory inspection, for it is not designed to be mistaken for the real thing. The pseudo-bill often presents itself as being of an implausibly large denomination (at various times there have been one hundred,

FIGURE 3.1: Bible tracts in the form of faux dollar bills. Courtesy of Taylor C. Nelms.

one thousand, and even one million and one trillion dollar variants). The quality of the paper, the feel of it in your fingers, is wrong. If you attend to the serial number on the facing side of the bill, that appears off as well, as if someone was engaging in only the laziest form of counterfeiting; the serial number starts off with "JS," which is notable because "S" is not one of the letters that is used in serial numbers of American paper currency.

It seems as if someone was not engaging in any attempt to counterfeit at all, only to trick the eye for a bare moment or two. When one flips the "dollar bill," the back of the bill is only vaguely reminiscent of US currency; all the design elements on the obverse have been either moved to the edges, or completely eliminated. (The amount of the supposed denomination and the phrase "IN GOD WE TRUST" are most strikingly retained.) In the place of the missing design elements, there is instead a rather lengthy text, roughly a hundred and fifty words long. One version of the text starts off in this way: "HERE IS THE MILLION-DOLLAR QUESTION: Will you go to Heaven when you die?" It then proceeds to argue, in a rather uncompromising manner, that you won't, at least not if you are relying on your own merits or moral character. It recites a story that the reader has most likely heard before, that Jesus died for your sins, rose from the dead, and paid off your debt of sin. In short, despite your sinful nature, you are in the clear. Of course there are terms and conditions that apply if the offer is to be valid: it closes with the admonition, "[t]oday, repent and trust Jesus, and God will give you eternal life as a free gift. Then read the Bible daily and obey it. God will never fail you."

The tract (we can call it what it is) is obviously an attempt at guerrilla proselytizing, a bait-and-switch tactic to steal someone's attention for just the brief time needed to make the pitch. One could see this as nothing more than an opportunistic moment of protected religious speech, or perhaps some mere pious fraud, and not as anything that actually conflated money and God's grace in a dangerous and confusing way (even if a sizable quantity of these tracts were once confiscated by the Secret Service, in what a judge declared was a warrantless, and hence illegal, search and seizure).[1] Alternately, it would be easy to read the pairing as offensive, as mixing the sacred with the profane (though which is sacred and which is profane may differ depending on who is making the judgment).

But then again, something about these bills suggests a kinship between the message and the class of objects it was camouflaged as. They both point to measures of value, albeit in different registers—one being more immediate "ultimate" value, the other exchange value. But there is also something about the way these objects function that suggests a kinship. There is an anonymous element to money, or at least there are affordances that allow money in its cash form to, at times, circulate anonymously and facilitate interactions between individuals with little preexisting relation, just as there is a depersonalized, minimalist edge to this generic evangelical message, which could be read as hailing anyone. (And good luck determining who the author, animator, and agent is with this bill, or deducing how one would properly follow the imperative to "read the Bible and obey it.") Perhaps there is something more to this pairing, something fitting about the actual religious message, as well as the monetary form on which it is mimetically leaning in this instance.

This chapter will argue that there is something telling about the pairing found in this bill. It will argue that money and religion, at least in their "modern" expressions, are both in a way anonymous, in the disturbing and destabilizing understanding of what "anonymous" can mean. Further, this chapter will argue that they share other features not unrelated to this anonymity: an indifference to all sorts of barriers and a tendency to be indifferent to or even erase the social fabric. But it will also argue that modern money and modern religion do something else. Just like the line from the book of Job that became a folk maxim—"God giveth and God taketh away"—at the spaces where money and religion work together at their closest, they also foster new structures, relations, and barriers. And given that these organizations are resistant to any easy quantification, it is impossible to say which side of the ledger, the destructive or the creative, has greater weight. But to make this argument, it is necessary to understand what is "modern" about modern religion, if one is to think of the modern as more than a mere temporal marker. And to make this argument for the period set aside by this book, it is necessary to see how what is arguably one of the most "modern" modes of religion has operated for over a century and continues to operate today.

THE HORROR OF IT

Discussions of periodization are always awkward; there are numerous false starts, obscured, dark precursors, and stubborn remnants of earlier forms. And this is especially the case when we are dealing with discussions of money; as some of the other chapters in this volume show quite clearly, new forms of money, exchange, and value do not so much replace earlier modes as appear parallel to them. They tend to proliferate (all at once), even as, at the same time, the newer forms work to retrospectively transform the apparent qualities and capacities of older modes of exchange.

But sometimes periodization works in a way that is right on the nose. At midnight of New Year's Eve, as 1900 came to a close and the last evening of the nineteenth century dissolved into the first morning of the twentieth, Agnes Ozman spoke in Chinese. This occurred during a vigil at Charles Fox Parham's Bethel Bible School in Topeka, Kansas. The school itself was a ramshackle structure known by the Topeka locals as "Stone's Folly" (Synan 1997: 90). The house, over three stories, was ornate to the point of being an effectively American Midwest rococo, if not flat-out byzantine. But while some parts were choked by ornate crown molding or other decorations, other parts, constructed after the exhaustion of either finance or ability, had a plainer feel, out of step with the ambition of the rest of the building. Among the more ambitious parts of the

FIGURE 3.2: The Bethel Bible School in Topeka, Kansas in the United States, *c.* 1900, one of the sites where modern Pentecostalism originated. Marion Doss, CC BY-SA 2.0.

building was a spire that was being used as a "Prayer Tower," a place "where a constant vigil of prayer was kept up day and night" (Ozman 1909).

This was more than a mere linguistic exercise. This was an effort at once to restore the Church to the state of primitive Christianity and also to "immanentize the eschaton," that is, to trigger the end of days. Parham was operating in a Holiness strain of the Methodist tradition, and he and his students had been seeking the infilling of the "Holy Ghost." Despite the Methodist inflection, this was not only intended for, or only of interest to, a Methodist argument. That is, these quintessentially Methodist concerns were no longer Methodist concerns alone. These ideas were "spilling outward to agitate other communions," as one historian has described (Blumhofer 1993: 26). Parham was not just seeking a higher intensity of being blessed; this was also an attempt to fast forward the apocalyptic narrative—or to at least take advantage of a reading of the narrative as rather close to its denouement. While there were those who labored assiduously for the millennium to come about through human will, at the end of the nineteenth century, it was also common to refer to the then-present era as the "evening light," signaling at once restorationist and apocalyptic expectations (Blumhofer 1993: 11). Parham's Bible School certainly had a millennialist sense of economic procurement. Their program was organized around "faith lines," where faculty and students "trusted the Lord to supply" all their needs (they actually refused to ask for offerings during services, preferring to procure all necessities through prayer) (Ozman 1909; Blumhofer 1993: 47).

Ozman's breaking out into Chinese (or at least into something that one of the people present recognized as Chinese) is seen by some as a pivotal moment—and in some tellings, *the* pivotal moment—in the birth of Pentecostalism, an expression of Christianity that would take on world-historical importance. The centrality of Ozman is debatable. People had been breaking out into glossolalia well before Ozman, and Parham and Ozman's breakthrough appeared at least initially not to come to much. After a small burst of local media attention and some small success in revivalist talks by Parham in Kansas City, Topeka, and Lawrence, Parham's school closed, and he was abandoned by his supporters, including Ozman, who left his tutelage and oversight for the "Holy Ghost and Us" Maine church where Parham had first heard furtive rumors about the rustlings of tongues (Blumhofer 1993: 52–53). Over the next few years, Parham would slowly rebuild a following as a minister of an "assembly" (he refused to use the word "church") and would run crusades in East Texas and help set up and preach at more Bible schools, but while doing so he had a tendency to "not emphasize unduly his innovative doctrines" (Blumhofer 1993: 54). His health declined in those later years, and he was dogged by rumors of sexual immorality with men, which resulted in an arrest in Texas, though not a prosecution.

It is for that reason that when Pentecostal believers argue as to when to set the inception of Pentecostalism, there are those who would rather alight on the equally symbolic 1906 Los Angeles revival that is metonymically referred to as "Azusa Street." Part of the attraction to Azusa Street is that it was an avowedly interracial happening. It was led by William Seymour, an itinerant Holiness Minister who had recently crossed over from his previous status as a Baptist. For part of 1905, Seymour attended a later iteration of Parham's Bible schools. While there, he supposedly had to stand outdoors while listening to Parham's lectures through an open door or window; sometimes this is presented as being mandated by Jim Crow laws in Texas, sometimes as being mandated by Parham's racism.[2] While under Parham's tutelage, Seymour adopted his beliefs concerning the importance of tongues as the sole indication of being truly baptized in the spirit, even though at the time Seymour himself was incapable of speaking in tongues. Seymour then went to Los Angeles to take up a position there in a black Holiness church; after his first night's sermon, where he preached the importance of tongues as a special and distinct third blessing apart from sanctification, he famously returned to his church the next day to find himself locked out, denied entry as a result of the perceived outlandishness of his claims (Synan 1997: 96). For weeks afterward Seymour preached out of the living room of the man who lodged him, until on one evening in early April he and seven others "fell to the floor in religious ecstasy, speaking in tongues." When this happened, the daughter of the man who was sheltering Seymour was so scared by this apparition that she reportedly had to escape through the kitchen door. News of this event got out, and Seymour found himself next moving to preach out of a "makeshift pulpit" on the front porch, with the throng growing so quickly that at some point the floor of the porch gave way under the weight of all those present (Synan 1997: 96).

This is the point in the narrative where Seymour moves his mission into an abandoned downtown church on Azusa Street, a building which had formerly been the first black Methodist church built within the city. The number of attendees continued to increase, until his revival (and this is the point at which a generic narrator starts describing Seymour's ministry as a revival) catches the attention of the *Los Angeles Times*. The first of a series of articles about Azusa Street runs this headline: "Weird Babel of Tongues—New Sect of Fanatics Is Breaking Loose. Wild Scene Last Night on Azusa Street. Gurgle of Wordless Talk by a Sister." The article reports that

> Colored people and a sprucing of whites compose the congregation, and night is made hideous in the neighborhood by the howling of the worshipers, who spend hours swaying forth and back in a nerve-racking attitude of prayer and supplication. They claim to have "the gift of tongues" and to be able to comprehend the babel.
>
> Such a startling claim has never yet been made by any company of fanatics, even in Los Angeles, the home of almost numberless sects.

FIGURE 3.3: On April 18, 1906, the *Los Angeles Daily Times* published an article headlined "Weird Babel of Tongues," which reported on the Azusa Street Revival led by African-American Pentecostal preacher William J. Seymour. Courtesy of the *Los Angeles Times*.

Later *Los Angeles Times* articles maintain the same tone, luxuriating in reporting details in a lurid shade of yellow. We are told of policemen monitoring, and sometimes shutting down for a night, this "queer mixture of rich and poor;" a later piece takes a more ethological turn, focusing on how members "bark like dogs [. . .] shriek all manner of strange words that mean nothing" and how "kickers" stomp out a "sanctified beat," only to later shift genres in the direction of a police procedural:

> Several women spent at least a part of the night lying flat on their backs on the dirty floor of the room, each endeavoring to kick her heels higher in the air than the others. As a result the fanatical and almost hysterical females were practically standing on their heads in the midst of a large audience.
>
> As such exhibitions are not allowed even in the rough resorts in the city, the police were forced to call a halt to this part of the "holy kickers'" rites. When the women were forced to desist they became wildly hysterical and screamed and preached until they sank exhausted and nearly unconscious to the floor.

Yet another article informs us that under the guidance of this "one-eyed negro leader," "[w]eird prophesies concerning the destruction of Los Angeles" were "shouted by several of the ranters."[3] "[D]ire calamity was foretold by negro fanatics who professed to see only destruction for this city ere many days." One subheading for a section of the article that reports on the apparent dissolution of racial and gender hierarchies and taboos sums up much of the attitude towards Azusa Street: *"The Horror of It."*

DETERRITORIALIZING RELIGION, DETERRITORIALIZING MONEY

The horror that so shook the *Los Angeles Times* was a horror of *mixing* that which should be kept apart—a mixing of bodies, languages, races, genders, enthusiasms, and poor and rich believers. Pentecostalism is admittedly just one mode of the many varieties of "religion" and just one of many varieties of Christianity. And considering the topic of this book, it may seem odd to lean into a discussion emphasizing race, gender, and language instead of fiscal practices. But without granting it any kind of causal role or privileged status, Pentecostalism as a form is a very productive avenue to think about the relationship between ritual, religion, and money between 1920 and the present.

The reason this is productive is because of the "horror of it all," the way Pentecostalism smashed both metaphorical and sometimes quite real social barriers. There is, in this "horror," first, a surprising resonance between how money and Pentecostalism are thought of and second, a resonance between what such thinking about money, religion, or both obscures or gets wrong. This is not to say that the resonances between the "horrors" of Pentecostalism and money are mistaken. But such thinking only captures one half of the story, misapprehending a partial operation for the totality of the work being accomplished. It thinks, in other words, of money and Pentecostalism as only being acid baths, pure instruments of destruction.

Pentecostalism *is* destructive; in the language of the early twenty-first century, it is a "disruptor," something that takes existing obstacles and hierarchies and rips them apart. Consider the various boundaries that early Pentecostalism crossed. The easiest is language. Just as Seymour preached, speaking in tongues is considered by many forms of Pentecostalism to be "initial evidence'" of being baptized in the Spirit; which is to say that it is the only guarantor that one is truly indwelled by what Parham and his kind would call the Holy Ghost. Speaking in tongues comes in two different forms, depending on what the local understanding of the phenomenon is. One form is xenoglossy, which is to say the spontaneous capacity to speak a foreign language. The other is to understand speaking in tongues as a divine, rather than human, mode of communication; this is usually understood as a love language to God, articulated in a language given by God, to which the subject does not have access (Bialecki 2017: 136–140; Samarin 1972). At one level, this difference is taken quite seriously. Early Pentecostal missionaries, for instance, would go to foreign countries convinced that they would be able to communicate with the people there through their xenoglossic gifts; this usually ended up working out just as well as one might expect. The later understanding of glossolalia as a love language to God ends up eroding language as sense, since speaking in tongues then becomes a phonetic stream over which one feels little conscious control, a kind of linguistic automaticity that is not only indifferent to referentiality, but acutely hostile to it. It is interesting to note, though, that when I did fieldwork with US American middle-class charismatic Christians, there was a slippery boundary between the two glossolalic instantiations; while there was never a claim that people themselves were engaging in xenoglossy, it was always a possibility for someone else, somewhere else. Language as a form lost its integrity; barriers were now at best notional constraints.

The same can be said about race and gender. While Parham's deep-set, nineteenth-century racism kept him from opening up the movement, what is surprising is how immune to racial barriers early Pentecostalism became once it hit critical mass in Los Angeles. Pentecostalism's racial openness is not a foregone conclusion, and over time many denominations have formed that, to various degrees of openness or completeness, are effectively racialized; but what is striking is that while this occurs, Pentecostalist churches or denominations often show higher degrees of racial integration than other comparable Protestantisms.

Similarly, Pentecostalism opened up gender roles, not only in allowing the sort of inter-gender fraternization that so disturbed the *Los Angeles Times*, but also in allowing women to take on positions of authority. Agnes Ozman would be followed by the likes of Florence Crawford (founder of the "Apostolic Faith Church" denomination), Aimee Semple McPherson (who built the Angelus Temple in the Echo Park neighborhood of Los Angeles, and who also instituted the International Church of the Foursquare Gospel denomination), and Kathryn Kuhlman (a successful leader of healing campaigns). Appearing as the public faces of organizations that they built, these women would become famous (and, in the eyes of some, infamous) US religious leaders. Again, there is a tendency for Pentecostalism to revert to a gendered mean and for markedly male and female roles, styles, and ethical obligations to emerge (Erikson 2012, 2014; Haynes 2017). But again, when compared to other forms of theologically conservative Christianity, Pentecostalism has an openness to gender that stands out. The reason why Pentecostalism was such a solvent in these areas was also the reason why it was corrosive of hierarchies based on education and institutional endorsement. Predicated on the logic that it was the Holy Spirit, and not human credentialization, that made one a pastor, many Pentecostals skipped the seminary training and denominational authorization; in short, anyone could become a pastor, as long as he or she could win over enough parishioners. This allowed Pentecostalism to self-replicate at a faster rate and in a more opportunistic and entrepreneurial manner, with fewer resources lost to maintaining the sorts of institutional mechanisms other modes of religiosity devoted to religious formation.

But our discussion has yet to exhaust the capacity for Pentecostalism to eat at social boundaries and dissolve social relations. Pentecostalism has been successful in the United States, with many of its ecstatic practices such as healing, speaking in tongues, and battling demons having been adopted by pre-existing Protestantisms or Catholicisms (see, e.g., Csordas 1997a, 1997b). But Pentecostalism's greatest levels of success have been as a good made for export, with about two-thirds of the roughly 280–523 million believers (estimates on the number of believers vary considerably) located in what is referred to as the global South (Robbins 2004). And here, adoption of Pentecostal religion almost always means reevaluating the local supernatural entities. This inevitably takes the form of now understanding what was before gods, spirits, or ancestors as actually being demons (Meyer 1999). With this comes a concomitant reevaluation of the sort of local ritualized social practices that are usually embedded within or inflected by local modes of religiosity as also being demonic. Social obligations, such as funerals, feasting, initiations, and labor cooperatives, are now cast as evil and must be resisted as such. Given how deeply these obligations are usually entwined with kinship, this act of "making a break with the past" (Meyer 1998) is sometimes seen as fraying the social fabric to a point beyond repair.

There are thus strong parallels between the way Pentecostalism works to uproot various binaries, practices, and conventions, and the way critics imagine that money, finance, and capitalism have destructively operated in the twentieth and early twenty-first centuries. Money, imagined as a neutral holder of value, is commonly seen as also breaking down social barriers and diluting social ties, a tradition that includes Marx's understanding of the switch to a monetized society as creating the conditions for which "all that is solid melts into air" (Marx and Engels 2002); Simmel's (2011) view that in critically dense population centers, money allows for effective anonymization, as people can disentangle economic action from any long-standing social ties; and Deleuze and Guattari's (1983) understanding of money and capital as operating as a system of decoding, transforming everything into abstract deterritorialized flows. This is not the only position, of course; money is often thought to supplement or even catalyze local practices (e.g., Bloch and Perry 1989; Akin and Robbins 1999; Sahlins 1999; Maurer 2006; Nelms and Guyer, this volume). But a conception of money as an engine of social and cultural flattening is common.

This relation between Pentecostalism and accelerated and destabilized monetary flow is sometimes imagined not as mere parallelism, but as some sort of causal relation. Sometimes it is imagined that the leading partner in this dance is finance and money, and the dance is seen as one of abstraction. One example of this is the "occult economies" argument presented by Comaroff and Comaroff (1999), which posits that a late twentieth-century rise in supernaturalist-leaning forms of Christianity such as Pentecostalism (as well as a rise in witchcraft killings and an interest in Satanism) around the world, especially in sub-Saharan Africa, was the fruit of new monetary regimes and flights of capital that came with neoliberalism. At other times, religion is given the lead, and more concretized causal logics are relied upon. In a widely circulated and commented-on *The Atlantic* article entitled "Did Christianity Cause the Crash?" (Rosin 2009), for example, it is argued that the Prosperity Gospel movement, a particularly fast-growing mode of the already fast-growing Pentecostal movement, accelerated the credit crisis that triggered the financial crisis of 2007–2008. The connecting fiber between the two is, supposedly, that the Prosperity Gospel's promise of exponentially larger wealth for faithful believers incited Christians to throw caution to the wind when it came to borrowing against their homes, reasoning that the generosity of a divine hand meant they were not actually exposing themselves to risk (but see Coleman 2011, 2017; Bowler 2013).

These are two of the main contemporary accounts, but they are not the only ones. There are others that see more complicated relations between Pentecostalism and capital. There is the argument, for instance, that Pentecostalism was not a direct expression of accelerations in finance and shifts in the forms that money takes; this argument instead sees this mode of religion as a form of modernism, an almost aesthetic response to the alienation emerging from the intensification of urban centers, which are themselves seen as money- and finance-driven developments in the structure of the modern world system (Shapiro and Barnard 2017). And there are even crude-logics of causation, which see early Pentecostalism as an expression of relative deprivation, the creation of supernatural powers and importance to compensate for a lack of worldly status and in particular for the injuries of poverty (Anderson 1979). We should also note that these accounts tend to focus on the Prosperity Gospel variant of Pentecostalism as their exemplar, and we will return to the various global permutations of the Prosperity Gospel later on when we try to think through the other side of these claims.

But it is not necessary to think of the Prosperity Gospel, or even to privilege Pentecostalism or Christianity, to theorize in this vein. Roy (1994, 2006) has argued that certain fast-moving forms of Islam are at once a symptom of, and a catalyst for, a deterritorializing secularization of Islamic society. He has suggested that this is part of a wider phenomenon, a stripping of "culture" from "religion," allowing at once a proliferation of religious forms and a simultaneous simplification, homogenization, and radicalization, since limits on the expression of religion caused by its being embedded in culture are no longer operative (Roy 2014). Roy sees this occurring as the result of a globalization of the "religious market," a concept borrowed from Stark and Finke (1988), which posits that different religious forms are understood as competing against each other for adherents. Roy's view of that market differs markedly from the optimistic self-maximizing exercise in choice that colors Stark and Finke; it is rather a clear race to the bottom. But there is another facet of Roy's argument that stands out in the present context. Roy's expansion of the idea of the "religious market" to a global stage also shifts the nature of the discussion from a metaphorical market, analogous to the capital and monetary market with which we are familiar, to something that has closer resemblances to actually existing markets. We no longer have just various religious entrepreneurs, forging new religious movements in their appeal to a preexisting market base. Instead, religions are caught up in various regulatory regimes resulting from different legislative approaches to the "freedom of religion;" the movement of religions is laminated onto the movement of participants in the global labor market; and religion becomes deeply embedded in different media ecosystems (particularly media ecosystems that are partially or completely monetized).

It is not necessary to swallow Roy's separation of religion from culture (a bone that he acknowledges many anthropologists will choke on) to see that his argument makes our discussion of Pentecostalism not a special case, but merely a particular exemplar; the same conclusions can be reached if one starts thinking the problem through from a different vantage point, that of Islam, as well. That does not mean that our choice of cases does not facilitate thinking through specific features in greater or lesser detail, however. While we will return to Islam in the conclusion, for the next leg of the argument I will concentrate our focus and lean into examples of the Prosperity Gospel. Since the widely spread Prosperity Gospel folds in money alongside other forms of supernaturally achieved thriving, focusing on it allows us, first, to think through the relation between "deterritorializing" money and "deterritorializing" religion in greater focus. But second, it will enable us to take up this effort with greater comparative ambition, as the Prosperity Gospel has found footing in places as widely dispersed as the slums of the Philippines, the conference centers of Sweden, the Zambian Copperbelt, and the US Appalachian hills. As we will see, the story does not end with deterritorialization.

Breakthroughs and points of contact

Roy's language of the deterritorialization of religion stands out in the context of this discussion in part because it is the same language used by Gilles Deleuze and Felix Guattari, two of the proponents of the acidic vision of money referenced earlier. Much as there are elements of Roy's argument that may go against social scientific sensibilities, there are also elements of Deleuze and Guattari's description of capital that strain plausibility. As Lowrie (2017) has observed, the vision of capitalism as nothing but deterritorialized flows suggests a capitalism that is purely mathematical, completely stripped of all cultural context and social barriers (see also Bialecki 2018). This scenario, of capitalism as unencumbered by either constraint or sense, is one that rhymes with Roy's view of modern religion as denuded of all elements of culture; and while there are few anthropologists who would unproblematically celebrate all the instantiations of culture that have been brought about by global capital, there are even fewer who would say that no culture (or whatever relexified signifier they use in the place of culture; see Brightman 1995) colors or participates in global capitalism at all.

Yet one could argue that there is almost something un-Deleuzian in Deleuze and Guattari's vision of capital. This is because complete deterritorialization is something that is very rare in their imagination; as they themselves insist, almost every deterritorialization comes with a concomitant territorialization (see Deleuze and Guattari 1999). For them, except for forays into total extinction, a disarticulation always implies some resulting re-articulation, either purposefully authored or as an emergent phenomenon. It need not have the complexity of what came before, and it may give rise to something almost reminiscent of the bland homogeneity that results from thermodynamic processes like heat death, but some form of order must insist or maintain. If nothing else, when discussing ever-intensifying processes—and the deterritorializing work of both money and religion as imagined by its critics seems to be a candidate—there has to at least be sufficient mechanisms remaining to allow these processes to double down on their labors. There must be chains of material entanglement that are left behind (see Swartz and Stearns, this volume).

The Pentecostal Prosperity Gospel is arguably constituted mostly of such chains, a series of metonymic links that have been there since the beginning that serve as both trace and engine. Most forms of Protestantism are set up to ethically valorize and attend to subjective human agency as opposed to material entailments (Keane 2007). This is not so with Pentecostalism, which breaks so decisively with this mode in its celebration of materiality as both ethical actant and sensuous object that it really can be categorized as its own separate religious mode (Meyer 2010). This can be seen clearly in both the pneumatology and praxis of the twentieth-century US televangelist Oral Roberts. It would be wrong to say that Oral Roberts invented the Prosperity Gospel. On the one hand, a sort of Pentecostal expectation that God will provide is baked into the very first moments of Pentecostalism, as shown by the lack of financial concerns found in the "faith lines" that funded Charles Fox Parham's and Agnes Ozman's early experimentations with the Holy Ghost. On the other hand, the Prosperity Gospel also drew from a variety of nineteenth-century sources that postulated that positive thinking and exercises of the will would lead to wealth (Bowler 2013). Still, Oral Roberts did much to staple these imaginings to Pentecostalism—theorizing, systematizing, and popularizing the idea that the rewards of Christianity were not merely spiritual but also temporal, and that physical wealth and fiscal success was part of what Jesus had won for those who believed in him.

As teased out by Blanton (2015) in his ethnography of materiality and media in Southern Appalachian Pentecostalism, part of Roberts's legacy was his understanding of how the Holy Ghost transmitted blessings by a "point of contact," his term for a bodily locale that was put into immediate physical touch with whatever vessel was transmitting divine healing, or whatever other blessing was being communicated. The simplest example is the practice of "laying on hands" when healing someone; the act of touching someone during healing prayer can be understood as an almost mechanically channeled transmission of grace. But the example that Blanton spells out in the greatest detail was a common scenario that involved a person listening to a Pentecostal service on the radio, who would physically touch the receiver so that the healing of the Holy Spirit could be imparted. As Blanton notes, for all the emphasis on belief that is a part of Pentecostal discourse, the necessity of tactile connection to an implement linking the recipient to the pastor through a complex web of infrastructure underscores the materiality of the process as well.

Roberts championed other forms of channeling mediation; one that particularly caught the Pentecostal imagination was prayer cloths. Small pieces of fabric, often cut with intentionally jagged edges so as to prevent them from fraying, serve as (literally) anointed carriers of a blessing from whoever originated them. These cloths did not fall from the sky; they were produced

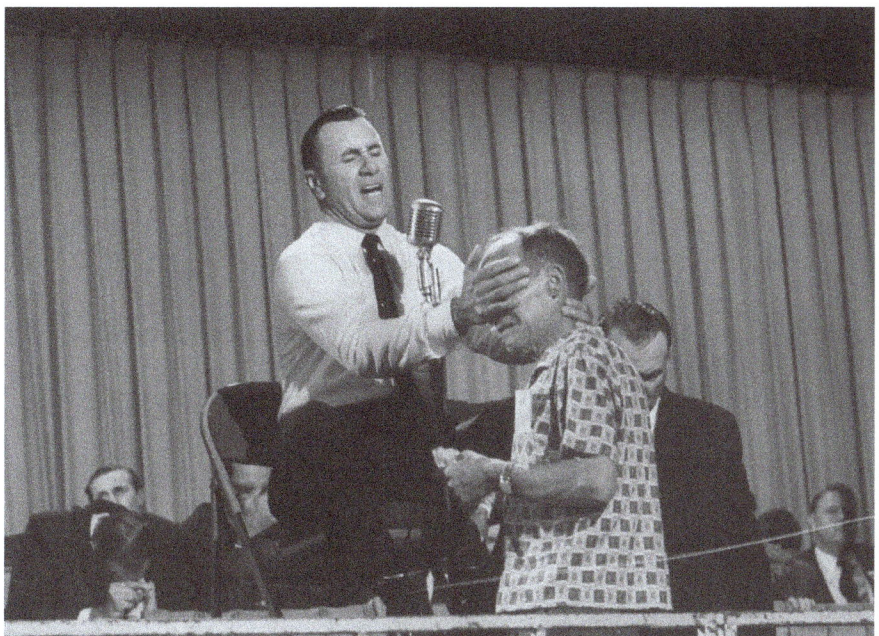

FIGURE 3.4: Pentecostal preacher Oral Roberts lays hands on the sick in his prayer line at evening service, July 1962. Francis Miller/The LIFE Picture Collection/Getty Images.

and circulated through a support infrastructure set up by Roberts and other pastors. As Blanton notes, they were normally imagined to function as divine prophylactics, warding off harm. However, they were also imagined as serving a different function, a form of augmenting "financial blessings," which was imagined as working both on "the sender and the receiver." These prayer cloths were not free. They were given in exchange for donations to the pastor; as Blanton parenthetically notes when discussing A.A. Allen, another early and influential Prosperity Gospel minister, "[t]hose members of the faithful who were unable to pledge the $100 for the 'Power Packed Prayer Rug' could settle for a 'Prosperity Blessing Cloth' at a much smaller price" (Blanton 2015: 66).

It is easy to see this in a cynical light, as someone producing multiple differentially priced apotropaic magic devices so as to maximally fleece the market. That framing, while tempting, ignores the fact that following most expressions of Pentecostal logic, this was not a fee-for-services operation, and the reason that a larger donation was associated with a greater blessing was not merely the avarice of A.A. Allen. As has been observed by Coleman (2004, 2006) in his work on a major Swedish prosperity church, Prosperity Gospel transactions operate under the logic of the gift, as outlined by Marcel Mauss: elements of the selfhood and agency of the giver adhere to the gift, circulating outward as it does its work. Coleman has shown that this is certainly the case for Pentecostal language. One example is how the speech of powerful Pentecostal pastors can become internalized as listeners learn the phrases and adopt the verbal tics associated with the speaker. This is no isolated finding: Reinhardt (2014) has shown how Ghanaian pastors-in-training engage in a process called "soaking in tapes," listening to recorded sermons for prolonged periods of time to gain some of the recorded pastor's anointing. And what is more striking is that money, despite its anonymous character, is itself also more capable of carrying that charge, serving as a conduit for the expression and circulation of charismatic blessing. So the money given out to A.A. Allen for the "Prosperity Blessing Gospel" was more than just a payment. As the word "pledge" suggests, it was a moral act that also created a bond as, in effect, something not unlike the "hau" of the believer—a kind of spiritual force (taken from the Māori language and conceptualized by Mauss as the power of return in gifting)—was mailed off, facilitating a "point of contact."[4]

Despite how nicely they fold into what anthropologists have discovered via their ethnographic engagement with the Prosperity Gospel, A.A. Allen and Oral Roberts, despite their prototypical nature, are outliers, as are the local AM station radio pastors in Blanton's research. This is not because their praxis is atypical; elements of their religious practice can be found in diverse places such as Sweden and Ghana. Rather, it is the distance implicit in the mediatic technologies that they make use of which sets them apart. The Prosperity Gospel television preacher may be a staple of American cultural imagination, but most of the time the Prosperity Gospel works at much more intimate scales, in distance, of adherents, and amount of wealth involved. This is important because the circulation of money and blessings does not just create nationwide or global networks of exchange, though obviously work on that scale does occur (see, e.g., Coleman 2000). Most of the time, what is achieved instead is the establishment of more local communities.

This small-scale community building can be seen clearly in the ethnographic work of Haynes (2017), who has studied Prosperity Pentecostalism in the Zambian Copperbelt. Famous as a place of rapid and unstable urbanization, as well as a place stripped bare by neoliberalism and the collapse of the global copper market (Ferguson 1999), one would expect to see deterritorialization at its greatest intensity in the Copperbelt. We find something else, though: a patchwork of small churches. Here, the kind of intimacy that comes with small size is actually a desideratum. As Haynes (2017: 61) reports, "When an older Pentecostal woman heard me talking about a church with nearly a thousand members, she clicked her tongue and tutted in disapproval, 'No access to the pastor.'" This intimacy is important, because it is necessary to build the cross-cutting ties that constitute Pentecostal sociality. Haynes shows how communities are built around the circulation of both charisma and money.

FIGURE 3.5: Joshua Magezi, a Ugandan Pentecostal pastor, touches a woman's forehead during a ceremony on April 5, 2010. Trevor Snapp/AFP/Getty Images.

These are expressed in multiple ways. There are series of hierarchical exchanges, through which congregants give to the pastors who can pray for them to have "breakthroughs"—moments of success when one's fortune changes as a result of the prayer taken on by their "father" or "mother." In the Copperbelt, at least, ties of religious obligation are cast in the very kinship terms that Pentecostalism is supposed to dissolve. These are not unproblematic ties; the gifts—often of commodities such as concrete power, sugar, maize meal, or oil, but just as frequently of money—are understood as ultimately being offered up to God as part of a "sacrificial economy" (Coleman 2011), but are given to men and women who are understood as "prophets." This gives rise to a sense that while God's beneficence is for everyone, particularly gifted spiritual emissaries will tend to expend more of their effort interceding on the behalf of more generous members of their flock. That this would give rise to tensions is foreseeable. But while these tensions are always present to a degree, they have to work against a different, egalitarian edge of valuation, in which it is not one's potential as an intercessor that stands out, but rather one's achieved prosperity, which acts as a sign confirming divine favor. This may sound like an anti-egalitarian value, but unlike holding a prophetic mantle, the position of achieved prosperity is one to which all believers can aspire. It also opens the way for complex webs of exchange, where events are held for individuals to donate funds or commodities for a pastor or his family, but also include redistributive aspects in the way of gifts given to attendants or as "leftovers" shared with the needy at the end. They are, furthermore, opportunities for the believers to perform their prosperity and ratify their pastor's charisma.

This suggests two things. In some circumstances, the transformation of money into a "hau"-bearing object can help facilitate new social forms, which might suggest that both Pentecostalism and money do nothing but fray social ties. Further, however, it also suggests that money and money beliefs and practices like the Prosperity Gospel can accelerate the production of cultural forms and practices that are in some ways specific to the swath of society or culture in which they occur. This may sound surprising; we have talked about Pentecostalism's destructive nature, and the similar bill of particulars offered up against money has been rehearsed here as well. It is because of this destructive nature that Christianity, at least as a foreign import, has been described as a form of social critique (Handman 2014, Haynes 2017). But critique is never total. In the case of the Copperbelt Prosperity Gospel, Haynes emphasizes that the forms of prosperity performed there are exquisitely Zambian (see similarly Lindhardt 2009, Weigele 2004). And what is more, this logic of a continuing-upward social trajectory via patron–client relations is a deep-seated Copperbelt value as well. So while the Prosperity Gospel does raze some social forms—transforming, for example, local gods into local demons, much like social critics have argued that money does—it can also produce a new engine for the ratifying of local aesthetics, ethics, and sensibilities. Money, expressed through religion, as well as religion, expressed through money, turns out in the end to not be merely erosive, but also socially and culturally productive at the same moment.[5]

CONCLUSION

Pentecostalism is only one religious mode; despite its breathtaking rise, there are still vast stretches of the globe where the Pentecostal seed of faith has been unable to find root. But it is not just Pentecostalism that reflects this dialectical parallel with money and its social effects. Recall Roy's articulation of the destructive nature of contemporary religion not as a Pentecostal phenomenon, but rather as a general malaise that he identified by focusing on fast-moving revisionist forms of Islam. These waves of "reformist" Islam are also presented as taxing many preexisting social ties.

But at the spaces where money and Islamic religiosity intersect, one also sees new forms proliferate; one form in particular that has been the recipient of anthropological attention is Islamic banking and finance. Islamic banking includes forms of finance designed to avoid the sharia prohibition of *riba*, or interest. In the past fifty years there have been concerted attempts in locales as diverse as the Middle East, South and Southeast Asia, and the United States to create protocols, networks, and institutions that can do the work of Western

FIGURE 3.6: Pedestrians pass in front of a branch of the Meezan Bank in Karachi, Pakistan, June 2012. Meezan Bank is Pakistan's largest Islamic lender. Asim Hafeez/Bloomberg via Getty Images.

FIGURE 3.7: Delegates talk at the Global Islamic Finance Forum in Kuala Lumpur, Malaysia, September 2014. Charles Pertwee/Bloomberg via Getty Images.

financial capital, while still staying within the bounds of this prohibition on interest. These efforts sometimes take the form of conventional financial contracts that are carefully drafted so as to avoid the technical definition of riba, while still in effect providing something very much like interest; these are sometimes critiqued as being Islamic in form but not in substance, and hence being a land of "trickery." But others in the Islamic banking world have been trying to form institutions based on profit-sharing (and also, of course, a sharing of risk), which could provide both capital and profit without interest (Rudnyckyi 2014, 2016). Much like the Prosperity Gospel, Islamic banking can occur at vertiginously different scales. Islamic banking can be consciously carried out as a state project, as is often the case in Southeast Asia and the Middle East. But it can also take the form of relatively small-scale critique of global finance through experiments in new fiscal forms animated by different ethical modes of evaluation (Maurer 2005). Regardless, none of these attempts to foster Islamic banking take the form of a simple return to a prior institution; if such institutions existed, they could simply be "ported" into the present day, either as continuing forms or even as ideational or social structures. The lamination of money onto religion once again compels invention.

If religion and money in their modern forms catalyze such invention in the spaces or moments where they co-occur, it may be worth asking if in some ways the affinity between these objects is so deep that, to be honest, it is best not to think of them as separate. Which brings us back to our original document, the faux dollar bill. The bill, in its insistence that one think of salvation as something that at least partially has a value (recall the "million dollar question"), seems to be calling for an act of conversion in a doubled sense—not only for the recipient to dedicate his heart to God, but also for a shift from one regime of value to another. It places money and religion in a hierarchical relationship. But as we have seen in the Prosperity Gospel, there are moments in which money becomes a religion. Not in the crass way that people worship money, of course (though there are certainly spaces and moments in the Prosperity Gospel where that occurs, just as there are surely actors in Islamic banking who see the project as entirely instrumental and conceive of it as nothing other than a new model for profit). Rather, it seems that, at times, money and religion imply each other to such a degree that they approach what Mauss called "the total social fact," a form that is supposedly lost to us in the modern age of differentiated social spheres. Institutions that stand as total social facts are generally thought of as being eaten away by money and religion; recall the vulnerability of the sort of rites and practices that were constructed in such as way that their kinship, religious, and economic aspects could not be disentangled. But it appears that at least in some circumstances, in the wake of their destruction, opportunities arise for new forms of conversion, making the monetary religious and the religious monetary. This operation does not give rise to the same forms that existed before, and much like a recipient of the faux dollar bill Bible tracts, there are many who may feel cheated when they find out what they actually have in hand. But again, just like a recipient of the faux Bible tract, there are those who might see these new forms as bearing value, and as good news.

CHAPTER FOUR

Money and the Everyday

Instability and Inventiveness in the Modern Age

TAYLOR C. NELMS AND JANE I. GUYER

INSTABILITY AND INVENTIVENESS, EVERYDAY

The near-century covered by the "modern age" may be one of the most turbulent and inventive in the world history of money. This may strike some as surprising, for the modern age is also the age of consolidated national money and territorial currencies (Gilbert and Helleiner 1999; Helleiner 2003b). Yet turbulence returned many times, in many forms: two world wars, and many localized ones. A Great Depression and Great Recession, both preceded by world-turning financial crises. Recurring lurches in economic life, including changes in the regulation of prices and access to commodities, especially under wartime rationing, shifts in systems of employment and wages, and turns and returns to austerity. Frequent disturbances to the value of money—and to public confidence in its everyday use—by inflation and devaluation, which varied widely from place to place and time to time, but fear of which became standardized in expert and popular imaginations. Later, changes in the very form of money, as financial instruments and payment technologies diversified and digitized.

The modern age also registered a shift away from colonial and national economic planning and regulation through the creation of international monitoring, measurement, and support systems at Bretton Woods, including institutions like the World Bank and International Monetary Fund and indices like the gross domestic product (GDP) and consumer price index (CPI). There followed several decades of dismantling colonial rule, which led to many new national currencies, some of which, like the *franc* CFAs in West and Central Africa, coalesced into regional blocs linked to the metropole. In the 1970s, the Bretton Woods system collapsed, and in 1989, the breakup of the Soviet Union inaugurated another wave of new national currencies—and renewed monetary instabilities—in newly independent postsocialist states. The interface between "hard" and "soft" currencies became more visible as reliance on the former in the latter's economies expanded.

Many currencies were also decimalized, where in the past they had varied in their mutual numerical composition (Tschoegl 2010). Until 1971, for example, British money was 4 farthings (or 2 ha'pennies) to the penny, 12 pence to the shilling, 20 shillings to the pound, and about 21 shillings to the guinea, reflecting past values of copper, gold, and sterling. Their values relative to each other and to state-issued paper currency were linked to metal only until after World War I, when governments could not afford to guarantee conversion. Decimalization in 1971 definitively eliminated the relationship in the UK between money's material and its value in exchange, while standardizing denominational categories. Now there are 100 pence to the pound, rather than 240, and "Decimal Day" came to mark "a new era designed to slip the bonds of imperium"—and, for some, the unfortunate passing of a premodern, but more poetic (and more properly English) system of "bobs" (shillings) and "tanners"

FIGURE 4.1: A little boy examines a display of newly decimalized currency at Harrods department store in London, in advance of the United Kingdom's Decimal Day, February 15, 1971. Photo by Frank Barratt/Keystone/Getty Images.

(sixpence) (Bayley 2011). Other areas of the Commonwealth—India in 1957, for example, or Australia in 1966—had already taken this step. Efforts to redenominate national currencies—lopping four zeros off the face value of the Ghanaian cedi in 2007 (Dzokoto et al. 2010) or the surprise demonetization of the largest denominations of Indian rupees in 2016 (Dharia and Trisal 2017; Guérin et al. 2017)—and other state-led currency reforms and ad-hoc interventions became increasingly frequent, especially in the wake of post-World War II decolonization and the collapse of the Soviet Union, adding to the modern history of monetary instability.

Exposure to turbulence shaped people's understandings of and approaches to money in their everyday lives. For many, instability became the norm, and practices evolved to fit expectations. As people found ways to make do with, and make sense of, uncertainty and unpredictability, the classic functions of money—as standard of value and unit of account; state-backed instrument for settling debts; medium of commercial and interpersonal exchange; savings vehicle through which value is preserved over time—were rearranged and redistributed across different forms of value, practices, and projections of futures. Sometimes these adjustments incorporated long-standing options: networks of friends and family, the perceived durability of precious metals, the promises of digital technology.

For much of the modern era, then, the practices of both formal authorities and ordinary people were inventive, to cope with—and sometimes take advantage of—recurring change in the political, economic, legal, technical, and social worlds of money. Money is always caught between the sovereign who bestows and maintains the unit of account and the people who then use it, taking it up to settle their debts with one another, make individual and collective investments, and much more (Hart 1986; Desan 2014). We concentrate here on the people, in the "everyday" mode of life, who adapted by making demands of their own, through creative popular cultures of commentary and management, which turned money—especially, but not only, in its cash form—to multiple ends. We focus, that is, on the social life of money in its linguistic and material vernaculars, across local, regional, national, and global contexts. Because they share this focus, we draw heavily on anthropological and sociological literatures.[1]

Modern money is sometimes thought to dictate its terms to those who use it, but the history of people's diverse practical engagements shows us something different. Examining what people do with money, in its many material forms, and how they do it, "foregrounds money's pragmatics, its uses, affordances, and entailments," alongside its meanings and moralities (Maurer et al. 2013: 52; see also Carruthers and Espeland 1998). Of particular importance is people's inventiveness: in the face of economic precarity and monetary instability, shifting political borders and mobilities across them, intertwined economic and moral thresholds, currency interfaces, and changing technologies. We mean "inventive" in the sense suggested by Lave (1993: 13): "open-ended processes of improvisation with the social, material, and experiential resources at hand," oriented to specific problems at the frontiers of what's known. If "the properties of money are not universal but historically constituted, socially mediated, and politically regulated," as Truitt writes (2013: 12), then those properties are always also subject to invention and innovation in practice.[2]

Indeed, modern money, with all its turbulence, necessitated the skillful administration of cash funds, and their deployment to multiple ends—social and economic—across varied and variable contexts, in combination with other media of transaction and reserve. Everyday money management thus depended on new and existing material and institutional resources (including technologies of budgeting and accounting, saving and spending, payment and exchange) and repertoires of practice and experience (both habitual and innovative); it was also shaped by cultural and moral commitments and expectations about the appropriate use and accumulation of value.

We devote the following sections to exploring money's everyday multiplicity while focusing specifically on the management of money through language, savings technologies, and exchange practices. We discuss the units and dynamics of money management—how people turn to creative customs and alternative institutions to deal with the everyday problems and moral quandaries of household finance—which reveals, for example, the ethics of small-cash generosities and skills in enabling and leveraging pots and flows of money. Then we consider conditions of instability in everyday monetary life, looking at how people confront poverty, mobility, and—finally, in the last sections— technological change. Throughout we track the inventiveness of people's practices in response to and in expectation of such instability.

MONEY, MULTIPLE

The "everyday" is one possible register for talking about ordinary or popular matters, as opposed to the elite or technical. Invoked as an appeal to a reality at once common (shared) and commonplace (banal), it offers a way to talk about the mundane, in its etymological sense: that which belongs to this (secular, profane) world. As scholarly preoccupation, the everyday is itself a modern invention. It reflects a turn in analysis away from, as de Certeau (1984: v) writes, "the actors who possess proper names and social blazons," and the macro-level abstractions they stood for, towards "the chorus of secondary characters." In late nineteenth- and early twentieth-century Europe, scholars sought to document the effects of capitalist modernization: Durkheim, for example, on the social and psychological effects of industrialization and urbanization, Weber on the secularization and rationalization of culture, or

Lukács on the commodification of everyday life. These concerns reflected a novel metonymic understanding of human behavior, in which the prosaic, habitual, and intimate provided traces of and clues to the systemic, structural, or global. The everyday became, as Debord (1962) put it, "the measure for all things."

In the modern age, it is *money* that is routinely described in this way. Writing in the context of these turn-of-the-twentieth-century transformations, Simmel (2011; see also Allen and Pryke 1999) suggested that money, in offering a single standard of abstract accounting, came increasingly to mediate the everyday mental and social lives of modern, metropolitan subjects. Yet the argument that money, as a result, engenders a certain "colourlessness" has been used as a *foil* for research on money in social and cultural context, which has emphasized the variety of everyday meanings, materialities, and uses of money across space and time (Nelms and Maurer 2014; see also Bialecki, this volume). The diversity and dynamism of monetary tokens, and the many—indeed, often colorful— uses to which they are put, is a central lesson offered by an everyday perspective on money in the modern age.

Money's multiplicity overflows strict categories of form and function. There is nothing guaranteed about money's divisibility or fungibility, its negotiability or liquidity, its number, its accounting, its capacity to draw equivalencies—nor about the meanings such qualities and capacities assume or the moral charge they spark. Examples abound: money in family, ritual, charity, travel, games of chance or fortune, practices of play and pedagogy. Money as sign of identity and difference, as marker of borders and boundaries (local, national; ethnic, racial, religious; of rank or status). As medium and measure of expenditure, consumption, saving, credit, and debt. As political technology and symbol of sovereignty, autonomy, and allegiance. As site of conflict and of imagination. As vehicle for cultural, spiritual, and ethical values: aspiration and ambition, virtue and vice, dignity and despair, respect and regret, honor and shame. Today, in short, scholars emphasize the specificity and provincialism, not uniformity and universality, of "modern" money's forms and functions. This is as true of aggregate indices of the money supply and instruments of high finance as it is of cash and coupons.

Anthropologists and sociologists have long emphasized this practical, material, and representational pluralism, both in the "developed" West and the colonial and postcolonial South. The anthropology of money was founded on comparative, even encyclopedic, descriptions of culturally and functionally specific forms of value and media of ritual and ceremonial payment, often classed as "primitive" money (e.g., Firth 1929). Mid-century work described the supposedly corrosive effects of the "modern" currencies of colonizers or ruling states on such "special-purpose" moneys, a term coined by Polanyi (1957; see also Dalton 1965, Codere 1968) to indicate forms of value that served a limited selection of functions. One famous account of the Tiv people in West Africa described the dissolution of customary divisions between morally ranked domains—each with its own measures of value and media of exchange—after the arrival of colonial currencies (Bohannan 1959).

Others challenged juxtapositions of "modern" and "pre-" or "non-modern" forms of value and the accompanying teleological stories of monetary modernization, showing how pre-colonial currencies could circulate generally and how "Western money" is itself "special-purpose, not general-purpose, money" (Melitz 1970: 1021; see also Parry and Bloch 1989). Multiple, intersecting, non-reducible forms of value have long traversed many parts of the world, from China (Martin 2015) to Atlantic Africa. Guyer (2004) shows that people like the Tiv had for generations operated within the shifting, uneven geographies of regional trade networks, conveying and converting value not just within and between culturally static "spheres of exchange" but across junctures and along pathways that reached across Africa and beyond. In the Pacific, meanwhile, as elsewhere, "social scientific expectations that global capitalist expansion would quickly overwhelm traditional Melanesian economies have been confounded by the latter's dynamism and resilience [. . .] and state currencies and imported goods mingle within formal exchange systems fundamental to social reproduction" (Robbins and Akin 1999: 1; see also Foster 1998). In some places, like Indonesia, new currencies did not flatten how "people imagine their horizons," but their "alienating power" still sparked "a wishful dream of utopia" (Rutherford 2001: 323, 321).

Monetary change, that is, is additive rather than substitutive (Maurer 2015), and the circuits among different forms and functions proliferate, necessitating inventiveness on and across political, economic, and social frontiers, especially in the postcolonial world. People do not simply "socialize" or "domesticate" official currencies but manage them alongside other forms and units of value—livestock and real estate, ritual tokens and community moneys, treasure and "imaginary" accounting units, promotional cards and coupons, airline miles and virtual game credits—in complex ecologies (Neiburg 2016; Maurer and Swartz 2017). These technologies and practices are no less "modern" than the colonial and national currencies with which they interfaced. They show, that is, the pluralism of *both* money *and* modernity.

Even with regard to state currency, everyday life for people around the world has been multiply monetized across scales, with national, regional, and local currencies each institutionalized in their own ways, assets distributed across different numerical denominations, material interfaces, and accounting thresholds. The mythical idea of "one nation, one money" has never held true, and international competition and complementarity between state currencies has a long history (Cohen 1998).[3] Indeed, the need to mediate more than one currency may be expanding (Cohen 2004; Dodd 2005). The distinction between "hard" and "soft" national currencies, the expansion of migrant and refugee populations, and the explicit effort to create alternative or complementary currencies have resulted in moneys that are multiple not only in the literal sense of "many." Forms of value and exchange work in separate

FIGURE 4.2: A kina shell necklace from the highlands of Papua New Guinea alongside a cropped Papua New Guinea five kina note, picturing shell valuables. Institute for Money, Technology & Financial Inclusion, CC BY-SA 2.0.

and situationally convergent ways as people's everyday inventiveness opens to new horizons, as it has for trading populations in the past.

The management of multiple currencies is frequently oriented to the distinction between "hard" and "soft" currencies (Guyer 1995, 2011). Throughout the twentieth century, dozens of new national currencies proliferated alongside new national political projects. Many of these postcolonial and postsocialist currencies, however, were devalued through structural adjustment and destabilized through the post-Bretton Woods establishment of foreign exchange markets—even as elsewhere policymakers and central bankers have privileged inflation control over other substantive economic priorities like growth or employment (see Beggs, this volume). Such instability recreates colonial geopolitical and socioeconomic landscapes once thought to be on their way to being flattened into a single capitalist world system.[4]

The modern world is thus one that is increasingly *both* multi-currency *and* dollarized, as demand for national currencies that remain stable sources of value—the US dollar in particular (Eichengreen 2010)—has grown steadily throughout the modern era, especially in parts of the world where money forms trade at unstable rates. Hard currencies are used internationally by governments (held in reserve by central banks to peg or protect their national currencies), banks and businesses (to denominate prices and manage cross-border payments), and ordinary people (who turn high-value bills into stores of value). The cultures and politics of de facto and de jure dollarization vary from place to

FIGURE 4.3: People wait in line outside a currency exchange, January 2002, in Buenos Aires, Argentina. Quique Kierszenbaum/Getty Images.

FIGURE 4.4: A supermarket employee in Rio de Janeiro, Brazil puts up new price signs as Brazil changes its currency from the "cruzeiro" to the "real cruzeiro" in an effort to curb inflation, August 1993. JULIO PEREIRA/AFP/Getty Images.

place.[5] They introduce new thresholds, which can be managed in hard currency and its "functional analogs to reserves and futures" (Guyer 2016: 222). People in soft-currency economies confront pragmatic challenges about how to save, earn, and spend with money whose purchasing power lurches according to often opaque logics; they also confront questions about what such instability means for state sovereignty and individual agency, or value and inequality *per se*. What kinds of *social* equivalencies and distinctions do people draw when they deal in dollars alongside such other instruments and assets?[6]

Migration routes, border zones, and refugee camps similarly offer challenges and opportunities for the everyday management of money, especially through the spatial and temporal pragmatics of commensuration and circulation (Bolt 2014; Yeh 2016; Trapp 2018). The conversion of value across political economic boundaries and associated transactional media—such as through cross-border remittances—often sparks conflicts around the social uses and moral meanings of money (e.g., Levitt 2001; Pribilsky 2012; Pedersen 2013; Paerregaard 2014).[7] Long-standing remittance flows, for example, can arouse aspirations and expectations in mediating kin networks across geopolitical divides—such as between migrants and their families back home (Singh 2013; Thai 2014; Small 2018)—or in mediating the division between this world and that of the gods or ancestors—such as, in many parts of East Asia, through the burning of "spirit money," denominated in the local currency or US dollars (Kwon 2007; Chu 2010; Truitt 2013). These questions took on critical importance in the first decades of the 2000s, as the most profound refugee crisis since World War II sent families and entire communities scrambling to new lives around the world. As we write, reports are gathering on the financial hardships of refugees: payment in dollars or euros for their travel, the impact of counterfeits and variable exchange rates on the streets, the prices offered for their "assets"— land and homes, precious metals and jewelry, even body parts.

Finally, people around the world have also invested in grassroots efforts to introduce local complementary or community currencies (Blanc 2010). These efforts cut across divisions between hard and soft currencies, sometimes emerging in response to crisis and thus offering a livelihood strategy in confronting shortages of currency or credit. Classic examples include Depression-era experiments with scrip, celebrated by none other than Irving Fisher (1933; see also Champ 2008)—from the stamps issued in 1932 by the Austrian town of Wörgl to the shells marked up and accepted by local businesses in Pismo Beach, California in 1933 (see Feingold 2015: 17). Parallels can be drawn to the use of alternative value forms and barter in post-socialist contexts (Woodruff 1999; Humphrey 2002; Pine 2002; Rogers 2005). Twenty-first-century Argentina offers another example: there, thousands of people joined barter clubs and circulated provincial bond notes after the breakdown of the

FIGURE 4.5: A woman burns "ghost," "spirit," or "hell money" in a fire in the street in Hanoi, Vietnam, June 2015. Jeremy Woodhouse/Getty Images.

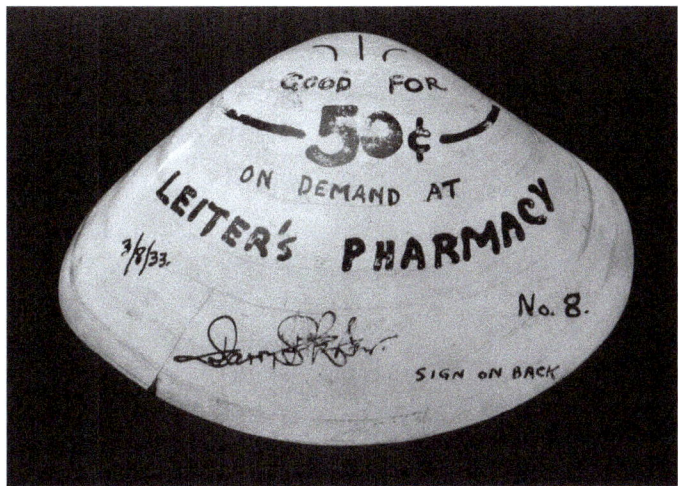

FIGURE 4.6: In 1929, the United States stock markets crashed, triggering bank runs and sparking the Great Depression. National Numismatics Collection, Division of Work & Industry, National Museum of American History, Smithsonian Institution.

country's convertibility regime, which had pegged the peso to the US dollar at a rate of one-to-one (Luzzi 2010; Ould-Ahmed 2010).

Many see local currencies not simply as substitutes for "failed" state money but as a "liberatory" political practice (North 2007: xv). Such is the case of the Ithaca HOURS or BerkShares experiments in the United States, the Bristol and Brixton pounds in the United Kingdom, the longstanding WIR system in Switzerland, or the interest-free microcredits offered by the Banco Palmas in Fortaleza, Brazil. Projects like these seek to reclaim money for social ends: by territorially delimiting monetary circulation, they encourage local consumption and promote local development. By providing an alternative medium of exchange and restricting outflows of local wealth, they obviate the need for external debt relations, and by strengthening local economic ties, they foster solidarity while promoting community autonomy. Some impose a carrying cost (known as demurrage) to discourage hoarding and facilitate a fairer distribution of wealth. Such grassroots currency reform thus emerges at the intersection of monetary instability and inventiveness, posing a challenge to the presumption of a one-to-one link between money and nation/state/market, even as the currencies themselves sometimes prove short-lived.

MONEY MANAGEMENT

Monetary multiplicity and instability invites and sometimes necessitates creative management. The units and dynamics of managing money, in the vernacular, under varying conditions of poverty and predictability were and remain a key preoccupation of everyday life in the modern age. In this section, we focus on the use of cash money, especially in the context of household management. As forms of wage labor emerged and spread through the Euro-American world, many people were paid primarily in cash—bills and coins. As a political and technical achievement, the widespread availability and acceptance of cash had important impacts on everyday life, and cash as a money form proved uniquely flexible and meaningful: terminologically, materially, and pragmatically. Cash in the modern age was thus central to transactional practices within and between family units and social networks, and it was shaped by long-standing moral philosophies and popular cultures of work and exchange, customs of household management, the practical impositions of recurring instabilities, and interventions by government and development actors.

Earmarking: economy and society

Money retains an ambivalent moral position in the modern era, when people feel torn between what appear to them as the conflicting logics of economy and society, capitalism and community, market and non-market domains of transaction and interaction. Anxieties—what Wilkis (2013) evocatively identifies as "suspicions"—abound about how money traverses the boundaries of economic and social life and "ushers in a world of moral confusion" (Macfarlane, cited in Bloch and Parry 1989: 17). Money takes on heightened social and moral significance as it circulates across domains through everyday practices of accounting and exchange. This traffic provokes tensions over the mingling of "hostile worlds": the vulgar economic with the traditional, the communal, the familiar, the intimate, or the personal; it also invites creative responses (Zelizer 2005; Rossman 2014; Bandelj et al. 2015; see also Bialecki, this volume and Haiven, this volume).[8]

A common creative response is to budget pots and flows of money according to source and/or intended destination—carefully designating and planning specific amounts, for specific purposes and people, on specific calendars. Zelizer (1997) made the important conceptual innovation of naming this practice "earmarking." Building on studies of life insurance and the valuation of children in the United States (Zelizer 2010), Zelizer writes about money in domestic transactions, gift-giving, charity, welfare, and discretionary payments like bonuses or prizes—which demonstrate how "people always introduce distinctions, doubts, and directives, that defy all instrumental calculation" (Zelizer 1997: 30; see also Zelizer 2010). In the process, they transform seemingly fungible "modern" money into special social and moral resources through mental, digital, and "tin can" accounting (4). Money, she concludes, is crucial to the creation and maintenance of interpersonal relations across supposedly separate "social" and "economic" domains: "everywhere we look people are creating different kinds of money [. . .] as they cope with their multiple social relations" (1).

Earmarking and enclaving practices are widespread forms of everyday monetary inventiveness (Carruthers and Espeland 1998; Carruthers 2010; Bradford 2015). The way this is done, in different contexts and languages, with different sets of rules and technologies, is a critical research frontier.[9] As Zelizer (1997: 30) points out, the moral practices of money become even more important in moments of economic change, such as the beginning of the modern age, when "an increasingly consumer-oriented culture" furnished many people with an expanding "world of goods and services" that "competed for th[eir] imagination and pocketbooks." The latter part of the era—when irregular and temporary employment conditions placed many in the "precariat" with respect to schedules and budgets, payday receipts, and long-term benefits, and when an increasing number of workers managed their lives in more than one currency, across geopolitical borders and fluctuating exchange rates, at long distances from kinsfolk—offers an important analog.

Language: words and sayings

Linguistic inventiveness is reflected in the many denominational terms for money and its divisions, numerical and material, which reflect local histories, cultures, and politics. Many monetary terms, including the name of certain denominations, originate in the very matter of money: borrowing historical, even ancient, vocabularies of weights and measures (Grierson 1977) or referencing physical composition (even if it has since changed; hence the five-cent "nickel"), inscription ("Benjamins"), or color ("greenbacks").[10] Other associations abound: in English monetary slang, a "quid" (one pound) is a term several centuries old, deriving from the Latin "quid pro quo" (a thing for a thing). In Ecuador, before that country's official dollarization, the one-sucre coin was called an "*ayora*," after the former President whose government issued them; in another period, 50-cent coins reissued during the tenure of a Vice-President famously fond of alcohol were sometimes called "*borrachos*" [drunks].

People have developed vocabularies to qualify types of money in other ways, too, often in concert with earmarking and enclaving practices. "Dirty" and "clean," "big" and "small," "hot" and "cold"—money's tangible qualities are mobilized to do the earmarking Zelizer has highlighted, drawing lines around categories of currency—and the people handling it—that would otherwise remain fungible, marking money's power, purchasing or otherwise (Lemon 1998; Cattelino 2009; Peebles 2012; Walker 2017). Linguistically, such terminologies often reflect anxieties about socially sanctioned vs. unsanctioned wealth (Roitman 2005). "Bitter money" (Shipton 1989), "hot money" (Walsh 2003), "polluted money" (High 2013), and even the "money of shit" (Hutchinson 1992) all refer to ill-gotten gains: profits of morally ambiguous or transgressive activities—mining, gambling, selling the land of one's lineage, laboring for a wage rather than traditional livelihoods—thought to be contaminating, corrupting, even ruinous, if not spent or invested appropriately. Bloch and Parry (1989) argue that such distinctions appear when money cycles between long-term investments in social reproduction, often centered on the family or community, and short-term forms of individual acquisitiveness and accumulation, usually routed through market exchange. The refusal to recognize money's connections to the collective can be construed as a betrayal. It is under these conditions, Peebles (2012) shows, that money is declared dirty and dangerous and must be "cooked" or "cleaned." These are the ubiquitous vernaculars of money's ritual regulations.[11]

As the digital and mobile infrastructures for money have expanded and diversified, so too have its languages. In the United States, for example, twenty-first-century payment applications PayPal and Venmo came to be used as verbs. The Kenya-based mobile money service M-Pesa, discussed below as a pioneer of cell phone-based financial services, borrowed the Swahili word for money [*pesa*], which is itself borrowed from the Hindi word *paisa*, a fraction of currency introduced to Kenya from British India in the late nineteenth century, when Indian migrant workers arrived to build railways there (Singh 2013). Money terms cross linguistic boundaries, as they always have, bringing with them practices and ideologies, but also leaving behind the voice of the authorities that originated them. Who now identifies "money" with the Roman goddess Juno Moneta, whose temple doubled as a mint?

Popular culture, especially literature and music, also offers resources for monetary vernaculars; these are often quite local. In mid-twentieth-century Britain, people still quoted Mr. Micawber, from Dickens' *David Copperfield*: "Annual income twenty pounds, annual expenditure nineteen nineteen and six,[12] result happiness. Annual income twenty pounds, annual expenditure twenty pounds ought and six, result misery." Small margins—and the ability to divert some cash into a store of value, by saving one year to the next—made significant differences to one's sense of life: between happiness and misery. Indeed, the idea that money should always be available, in small amounts, to be skillfully deployed, is embedded in other sayings, such as the value ("a penny") given to one's thoughts or the warning "Don't spoil the ship for a ha'p'orth of tar" (half-penny-worth). Other traditions offer other lessons. Midcentury Caribbean calypso, for example, offered cultural commentary on everyday life under the threat of devaluation, while in late twentieth-century US hip hop, descriptions of wealth and informal money practices became declarations of economic independence and reflections on the economic aspects of racial inequality. In all these cases, the assumption that money works to quantify is reversed as the qualities of money's quantity are foregrounded.

Storage: containers and concealment

The materiality of bills and coins produces problems and possibilities for daily management. Carrying and storing money—on one's person, in one's home, or with a trusted third party, such as a small business or employer—offers opportunities for creative everyday practice, as people seek to keep cash safe from theft, loss, or damage from fire, flood, or more mundane physical deterioration. The diverse dedicated storage items are illustrative. In post-World War I Europe, people stored paper money in cigarette tins and hidden in alcoves behind chimneys; as smoking expanded amongst the lower classes, the tins were recycled into daily use. The need to keep cash "safe" made its way into vernacular vocabularies: "piggy banks," money kept "under the mattress," or the "pocket money" kept in undesignated slush funds or given to children as an allowance. In Britain, as the danger of small-scale theft, especially in crowded places, became more routine and "pick-pocketing" became a recognized activity, pockets themselves became a liability and were replaced by bags. Some pockets were refashioned for safer carrying. Blue jeans were cut tighter to the body than trousers of the past, and their back pockets were made wallet-sized and riveted to prevent tearing; these smaller pockets were also possible to cover with a jacket, making theft a greater challenge to dexterity.

The physical vulnerabilities of cash have also played a role in money's digitization, especially through cell phone-based financial services. As we discuss below, such services have not displaced cash entirely, instead reshaping its meanings and uses while introducing new instabilities. (Whether hacking mobile accounts will become a new version of pick-pocketing remains to be seen.) The mattress still figures prominently in the popular imagination. So too does the local corner store, which can act as a custodian of everyday money by allowing customers to save their wages or receive goods on credit.

Still, the emergence of the mobile phone as a technology of money management foregrounds an important aspect of money's containers: the cultural—gendered, raced, and classed—politics of concealing and revealing money. The cell phone is a portable communication technology uniquely suited to mediate the play of transparency and secrecy, display and discretion—both in terms of what can be communicated *over* the phone (information, monetary value) and what can be communicated *by* the phone, as a sign of status or proximity to power. Cell phones can be used to make interpersonal demands, heightening expectations of increased accessibility by "allow[ing] one to access and command reciprocal obligations and intimacies without being physically present" (Kenny 2016: 258; see also Singh 2013). As a way to manage one's finances, however, cell phones can also be used to limit the publicity of transactions, thus mediating kinship and community pressures to share or redistribute wealth—and potentially expanding, for example, women's autonomy over personal savings. But mobile money can also heighten fears about privacy and what such privacy might hide, activating gendered and generational tensions over the display of wealth (Kusimba et al. 2015).

These are old anxieties—about money transferred "under the table," concealed in order to facilitate illicit romantic relations, or used in conspicuous displays of social power and status—inflected by new technologies. In twenty-first-century Papua New Guinea, similar dynamics can be found around that "old" technology of the pocket (Pickles 2013). Pockets can be used to conceal and reveal wealth and thus control how one's redistributions of value are received (stingy or generous). They also become (like the cell phone) objects of speculation and complaint: stigmatizing for some (suspected gamblers and prostitutes), celebrated for others (churchgoing men). Local logics thus offer different understandings of how to manage "pocket money," but they reveal a commonality: storage and concealment are not just about protecting cash, but accounting for it. Pockets and cell phones are technologies for both financial and moral budgeting.

Futures: giving and gambling

Much everyday money management, especially by the poor, has been historically devoted to the use of cash income left over after taking care of larger obligations to debts and taxes, paid off on a more regular calendar. The remainder had to be divided between the immediate necessities of life (the boundaries of which shifted and expanded throughout the modern age even as available resources stagnated with incomes) and investments, through both saving and speculation, in the planning of futures, both individual and collective. These investments do not fit neatly into the functional categories through which money is typically defined. Gifting and gambling, which lurk within the popular cultures of modern life, offer examples.

Throughout the modern era, gifting has been considered a privileged alternative to supposedly asocial or even anti-social commerce. But people give money for many reasons and to diverse ends (Yan 1996; Wilkis 2013). Think of small voluntary donations (which remained common long beyond when tithing demanded morally justified payments to sovereigns): coins given to beggars and panhandlers, collection money for church services, or customs like "a penny for the guy" (for Guy Fawkes' Night celebrations in the UK) and "alms for the poor" on certain holidays. Throughout the modern age, small cash gifts—like *Trinkgeld* (drinking money) in Germany or *ekmek parasi* (bread money) in Turkey—was the customary response to plaintive requests for assistance on streets or public transportation. Before the establishment of the modern welfare state, philanthropic giving among the working classes was even more common; Engels (1993: 284), for example, noted that "the poor are relieved much more by the poor than by the bourgeoisie [...] such help has a wholly different ring to it from the carelessly tossed alms of the luxurious bourgeoisie." People gain a sense of their own ethical value through such donations, however small, even if, as Engels suggests, it also invites worries about how such giving is more an assertion of inequality than solidarity.

Outside Europe, there are similar customs, revitalized by postcolonial independence yet still rooted in ancient scriptural prescriptions about tithing: giving away a portion ("one tenth") of one's income. Alms-giving is an important practice in Abrahamic traditions, from the Quranic *zakat*, one of the five pillars of Islam, to Christian charity, whether understood as selfless spiritual love or a charismatic investment in one's future financial empowerment (see Bialecki, this volume). South Asian religious doctrines and communities make analogous demands. When not in response to religious imperative or expectation, giving shifts in character. For example, when it flows through interpersonal networks of mutual aid among family and neighbors, it can become "care." When it is institutionalized in state assistance programs like government cash transfers or welfare payments, it can be embroiled in debates about the "rights" or "dependency" of citizens and the "responsibilities" or "profligacy" of the state.[13] When it is channeled through private philanthropic and humanitarian organizations, it is framed as "development." And when it is embedded in relations of political patronage (Ansell 2010; Bjorkman 2014) or wrapped up in an envelope informally exchanged (Praspaliauskiene 2016), it can become "corruption" or "bribery" to some, "reciprocity" or "obligation" to others (Humphrey 2002; Sneath 2006).

Moral philosophies and spiritual ideologies of giving stress the importance of purity of motive or intent. Yet across these domains, scholars have highlighted the social and ethical calculations and entanglements of giving. However "free," however important the display of disinterestedness, gifts entail obligations and can be used to reinforce hierarchy. Still, as Bornstein (2009: 643) argues (echoing Mauss and Engels), giving cannot be shuttled off in either direction: "To coerce the impulse to give into rational accountability is to obliterate its freedom; to render giving into pure impulse is to reinforce social inequality." Far from destroying or desacralizing relationships, then, cash giving does meaningful social work: discharging debts, fulfilling sacred obligations, cultivating an ethical sense of self, investing in the public good, building community, or tending to social relations that can be activated later for other purposes.

Gambling is a different kind of investment, reflecting a different kind of hopefulness, especially during periods of unpredictability. Historically situated between culturally specific epistemological regimes of speculation, risk, and probability (on the one hand) and luck, chance, and magic (on the other), gambling has long served as a model to understand—or simply denigrate as imprudent or immoral—many kinds of financial practice and speculative

FIGURE 4.7: Coffee pickers gamble in a game after getting paid in Ciudad Bolivar, one of the most productive coffee towns in Colombia, at the peak of the coffee harvest season, October 2017. JOAQUIN SARMIENTO/AFP/Getty Images.

FIGURE 4.8: Patrons of the MGM Grand Hotel & Casino in Las Vegas, Nevada, gamble on US college basketball games, March 2013. Photo by Chris Farina/Sports Illustrated/Getty Images.

accumulation. Yet gambling as an everyday practice is not cross-culturally universal (Binde 2005; Pickles 2016). In Europe, the wealthy had long gambled in games of chance, but in the early 1920s, gambling small amounts of money—for example, in football pools or on horse racing—became more common among the working classes. In the United States, gambling in the modern age is both mundane (office sports pools, family poker night) and restricted to special liminal spaces of excess (Las Vegas, riverboat casinos); discussions are inflected by these local dynamics.

In much of the postcolonial world, everyday gambling practices have emerged within living memory: from cock fighting, to card games, to underground lotteries. In these settings, gambling is often gendered, embedded in local customs and expectations about how men use their earnings in pursuit of uncertain gain, while women—judged as caretakers of household or community finances—are supposed to be more circumspect about risk. It is also often associated with socioeconomic inequality; arguments that it exacerbates or ameliorates such inequality through redistribution are both common. As a result, it is also often connected to "fast money" pyramid schemes (Cox 2018; see also Verdery 1995; Musaraj 2011) and to "occult economies" of magic, witchcraft, and divination through which people navigate the co-occurrence of wealth and poverty (Comaroff and Comaroff 1999; Klima 2006).

Households: poverty and pedagogy

How poverty is lived, through what kinds of money, mediated and managed by whom, became, over time, a central question of the modern age—one typically focused on the household in both public life and private budgeting. Steedman's (1986) personal family history from post-World War II Britain offers an example of the latter, highlighting challenges regarding income. Her parents, though employed, failed to bring in enough money, so her mother took in lodgers. She taught the children a lesson common to modern middle-class ethics: "If you want something, you have to go out and work for it. Nobody gives you anything; nothing comes free in this world" (37). Even a tip was assessed in terms of affordability and inequality, as her mother flung a sixpenny piece back at a titled customer: "If you can't afford any more than that, Madam, I suggest you keep it" (37).

An often-overlooked everyday use of money is as a pedagogical tool. As Steedman suggests, money is often central to teaching children not only the mechanics of budgeting and economizing, but the ethics of saving and spending (Zelizer 2002; Pugh 2009). Sometimes parents turn to old coins and notes, such as the gold guinea Guyer's own mother kept in an embroidered purse, to convey historical lessons about thrift, wealth, and instability. Such relics of the monetary past are collected in savings jars and tins, distributed by banks as promotional items, or purchased from craft stores, earmarked with phrases like "vacation fund" or "college savings." Money has also been incorporated into board games—think of *Monopoly* (the first version of which was intended to show how private property enriched owners at the expense of tenants), *Life* (in which the objective is simply to earn more over one's "lifetime" than other players), or *Mall Madness* (in which players compete to buy goods from different stores as quickly as possible). Indeed, many children's toys are simply

FIGURE 4.9: Taylor Nelms's son plays with a functioning toy calculator and cash register, made by the Swedish company, Ikea, 2018. Author's own.

facsimiles of bills, coins, and (increasingly) other technologies of payment, like the calculator cash register Nelms gave his son.

In her account of growing up poor, Steedman shows how valuable it is to collect "stories" about money, mediated by particular people in particular situations of life. Household stories of money are also important in accounts of impoverishment and inequality in the contemporary United States. Such accounts—of the subprime mortgage and foreclosure crisis; of factory closings and postindustrial landscapes (Walley 2013); or of people's turn to fringe financial institutions in the face of financial exclusion, stagnating wages, income volatility, and inequality (Rivlin 2010; Aitken 2015; Baradaran 2015)—echo lessons of past economic reporting in the tradition of Ehrenreich (2001). They tell, for example, of the effects of crisis and deindustrialization on labor precariousness, indebtedness, and financial insecurity. They also show how those effects are embedded in struggles over class identity, gender politics, and racial inequality, which are themselves shaped by national myths of work and homeownership, progress and economic democracy. Foregrounding the family as the hub of financial decision-making, they finally describe the creative practices of people caught up in these shifts: how they manage the uneven temporalities of wage supply and consumption demands through alternative financial services like check-cashers and payday lenders (Servon 2017) or confront the moralities of debt through new discourses of reciprocity and refusal (Stout 2016a, 2016b).

In sum, how money enters people's lives, and how it is then managed, is often mediated by boundaries of the household, formally defined and socially lived. While the household long served as a unit of governance, it took on new meaning as socioeconomic mobility shifted from collective project to individual responsibility. It became, for example, the basis for Consumer Price Index data collection, used to evaluate the effects of changes in money's value on purchasing power. Later, states and non-governmental organizations developed standards for personal and household income, such as the World Bank's international poverty line (US$1.90, updated in October 2015). The household, that is, has become a frame both for managing everyday financial relations and for evaluating such management. Even as the financialization of diverse spheres of life has continued apace before and after the twenty-first-century global financial crisis, attention to the household—to the intimacies of wages, budgets, debt—shows how financialized capitalist economies rest on, even as they disavow, the everyday relational worlds of home and family (Martin 2002; Allon 2010; Langley 2010; Adkins 2015; Bear et al. 2015).

Development: everyday finance

In the early twenty-first century, a new science and project of development grew up around studying the financial practices of poor households, especially in the global South. Bringing together research on poverty and everyday money practices, this paradigm echoes ethnographers' past findings in insisting that, far from living unsophisticated financial lives, the poor make calculated decisions about how to save, invest, and consume by managing diverse "portfolios" of monetary and non-monetary assets and instruments (Bannerjee and Duflo 2011). "Financial diaries" documenting these "portfolios of the poor" show multiple savings, credit, and debt commitments on the go all the time, in varied forms that are not strictly monetary, even if they can be re-assessed in monetary terms (Collins et al. 2009). Indeed, while the poor express a preference for cash in some contexts (Stix 2013), many work through in-kind obligations and non-money savings vehicles, an echo of the monetary multiplicity described above.

Among the financial challenges poor households face, "the most fundamental is that households are coping with incomes that are not just low, but also irregular and unpredictable and that too few financial instruments are available to effectively manage these uneven flows" (Collins et al. 2009: 16; see also Rutherford 2000). Expenditures, too, are often irregular and unpredictable, and as poor households deal with these cash-flow difficulties, they may find themselves suddenly in need of substantial funds. They must therefore find ways (through the advance sales of crops or by drawing on interpersonal and kinship networks for informal loans) to deal with risk and quickly raise lump sums. James (2015) similarly describes the link between the unpredictability of cash income and the turn to alternative financing strategies, highlighting the effects of indebtedness among the South African middle class.

The economics of poverty, in other words, is complicated by the relational temporalities of money, especially as they are implicated in everyday kinds of economic improvisation or making-do, including claims-making on kin, neighbors, employers, the state, and others. Ferguson (2015) in sub-Saharan Africa and Han (2012) in Chile document these "mutualities of poverty" (Ferguson 2015: 119): the solidarities and dependencies constituting crucial channels of distribution and networks of support for the poor, as they are managed in cash and credit. There are also often financial self-help groups and solidarity organizations of the people's own making, based on local cultures of credit and obligation, tied to systems of kinship, patronage, or community in

FIGURE 4.10: Roadside signage advertises money transfers, check cashing, and short-term payday and title loans in Birmingham, Alabama, in the post-GFC (Global Financial Crisis) US, 2015. Gary Tramontina/Bloomberg via Getty Images.

which households are embedded, sometimes based on centuries-old experience, sometimes rediscovered by development actors.[14]

Efforts are being made to import modes of evaluating "financial wellbeing" from the global South to the United States, bringing to light new understandings of post-financial crisis impoverishment. Edin and Shaefer (2015; see also Halpern-Meekin et al. 2015), for example, bring the World Bank $2/day poverty standard to bear on the United States, with greater emphasis on the grinding persistence of daily needs than the intermittence of urgent demands. Under precarious working and living conditions, they find that a high proportion of households must move around incomes and expenditures in highly changeable and responsive ways. People mix their earnings, sell blood and plasma, enter the sex trade, tap into free distributions, and find ways to be inventive with budgets. Morduch and Schneider (2017) similarly track household experiences of financial insecurity, using financial diaries to document the ways people save, borrow, and draw on communities of support to make ends meet. We add that struggling with inadequate and uneven household finances falls disproportionately on women and people of color. Feminist research has long described the gendering of care work, for example, while early twenty-first-century social movements such as Black Lives Matter revealed again the racialization of poverty and the ways it intersects with the politics of policing and incarceration.

MONEY, MOBILE

The rapid adoption of mobile phones around the world has offered another resource for everyday monetary innovation—provoking questions about the intersection of new technologies with people's existing money practices, while further multiplying money's forms (Maurer 2015). Using mobile technology as a platform for moving, saving, and accounting for money was pioneered in southeast Asia and sub-Saharan Africa. No "mobile money" initiative has been as successful—or as talked about—as Safaricom's M-Pesa, launched in Kenya in 2007. Its immediacy and liquidity allows mobile money to serve important livelihood functions, as well as being a resource in coping with people's shifting financial demands (Suri and Jack 2016). These include regular variations, like seasonal agricultural fluctuations, and unforeseen events, such as the late 2007/early 2008 post-election violence in Kenya, during which many turned to M-Pesa agents for cash to escape the violence or buy food and water (Morawczynski 2009). Unprecedented in the rapidity and scale of its uptake, M-Pesa captured the imaginations of development, philanthropic, industry, state, and scholarly actors as a model of the potential of mobile technology to extend formal financial services to the poor. The dream of providing basic banking functions through the cell phone, starting with the simple storage and transfer of value, quickly spread around the world.

FIGURE 4.11: An M-Pesa agent in Kenya checks a customer's identification, July 2013. Ivan Small/Institute for Money, Technology & Financial Inclusion, CC BY-SA 2.0.

Mobile money originated not in the plans of businesspeople or philanthropists, however, but in an inventive, everyday practice. Designed to facilitate microcredit bookkeeping and repayment, M-Pesa was inspired by the way Kenyans, like people around the world, had begun to trade prepaid cell phone minutes, known as "airtime"—using it to send gifts or for short-term savings, converting cash into electronic credits in one location and converting it back in another. Airtime was uniquely flexible: a commodity that could be bought and sold like any other, but also a medium of exchange, store of value, and—as talk and text—literally a form of communication and thus "social life" itself (Maurer 2012: 601). Mobile money is thus a "repurposing" of mobile technology and telecommunications networks—for profit and development, but also for everyday social and economic life. It thus also mobilizes and relies on existing social relationships—such as those between customers and the retailers who serve as cash-in/cash-out points—and existing patterns of practice and repertoires of meaning people have developed for money and cell phones (Maurer et al. 2013; Taylor and Horst 2013).

Wherever it is adopted, mobile money intersects with local cultures of savings and exchange, becoming embedded in kinship systems, status hierarchies, and associated expectations about the uses and abuses of wealth (Rea and Nelms 2017; Maurer et al. 2018). For example, Kusimba and her colleagues (2016) argue that in Kenya, M-Pesa has been used in culturally identifiable ways to circulate wealth through ties formed by women—between, for example, mothers and their married daughters, or between a grandmother in Kenya and her sister's daughters in Chicago. These ties fall outside, and are sometimes concealed from, patrilineal relations of male exchange and inheritance. The money is put to diverse ends: not typically as entrepreneurial capital (as development practitioners had hoped), but to pay for school fees, church donations, or coming-of-age and bridewealth rituals. As Zelizer might have predicted, specific transactions take on specific social meanings: as a sign of love, as a substitute for physical presence at weddings or funerals, as a way for children who have migrated to remain "useful" (Kusimba et al. 2015: 10). The mobility of mobile money—as it is channeled through bonds of kinship, friendship, partnership, and companionship—is both enabled and constrained by inventive everyday practices.

As the mobile money phenomenon has grown, it has also fed into a novel "financial inclusion" agenda, which sees the extension of formal financial services as key to poverty alleviation and seeks to harness mobile technologies to this end (Schwittay 2011; Gabor and Brooks 2016). Such endeavors to "bank the unbanked" overlap with marketing strategies seeking to leverage poor people's social networks and economic resources to access new revenue streams at the so-called "bottom of the pyramid" (the phrase is from Prahalad 2006; see Elyachar 2012; Roy 2010). These varied commitments to financial inclusion—as a business proposition, development program, and philanthropic endeavor—have profound implications for the everyday pragmatics of money, especially because proponents have increasingly framed cash as an "enemy of the poor" (Donovan 2015: 625). If mobile money was once imagined to provide "bridges to cash" (Eijkman et al. 2010), it is now understood to be "better than cash."

THE END OF CASH?

Newly consolidated national currencies were crucial to everyday life at the beginning of the modern era. Yet the following century was marked by expanding, if uneven, projects of "inclusion" linked to efforts to displace cash and build non-cash financial systems. These ranged from the promotion of deposit banking to the introduction of charge cards and later credit and debit systems (O'Dwyer 2018; Swartz and Stearns, this volume). Bank deposits and use of non-cash payment instruments like credit/debit cards have grown since the middle of the twentieth century, especially in the United States and Europe. The banking industry targeted the middle class and working poor in the second half of the twentieth century, after post-World War II shifts in housing policy and mortgage regulation. People's access to institutionalized credit was elaborated in ways that made personal and household indebtedness increasingly widespread, although sometimes—as in the lead up to the 2008 mortgage crisis or in the selling of student debt—also predatory. Digital financial inclusion was embraced in the service of such credit expansions, specifically efforts to grow microfinance in the global South, even as critiques grew of microfinance as a project of personal empowerment and social progress (Karim 2011; Taylor 2012; Schuster 2015). Still, microfinance, like subprime lending and student debt, was initially billed as a democratic project of socioeconomic inclusion (Copestake et al. 2016).

At the end of the modern age, the spread of mobile technology and the rise of the financial inclusion agenda threw the future of cash into doubt. As the mobile money phenomenon migrated back to the Euro-American world, it joined other experiments with digital payment and financial technologies, many of them backed by venture capital (Tiessen 2015; Kremers and Brassett 2017; Nelms et al. 2017; O'Dwyer 2018). These include consumer-facing applications for online purchases or person-to-person transfers, which typically rest on existing payment and communication infrastructures (think PayPal or Venmo in the US or AliPay and WeChat Pay in China); electronic tokens or coupons issued by private companies for use in closed circuits (like virtual world currencies); and cryptographically secured, decentralized accounting platforms (like Bitcoin; see Vint, this volume). These experiments were inserted into existing ecologies of value, from airline miles and loyalty cards to precious metals and cash itself, and existing repertoires of practice, like sending and receiving cross-border remittances.

The proliferation of such diverse "fintech" experiments shifted focus onto the costs and benefits of cash itself (Scott 2016). Critiques of cash circulated widely at the beginning of the twenty-first century, mainstreamed through organizations like the Better Than Cash Alliance, a United Nations-based partnership of governments, companies, and international institutions formed in 2012 that "accelerates the transition from cash to digital payments" (Better than Cash Alliance 2018). Cash, critics argue, imposes inherent costs due to its materiality; it can be difficult or dangerous to transport and store, because it is vulnerable to theft and decay; it has outsized environmental impacts. Cash can be useful for money laundering, tax evasion, corruption, and other black-market criminal or illicit transactions; it is cash, we are told, that funds terrorism and is used in drug and gun markets. Some experts suggested that in a post-financial crisis world, in which central bank interest rates hovered near zero but wages remained stagnant and growth low (roughly 2009 on), cash creates a "lower bound" prohibiting economic stimulation through rate cuts, since people can simply hoard cash to avoid negative charges (Rogoff 2016).

These critiques seek to reinforce both the benefits of cashlessness and its inevitability, reviving midcentury dreams of a world without cash (Swartz and Stearns, this volume). Anti-cash arguments provided justification for policy interventions, such as the European Union's decision to phase out the 500-euro note or the Indian government's surprise demonetization. At the time of writing

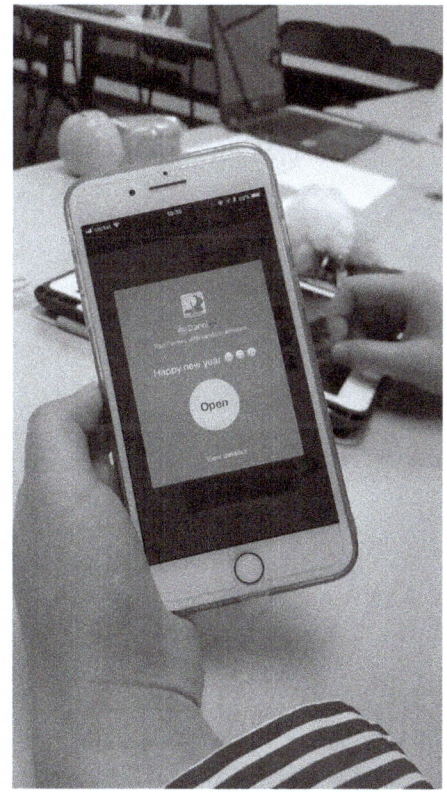

FIGURE 4.12: Red envelopes with money (known as hóngbāo in Mandarin) are given to friends, family, and others during Chinese New Year or for special occasions like births, weddings, and graduations. jyppe.com, CC BY-SA 3.0. Below, a student uses WeChat Pay to send a digital red envelope to friends, 2018. Chendanni Liu and Taylor C. Nelms.

this chapter in 2017—the fiftieth anniversary of the invention of the ATM—many suggest that the future of money can be found in the example of a country like Sweden, where most bank branches no longer take or hold cash deposits, where more people have access to cards than cash, and where churches accept Sunday collections via a real-time P2P mobile payment app called Swish (see, e.g., Henley 2016).

Yet there are new risks, too, and a pro-cash lobby is forming to highlight them (see, e.g., Lepecq 2016).[15] The business models of contemporary experiments with money rest on a combination of assessing fees on the movement of value through privately owned infrastructures (already the primary way card companies and banks turn a profit) and speculating on the uses of personal and transactional data, usually for marketing. As more money flows through these channels, new questions will be provoked about infrastructural breakdown; about fraud, cybersecurity, and identity protection; and about privacy, data security, and vulnerability to third-party surveillance.

Cash, in short, has redeemable qualities that motivate its "surprising resilience" in everyday life (Bagnall et al. 2016: 2). Cash is publicly issued, state-backed, and state-maintained; it is widely accepted and has no significant technological barriers to use; it is free insofar as no fees are imposed on its passage; and its transactions settle immediately. Cash's portability makes for low handling costs, and its fungibility allows for straightforward budgeting. While the costs to store cash are real, they are progressive, in that they increase the more physical currency you save. Thus, even as it has become more common to save and transact online or on one's phone, even as most of the total monetary value in the world exists in digital form—entries on the ledgers of banks and central banks—cash is not disappearing.[16] It remains useful for low-value transactions (such as, to return to an earlier theme, for gifts); in a contingency role as back-up payment instrument; for those seeking out an ethics of connection alongside the instrumentalism of exchange; and as an accessible store of value for the poor, for informal workers, for migrants and refugees. In the modern age, this is a substantial proportion of the global population.

We should thus question claims about the inclusiveness of cashlessness (Dalinghaus 2017). New concerns have emerged about a hierarchically segregated world, in which (as one report put it) "those on the lowest incomes become disconnected from mainstream commercial life by their dependence on traditional forms of currency" (Forrest 2017). The role of cash in living together becomes a new frontier to explore: "If we cannot find a common payment ecosystem, we may find ourselves wandering through divided cities, separated by the sound of bleeps and the shuffling of cold, hard cash."

CONCLUDING DIRECTIONS FOR THE STUDY OF MONEY AND THE EVERYDAY

The turbulence of the modern age continues into the twenty-first century, which offers a variety of frontiers and new directions for the study of money and everyday life. Ongoing shifts in employment, household management, access to basic services (including financial services), and technological change have all made everyday life less amenable to planning and prediction than they were even after the chaos and trauma of World War II and in the national creativity in the postcolonial era. Budgeting and calculation are quotidian challenges in the face of intermittent unpredictability, while simultaneously providing an imperative for popular inventiveness. The play between national currencies and international exchange rates remains profoundly important, while people have also, again and again, recuperated their confidence in money by combining and shifting between different forms of value, practice, and institutional and cultural resources; by appropriating and adapting local customs, from forms of mutual aid, to relational earmarking, to bundling together of multiple income sources in patchwork fashion; and by inventing other ways of managing family and community economies.

New everyday cultures of money management are emerging that depart from what had become the pillars of the modern age, when states consolidated territorial currencies and when central banks and private banking systems exercised control over the supply and circulation of money. Monetary multiplicity and mobility remain key lessons in our era of transnational trade and migration alongside renewed nationalisms, and nativisms increased corporate and development interest in money and finance, technological change and the pushback such change provokes. The growing prevalence of digital and mobile financial systems, in particular, introduces new opportunities for inventiveness, as well as new instabilities.

As the technologies and institutions of money change, so too do the ways people use it and understand it, every day. Monetary authorities and ordinary people are both still working out how new financial technologies and privately issued tokens of value will coexist with national, foreign, and customary moneys—including cash. Indeed, a key surprise of the modern era is that even when money goes mobile, cash remains—and it remains especially as a part of the everyday. If efforts to implement mobile money services in places like Kenya teach us anything, it is that in everyday practice, money is extraordinarily diverse in form and function. How such diversity will manifest along the digitization of money and finance—how there will emerge new transactional forms, pricing dynamics, budgeting practices, and multicurrency mediations—is a question at the leading edge of monetary change.

These are important questions to be placed in the exploratory ethnographic mode—to track, study, and interpret the life of money in the everyday. In this experimental moment, the ways people earn and spend, make and maintain stores of value, earmark and budget, invest and donate, gift and gamble are all at stake. We thus return also to people's confidence in money and to their moral philosophies and popular cultures. The opportunities are still being crafted and experimented with. How it will work within—and potentially transform—existing social units (households, family networks, donation communities) is an open question. How will irregular incomes from precarious work be pooled and managed? How will they be earmarked, saved, insured? Or has the everyday management of money become literally "every day"? Each day, each household, each person must now confront whatever challenges appear in front of them, with whatever resources are currently at hand. What the future—of money, of life—looks like in such a situation is profoundly uncertain.

CHAPTER FIVE

Money, Art, and Representation

Six Artists, Two Crises (1973, 2008)

MAX HAIVEN

INTRODUCTION

While in the modern age it has usually been supposed that money and art are diametrically opposed, they are mutually reinforcing. While allegedly unrelated, they are in fact intimates brought into critical proximity by the institutional and systemic particularities of late capitalism. While both art and money predate (late) capitalism, the unique forms they take on in and as part of that system share important mutualities. If money can claim to be cool, rational, base, and worldly, then art can be passionate, imaginative, virtuous, and transcendental. Indeed, art's monetary value relies precisely on offering the buyer the chance to acquire a commodity whose value is in some sense non-commodifiable, resilient to money's influence. Conversely, the great claim of modern money management is to eschew any pretense of artfulness and insist upon the scientific dispassionateness of economics and financial risk management (see Beggs, this volume). It is a surplus of temperament and imagination, we are told, that throws an otherwise rational clockwork into disarray. It is not only that the single largest demographic of collectors of contemporary art are financiers, or that the heart of the art world has pulsed so enthusiastically in the great financial metropoles of the modern era. It is that money and art share a strange and fateful symmetry.

FIGURE 5.1: Evening sales at Christie's London headquarters, June 2014. Lionel Derimais/Getty Images.

In this chapter, I describe one part of that symmetry, focusing on how this entanglement has evolved through the advance of financialization. I have selected six works by radical artists from two key moments of crisis in the modern history of financialization: 1973 and 2008. All six directly engage with money, either as a tangible medium or as a prompt for artistic, political, and cultural critique and invention. By critically examining this work, we can see how artists understand the broader economic conditions in which they find themselves, gain an understanding of those conditions, and trace the fate of money itself. Artists like these seize upon the contradiction with which I opened this chapter: money and art appear as sworn enemies but in fact share deep affinities. It is these affinities that give money-art, and especially radical money-art, its aesthetic and its critical heft. Such approaches are especially important today, in our moment of financialization (Velthius and Coslor 2012).

I have selected 1973 and 2008 as pivotal years for reasons that will become clear below. Two years after Nixon severed the US dollar from the gold standard, 1973 was marked by OPEC-triggered oil crises that threw the petroleum superpower into economic extremis. Meanwhile, a US-backed coup d'état in Chile made possible experiments in neoliberal free-market policies that would radically transform the world in the following decades. In the world of finance, 1973 saw the invention of the Black-Scholes formula for pricing derivatives, which revolutionized risk management; the construction of the digitized World Trade Center in New York; and the opening of the world's first dedicated options exchange in Chicago. Meanwhile, the thawing of tensions between the United States and Russia and China signaled the softening of state socialism. 1973 is also about the year (depending on measurements) that the purchasing power of US workers reached its peak, holding steady or (in aggregate) declining since then. It also represents a high-water mark in a cycle of social movement struggles against the order of capitalist reproduction. For these reasons and more, 1973 here represents a convenient date for periodizing the emergence of financialization.

Critical, activist-oriented art has much to teach us—not only about aesthetics and culture, but also about politics and economics. I have previously explored the connections between finance and the imagination (Haiven 2014). I argue, first, that the rise of "fictitious capital" depends on creating systems capable of sustaining the dominance of "imaginary wealth"—where "imaginary" does not mean "unreal" but rather, in the spirit of Castoriadis (1997), the solidification of a shared social process of meaning-making into durable social institutions and, more broadly, forms and orders of value. Second, I argue that financialization has both fomented and depended on a more profound transformation of the discourses, affects, subjectivities, and habituses of daily life, even for those who

FIGURE 5.2: Police officer stands guard outside the New York Stock Exchange, March 2003. Stephen Chernin/Getty Images.

FIGURE 5.3: Father and son with a warning sign during the 1973 oil crisis. Photo by Smith Collection/Gado/Getty Images.

have little experience with or understanding of the financial services industry. In other words, financialization is not only a political economic transformation; it is also a sociological and cultural one in which the measurements, metaphors, ideas, value-paradigms, logics, and affects of finance become increasingly useful—indeed, dominant—tools in the governance of social institutions and the reproduction of social life. Finally, I pose the idea that "finance" is itself a technology of the imagination, a set of techniques by which capitalism as a whole and its privileged functionaries gain a sense of an increasingly complex world system (Haiven 2011).

This work has led me to an interest in art (Haiven 2015a; 2015b), especially critical and radical contemporary art that mobilizes money as a creative and critical medium. Such art can be approached as offering a crucial moment of reflexivity within financialization, which can be studied for clues as to financialization's otherwise opaque contradictions. I approach such art as singular works, capable of critical reflexivity, and also as symptomatic of the systems of which they are a part.

THREE THEORIES OF REPRODUCTION

My analysis of the six artists over the two periods covered in this chapter mobilizes a three-pronged theorization of capitalist reproduction (and reproduction under capitalism), which I have elsewhere (Haiven 2014) discussed at greater length. The first analyzes the ways capitalism seeks to reproduce itself; the second seeks to explain the reproductive cycles between capitalism as a system, social institutions, and individual actors; the third centers the (typically feminized) labor of reproducing life and society as a means to reframe exploitation and resistance. These three theories offer critical approaches to struggles within and against capitalism, creating a triangular frame that allows us to attend to the historically and geographically specific nature of capitalist accumulation and its transformations. They sensitize us to systemic contradictions that offer opportunities for resistance, while also prompting the reorganization of capitalism in the name of its own reproduction. Finally, I find in this triangular framework an accounting of culture not as a secondary, residual, or contingent element of economics but as an integral, dialectical force.

Importantly, this three-fold approach to reproduction encourages us to see capitalism less as a total system and more as a crisis-prone and -driven constellation of shifting forces. As Cleaver (2000) makes clear, these crises, while they may appear structural or internal, always stem, ultimately, from resistance and rebellion. What Harvey (2006) calls the "fixes" for these crises never solve the underlying contradictions but elevate them to a new level, posing new contradictions and challenges for social struggles. The three-fold approach to reproduction allows us to see that, in each historical moment, the tensions between different forms of reproduction can fruitfully be read as key fault lines of crisis, contradiction, and struggle—in particular, over money.

The reproduction of capitalist circulation

The first realm of reproduction builds on Marx's (1981, 1992) analysis of capitalist accumulation. Taking up the work of classical political economists, Marx agrees that "capital" under capitalism is not given. It is a force always in motion, based not on the stability of land or precious metals but on the society-wide orchestration of labor (Itoh and Lapavitsas 1999; Nelson 1999). Marx's signature contribution was to identify that this orchestration of labor was fundamentally based on exploitation and thus inherently riven by recurrent crises, stemming from the internal contradictions of the system or from workers' struggles. Most of these crises are connected to contradictions that interfere with the circulation of capital, where money plays a key role (Harvey 2006). Examples include: the falling rate of profit, where competition between capitalist firms forces prices so low it becomes perilous to the reproduction of individual firms; the overproduction (or underconsumption) of goods based on the system's productive priorities being driven by exchange values, rather than use values; the over-exploitation of the working class, leaving them without enough money to reproduce themselves through the purchase of the fruits of capitalist productivity (i.e., their own productivity sold back to them); and manifold contradictions having to do with temporal and geographic limits to capitalist circulation. The list goes on—and this framework has been a centerpiece of understandings of money and finance in the modern or late capitalist era.

Two things are vital for our purposes. First, whatever the root of these crises, they tend to manifest in capital's circulatory medium, money (Lapavitsas 2013). Second, as Luxemburg (2003), Lenin (1948), and others (Harvey 2003, 2006; Panich and Gindin 2012) have illustrated, capitalism's response has been to displace or elevate the contradiction to a higher level through institutional developments or systemic transformations. For instance, as Harvey (2006) elucidates, the banking and finance sector emerges to help capitalism "fix" the problem of the temporal and geographic contradictions of circulation, providing an institutional basis for geographically mobile commercial paper (bank scrip, credit notes, etc.) and temporally secure investments (which redistribute profit among capitalist enterprises) (see also Lapavitsas 2013). As Luxemburg (2003) notes, colonialism and imperialism are also means to reproduce capital in circulation once it has accelerated to terminal velocity within a specific country— not only freeing up new sources of labor and materials, not only opening new markets, but also offering opportunities to waste ill-begotten wealth on military expenditure, relieving the tensions of over-accumulation and conscripting the working classes under nationalism (Harvey 2006). In short, as capitalism's inherent contradictions manifest as crises in the circulation of money, these crisis offer opportunities both for struggle and for (often violent) capitalist restructuring.

The reproduction of class institutions

The second realm of reproduction emerges from the work of French sociologists and social critics (e.g., Foucault 1978a, 1978b; Bourdieu 1990, 1993, 2005; Althusser 2014) and the England-based progenitors of the field of cultural studies (e.g., Hall 1996a; Hoggart 1998; McRobbie 2005; Williams 2005; see also Giroux 2001). Both schools of thought sought to break with doctrinaire Marxist interpretations of the reproduction of capital, which gave short shrift to the agency of individual actors and to the centrality of state institutions, especially in the postwar industrialized West, where mass media and the regulatory state had risen out of class conflict to reproduce and mediate capitalism (Hall 1996b; Williams 2005). The importance of social institutions in mediating capitalist accumulation while generating complicit, docile, or specialized subjects was of central importance to a generation of critics who likewise witnessed a new cycle of grassroots struggles by workers, students, prisoners, psychiatric patients—and artists (Katsiaficas 1987; Ross 2002). Also of critical importance was the emergence of a larger postwar middle class, which conscripted increasingly isolated citizen-consumers by preoccupying their personal hopes and ambitions (Plant 1992). These theorists were concerned, in part, with how a traditional understanding of capitalist cultural politics was shifted by the increased availability of money to workers, without any real change in ownership of or control over production.

Thus these scholars were concerned with how class identities and institutions were reproduced and how class, in turn, reproduced social institutions. For these scholars, institutions were fields of power that, while not directly subjugated to capital, nonetheless helped reproduce it and its subjects. Their analysis focused on semi-autonomous hierarchies and circuits of value at work within schools, the media, prisons, galleries, bureaucracies, the military, and public space and the various institutions of what has come to be called the "art world" (including museums, galleries, auction houses, dealers, art schools, periodicals and philanthropic foundations). Differential forms of "capital" (symbolic, cultural), in Bourdieu's terminology, circulated semi-autonomously through these institutions in ways that could not be understood as simply due to the machinations of ("big C") Capital (Beasley-Murray 2000). These authors sought to understand, then, how power might be exercised and reproduced outside of, or alongside, money through institutional environments and subjectivities. They also sought to describe how the logics and codes of money might be infiltrating and reorganizing spheres of social life initially thought to be immune or allergic to them.

The reproduction of social life

The final realm of reproduction surfaced out of materialist feminist critiques of Marxism that emerged in tandem with broader Second Wave feminist movements of the late 1960s and early 1970s. Rejecting both a liberal feminism that sought reforms within capitalist institutions and a culturalist feminism that understood gender-based oppression as a matter of attitudes and dispositions (natural or nurtured), these critics sought to understand women as uniquely exploited workers whose labor was central to capitalist accumulation and reproduction (James and Dalla Costa 1979; Mies 1986; Fortunati 1995; Firestone 2003; Federici 2005, 2012; James 2012; see also Fraser 2013). In contrast to traditional Marxist approaches focusing on the commodification of the energies of formal wage workers, materialist feminists turned their attention to the production of this laboring commodity itself—the worker—and identified the patriarchal home as the workshop. Reproductive labor—bearing and raising children, cooking and cleaning to maintain the home, and caring for and reproducing working-class community, all of which have traditionally been expected of or forced on women—became a central axis of struggle (Ferguson and McNally 2015). The Wages for Housework campaign, for instance, aimed at the contradiction between capitalism's reliance on women's reproductive labor and the exclusion of such labor from the waged economy (Weeks 2011).

FIGURE 5.4: Undated poster for the Wages for Housework campaign, deposited in the MayDay Rooms in London by feminist scholar, teacher, and activist Silvia Federici. January 28, 2013, CC BY-NC-SA 4.0.

This theoretical paradigm's emergence was timely. By the late 1960s, laws and customs that had prohibited or constrained (white) women's economic participation in capitalism were slowly diminishing, thanks to stalwart activism. The prospect of women's economic and legal self-sufficiency presented a quandary for feminist thinkers: to what extent should women's access to money be pursued as a means towards empowerment and fulfillment, and to what extent should it be distrusted? Could capitalism survive without the exploitation of women's reproductive labor?

In recent years, as affective, care, and other kinds of reproductive labor have been increasingly commodified (through, for example, the formal and informal "service sector"), theories of social reproduction have been more widely applied to understand the changing nature of work and life in an era defined by precarious work, the decay or weaponization of the welfare state, and the subtle, unsung, unpaid, and essential micro-labors that reproduce bodies, minds, and souls within organizations and institutions (see Luxton and Bezanson 2006; Haider and Mohandesi 2015; Stakemeier and Vishmidt 2016).

THREE WORKS OF MONEY-ART, 1973

Art's special place under capitalism gives artists who work with money the potential to offer unique and provocative insights. Art is a form of labor and a commodity that, to maintain institutional legitimacy and market value, must constantly and in new ways reject its own commodification—even when this rejection takes the form of a crass, iconoclastic embrace of that commodification, as in the work of superstars like Damien Hirst, Takashi Murakami, or Jeff Koons (Taylor 2011). Money itself, when incorporated as a medium (coins, bills, credit, debt) or as a theme, can superheat these tensions in such a way that the otherwise seemingly rigid cultural politics of money become pliable or ductile.

One of the "functions" of money—in addition to medium of exchange, unit of account, store of value, and so on—is as a medium of the imagination (Haiven 2015b). Coins and banknotes have long been aesthetic canvases, although usually monopolized by the powerful and used to circulate images of rulers and nations aimed at reinforcing political legitimacy and sovereignty (Helleiner 1998; Hymans 2004, 2010; Lauer 2008; Papadopoulos 2015). Yet money is available to others, too. A full genealogy of the critical artistic use of money is beyond the scope of this chapter (see Haiven 2015a). But art and artists have consistently sought to understand and in some cases challenge the power of money in their work (Shell 1994; Crosthwaite, Knight, and Marsh 2014). There have been many artists drawn to the theme (Siegel and Mattick 2004), and in the post-2008 moment, the role of art and artists as radical critics of the capitalist economy has become even more clear (see Sholette and Ressler 2013).

The following three radical artists and artworks work directly with money as a means to address and challenge contemporary conditions of capitalist reproduction. Each is inspired or agitated by a central contradiction of the 1973 moment while also pointing towards changes to come. Furthermore, each focuses on a particular realm of reproduction; between them we can triangulate the forces shaping the emergence of financialization and the transformation of money in the modern era.

Joseph Beuys, KUNST=KAPITAL *(197?–198?)*

Starting in the early 1970s (dates are difficult to ascertain), West German sculptor and pioneer of performance and conceptual art Joseph Beuys used banknotes of various nations as a canvas and a distribution system for a series of provocative messages (Rösch 2013: 21–23; Opitz 2015). Primary among them was KUNST=KAPITAL (Art=Capital), which he scrawled in pen, crayon, marker, and paint on an unknown number of notes before passing them back into circulation. The technique was not new. Since at least the early nineteenth century, circulating legal tender has been used as a medium of political expression, from the coins engraved by suffragettes with the message "VOTES FOR WOMEN" to the convict love tokens of incarcerated working-class Londoners, who—convicted of petty crimes (including counterfeiting or handling counterfeit currency) and awaiting colonial transportation and indenture—inscribed messages to loved ones on coins (Shell 1994; Field and Millet 1998). In fact, the Nazis also used this technique to spread anti-Semitic propaganda on devalued German Marks during the Weimar period (Sandrock 2007).

It would be tempting to read Beuys' intervention as merely a cynical reaction towards the increasing commodification of art in the 1960s and 1970s, a topic of furious conversation at the time in the United States and Germany. There, thanks in part to postwar prosperity, in part to government support for abstract expressionist art as a Cold War strategy to promote "Western freedom," art markets were booming and "contemporary" or "modern" art was becoming a known quantity and a desirable designation (Saunders 2001).

Yet although Beuys in some ways embraced and leveraged the persona of the romantic artist, cultivating a cult of personality and designating himself a neoshaman with vast social responsibilities, Beuys' KUNST=KAPITAL message, a frequent topic of other work and lectures, was not some melancholic or furious denunciation of art's growing proximity to money. Rather, the formula represented the irreducible kernel of an expansive quasi-Marxian theory of value that Beuys thought could become the basis of a socialist-humanist

FIGURE 5.5: Joseph Beuys's "KUNST=KAPITAL" (1979). Estate of Joseph Beuys/SODRAC.

FIGURE 5.6: British penny inscribed with the words "VOTES FOR WOMEN" by suffragettes in the early 1900s. The British Museum, CC BY-NC-SA 4.0.

philosophy capable of transcending the bad infinity (or false dialectic) of Western capitalism and Eastern communism (Beuys 2010).

Beuys coined the term "social sculpture" to describe works that incorporated human actors, joining other postwar artists in dissolving the distinction between artist and audience. In this piece, each banknote is transformed into a social sculpture consummated through its return to monetary circulation. Beuys famously believed that all human beings were inherently artists, entitled to use imagination to transform the world. But following Marx (and also, perhaps, channeling anthropologist Marcel Mauss), this imaginative potential, under capitalist relationships of exploitation, was not so much lost as subsumed or redirected in the interests of reproducing commodities, the same commodities the worker was compelled to purchase. The chief mediator and medium of both the exploitation of labor and the circulation of commodities was money—a substance whose value was, especially in the case of paper banknotes, largely imaginary. Yet Beuys was not making a simplistic argument that money is an illusion. He was appropriating money's functions to critique them. As a means of circulation, he compelled money to circulate a radical message (radical in the sense that it seeks to destabilize the root); as a unit of account, he made money account for a shared humanist ledger wherein imaginative energies are transmuted into (alienated) material wealth; as a store of value, he summoned money to reveal what is encrypted within it: humanity's own collective imaginative potential, cruelly subverted. Beuys might be said to be translating Mauss's observation that money is the "false coin of our dreams," our own inherent imaginative power returned to us as a worldly token (Graeber 2001).

Beuys leverages several contradictions inherent in the moment. For example, the nation-state's reliance on currency as a vehicle for the reproduction of an imagined community can at times contradict the needs of capitalist interests, which—as in both the United States and West Germany in the late 1960s—experience territorial limits accumulative expansion (Cleaver 2005). The late 1960s also represented a moment of profound crisis for the Keynesian, regulatory state, which had seen profits and capitalist wealth-share dwindle relative to workers' economic power. Occupying the object (banknotes) where state power and capitalist circulation intersect was a crucial gesture for Beuys in his efforts to stimulate the radical imagination. Indeed, Beuys identified money's vulnerability at a moment when its claims to accurately represent value were tenuous.

Hans Haacke, MoMA Poll *(1970)*

Another West German artist, Hans Haacke (2016), likewise leveraged the contradictions of capitalist reproduction to produce incisive radical work. The work in question, *MoMA Poll* (1970), is an early and influential part of what would, by the late 1980s, be identified as "institutional critique," through which the artist calls conspicuous attention to the ways broader systems of power are at work in the institutional environment of the gallery or museum, in their work itself, or even in their own subjectivity or economic participation as an artist (Osborne 2002; Metzler 2013).

Haacke applied to a juried exhibition of works from emerging artists to present a piece that would encourage audience participation, something relatively new and daring at the time. MoMA had become a popular recreational and educational destination, thanks to a growing educated urban middle class, tourism, and the largesse of the US government and capitalist class eager to promote the freedom and individualism of "Modern Art" as a form of Cold War propaganda. Visitors would be asked to cast a vote in a transparent YES or NO ballot box regarding a topical current event. After being accepted into the show Haacke revealed at the last minute that the question would be "Would the fact that Governor [Nelson] Rockefeller has not denounced President Nixon's Indochina policy be a reason for you not to vote for him in November?" and invited the audience to "Answer: If 'yes' please cast your ballot into the left box if 'no' into the right box."

In addition to being a scion of the Standard Oil and Chase Bank corporate empire, Rockefeller was a major Republican politician, a three-time candidate for the party's presidential nomination and a frequent appointee to leading security and military committees under the Nixon administration (Smith 2014). Before taking up duties in Washington and Albany, Rockefeller had served as a longtime governor of MoMA, and at the time of Haacke's poll, both his brother and sister-in-law were trustees (Haacke 2009). The considerable pressure they collectively brought to bear on the curator was not sufficient to convince him to remove Haacke's piece, but it did lead to the curator's dismissal several months later, after the piece was displayed. Haacke kept records of the visitors to the museum and the piece, as well as the vote tallies. "Yes" won handily.

Haacke's intervention set an ideological trap: to force money to reveal itself as the *sine qua non* of the museum, to goad what is usually invisible to come into the light. It was also part of a series of actions that targeted MoMA during the Vietnam War, which sought to call attention to the complicity of art and culture in the reproduction of American capitalism and imperialism abroad (Bryan-Wilson 2009). Yet it was also a moment when "contemporary art" further developed an appetite for social critique; hence the inclusion of Haacke and other radical artists in the exhibition. Their ability to occupy that space and make their interventions was due to contradictions in the institutional reproduction of capital that Haacke's piece sought to illuminate.

As Bourdieu (1984, 1993) famously argued, artistic taste is by no means a natural or purely intuitive affair. Especially in the modern epoch, taste is educated, refined, and manipulated as a means to generate and accumulate cultural and social capital, largely among the wealthy classes. As capitalism emerged in Europe, art too emerged as a distinct and secular category (Wolff 1984). Whereas once art might have been embedded in religion or craft, an emerging bourgeoisie—who, as opposed to the aristocracy they displaced, enjoyed no class legitimation outside of access to money—developed an appetite for singular, commodifiable art objects whose purchase and collection served as proof of intellectual and spiritual superiority (Haiven 2014). Ironically, it was precisely a class obsessed with and wrought from the base and worldly circulation of money that demanded artifacts that allegedly emanated from and reflected the transcendental realm of romantic imagination (see Bürger 1984). Art connoisseurship, organized around the acquisition of commodities and public rituals like gallery-going and auctions, became central to the reproduction of the capitalist class (Baudrillard 1981; Clark 1999).

The rewards are not only subjective and communal. Sitting on the same boards or going to the same events offers otherwise competitive capitalists an opportunity to collaborate and make common cause, form alliances and agreements in the interests of their class (Currid 2007; Thompson 2008; Thornton 2008). Meanwhile, presenting themselves as patrons of the arts and

FIGURE 5.7: Installation view of Hans Haacke's "MoMA Poll" (1970). © Hans Haacke/Artists Rights Society (ARS), New York. Courtesy the artist and Paula Cooper Gallery, New York.

therefore facilitators of the higher human ventures and defenders of the artistic pursuit of unalienated labor might all be seen as buying capitalists a kind of indemnity or absolution for the fundamental exploitation of alienated labor in factories and fields that begat their wealth in the first place. Further still, the canon of art, focused on the products of elite white European men, creates a field of ideological legitimacy around this demographic's right to rule; the monopolization of the narrative of artistic triumph justifies supposedly benevolent rule over women, people of color, colonial populations, and the working class (Fanon 1963). Finally, art collecting and connoisseurship offers a number of financial rewards. While art objects are notoriously illiquid assets, they have long been used as long-term investments, as savings instruments or as collateral for loans or components of estates (Horowitz 2011). Donations or loans of works to museums not only earn self-congratulation and the admiration of one's peers, they also offer tax breaks and opportunities for tax fraud (Davis 2015; Steyerl 2015). More generally, investment in art (especially contemporary art) offers the wealthy a sort of para-financial game, a parody version of "real" markets, where psychosocial muscles of financial speculation get to stretch in a gymnasium of the imagination (Velthius 2007; Malik and Phillips 2013).

All these motivations were certainly at play for the Rockefellers and helped shape the institutional ecology of MoMA in the early 1970s. Since its founding by New York financiers in the 1920s, the museum had served their interests, while claiming to promote those of the public and of art. But MoMA was unique in ways that are highly demonstrative: from its outset it was dedicated to collecting and showcasing the "modern" (Wilson 2009).

But by the late 1960s, artists had begun to realize and question their culpability in the reproduction of capitalism and imperialism, while also seeking to escape and reject the circuits of cultural capital and commodification that had begun to embrace them (Bryan-Wilson 2009). At the same moment that capitalism created new institutional frameworks for the collection and exhibition of modern and contemporary artwork, it also opened the door to forms of political and aesthetic radicalism diametrically opposed to it.

This contradiction was only a particular reflection of a broader crisis of reproduction in the late 1960s, one in which many oppressed and exploited populations rebelled against the capitalist and imperialist system they were being reproduced to serve (Katsiaficas 1987). As the Civil Rights movement morphed into the Black Power movement, racialized subjects of empire rejected the reproduction of racial hierarchies in the institutions of prisons, law enforcement, schooling, health, housing, and universities. Second-wave feminism and queer liberation likewise rejected the institutions of gender, marriage, and sexuality that were central to the postwar mythos of middle-class suburban happiness. Students rose up against conservative educational institutions. This was a moment when the bluff was called on the forms of "freedom" and "prosperity" promised as part of the postwar "deal" that had supposedly saved capitalism from collapse and uprising (Day 2005). The compromise was falling apart. Put otherwise, the institutions and identities germane to the reproduction of capitalism were on the rocks.

Haacke's intervention at MoMA, then, capitalized on these contradictions not only to tweak the nose of power in its own temple, but also to suggest a new set of priorities for art: politically engaged, participatory, explicitly challenging social norms, aesthetically blunt. His is a reflection of and contribution to a revolt within and against institutions central to the reproduction of capitalism, insisting they serve instead the reproduction of democracy.

Lee Lozano, REAL MONEY PIECE (1969)

Lee Lozano was a path-breaking, erratic, and enigmatic figure in the history of feminist and conceptual art. Central to Lozano's practice were experimental pieces of interactive, durational performance art, based on a set of brief, strict instructions to herself or to others (Molesworth 2002; Koch 2011; Spears 2011; Lehrer-Graiwer 2014). Paradigmatic is her 1969 *CASH PIECE,* also known as *REAL MONEY PIECE*, whose physical trace takes the form of pages of her notebook that begin with the following instructions:

> NOTE: AT BEGINNING OF THIS PIECE THE JAR CONTAINS BILLS OF $5, $10, $20, ABOUT $585'S WORTH, COILED IN TWO OR THREE PACKETS AROUND THE INSIDE OF THE JAR, UNBOUND. THE MONEY COMES FROM ROLFE RICKE FROM SALE OF PAINTING "SWITCH." OFFER TO GUESTS COFFEE, DIET PEPSI, BOURBON, GLASS OF HALF AND HALF, ICE WATER, GRASS, AND MONEY. OPEN JAR OF REAL MONEY AND OFFER IT TO GUESTS LIKE CANDY.
>
> —APR 4, 69

These instructions to herself (and perhaps future artists wishing to replicate the piece) are followed by a day-by-day journal of the results of the experiment from April 4 to July 9, 1969, documenting the responses of visitors, friends, and other artists. These responses range from whimsical to avaricious, mirthful to furious. On April 27, "KALTENBACH TAKES ALL THE MONEY OUT OF THE JAR WHEN I OFFER IT, EXAMINES ALL THE MONEY & PUTS IT ALL BACK IN JAR. SAYS HE DOESN'T NEED MONEY NOW." On May 1, "WARREN C. INGERSOLL REFUSED. HE GOT VERY UPSET ABOUT MY 'ATTITUDE TOWARDS MONEY.'" On May 23, "PAULA DAVIES AND MARILYN LEARNER DROP IN UNEXPECTEDLY. NEITHER TAKE ANY [MONEY] BUT PAULA SAYS LATER SHE WAS 'CONTROLLING HERSELF.'" And on June 6,

> ALAN SARET VISITS AGAIN & MAKES A PIECE OF THE MONEY WHICH IS NOW IN TWO PILES ON THE FLOOR, EACH SHAPED SIMILARLY TO A 'FOOTSTEP' BY FOLDING & MOLDING TO HIS HAND. IT LOOKS GOOD LIKE THAT & I'M GONNA LEAVE IT ON THE FLOOR FOR A WHILE.

REAL MONEY PIECE developed several months after/into Lozano's *GENERAL STRIKE* piece, which involved these instructions:

> GRADUALLY BUT DETERMINEDLY AVOID BEING PRESENT AT OFFICIAL OR PUBLIC "UPTOWN" FUNCTIONS OR GATHERINGS RELATED TO THE "ART WORLD" IN ORDER TO PURSUE INVESTIGATIONS OF TOTAL PERSONAL AND PUBLIC REVOLUTION. EXHIBIT IN PUBLIC ONLY PIECES WHICH

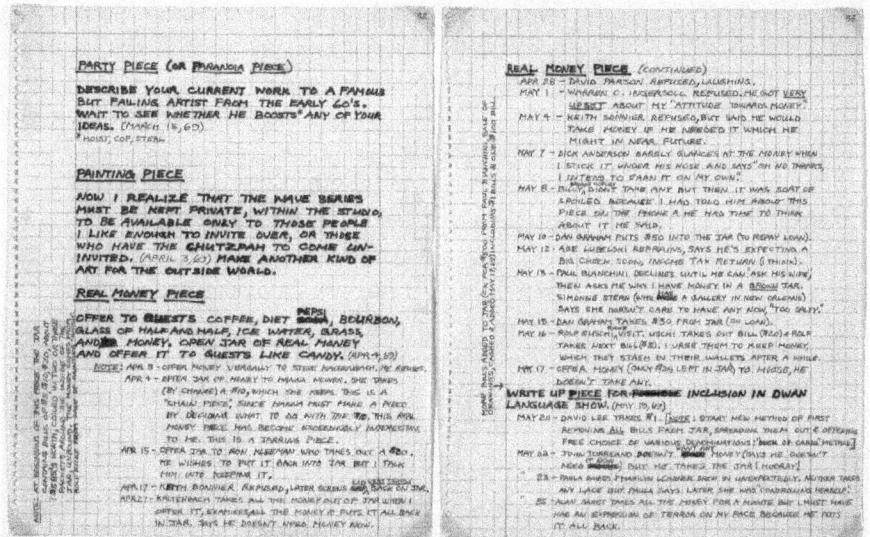

FIGURE 5.8: Two pages from Lee Lozano's notebooks concerning her *Real Money Piece* (1969). Wadsworth Atheneum Museum of Art.

FURTHER SHARING OF IDEAS & INFORMATION RELATED TO TOTAL PERSONAL AND PUBLIC REVOLUTION.

It also came several months before Lozano's more extreme and ultimately self-destructive "DECIDE TO BOYCOTT WOMEN" piece (in which she refused to communicate at all with women) and "DROPOUT PIECE" (in which she not only severed ties to the art world but also sought to break herself of all artistic habits, often with the assistance of powerful narcotics). 1969 was arguably the height of Lozano's career by conventional measurements, culminating the following year in a solo show at New York's Whitney Museum. Yet it preceded a period from 1972 to 1981 during which she disappeared and after which she did not exhibit art or communicate with anyone outside her family until her death in 1999.

While feminist art and art criticism was not to emerge in earnest until later in the 1970s, Lozano was among a number of female-identified artists who made gender, sexuality, and the body central to radical art practice (Wark 2006). In so doing, she adopted and critiqued masculinist trends in performance, conceptual, and minimalist art, all of which had emerged in the 1960s (and prior) as approaches by which to avoid and critique the increasing commodification and imperialist uses of American postwar contemporary object-based art. For

Lozano, a "TOTAL PERSONAL AND PUBLIC REVOLUTION" meant more than just solidarity with particular causes or groups and also more than creating propaganda for a cause. It implied a brutally rigorous personal practice of reflexively interrogating power as it worked through everyday life, social intercourse, habitual patterns, evaluative expectations, and the gendered body. Lozano's work was a sort of militant research into the field of social reproduction and an almost desperate seeking-out of the contradictions therein.

In *REAL MONEY PIECE*, Lozano addressed these challenges explicitly with money, avoiding more philosophical or conventionally "political" approaches to currency. Lozano isolates money as a social medium—both in the sense of something that *mediates* human social affairs, creating striations and complications within the field of relationships, affects, and perceptions, and also in the sense of an *artistic medium*, a set of materials of creative expression (Haiven 2015a, 2015b). Lozano's quasi-scientific isolation of cash as the "independent variable" in a series of experiments makes visible its typically invisible impact on social relationality.

This piece revealed that, behind the embattled camaraderie of the New York radical art "scene" lay vast inequalities: Lozano herself constantly struggled economically, in part because she was an experimental and radical artist fundamentally opposed to commodification, in part because gender oppression militated against her success even amongst similar artists. Meanwhile, many of the visitors to her studio were wealthy collectors and benefactors, or artists enjoying some degree of monetary success. The piece revealed otherwise overlooked fault lines among these individuals' relationships with money.

REAL MONEY PIECE also illuminated the role of money in social reproduction more broadly. Lozano's financial difficulties as a divorcee living alone in New York spoke directly to the reliance of women on men's access to higher wages and more desirable occupations. While money was still off-limits as a topic of polite conversation—even in the more radical realms of the art world—it continued to structure and delimit social relationships. Offering money "like candy" to visitors not only undermined its value; it also transfigured an icon of private competition into a sacrament of the gift, undercutting the conventional logic of money and setting the scene for a very different social interaction.

At work here is the contradiction between money as the earthly representative of capitalist circulation and money as a medium of daily life. From a conventionally economic perspective, money's only role is to mediate commerce in the public sphere, to act as a measure and token of value in exchange. Yet as we know, money also has multiple uses and resonances in the private sphere as a cipher or surrogate for interpersonal and cultural values (Zelizer 1997; Bialecki, this volume; Nelms and Guyer, this volume). For Lozano, a TOTAL PERSONAL AND PUBLIC REVOLUTION thus required interrogating money as *both* the medium of capital's reproduction in circulation *and* the medium of social reproduction, questioning its power to orchestrate productive labor in the public sphere and reproductive labor in the private.

THREE WORKS OF MONEY-ART, 2008

The three artists above all seized on—thus illuminating—capitalist contradictions and crises of reproduction that, while opening opportunities for social and artistic movements, would trigger systemic transformations in the nature of capitalism. Before exploring the work of three artists responding to the crisis of 2008, let us briefly review three seismic changes that followed 1973 in our three spheres of reproduction.

On the level of the circulation of capital, 1973 was the year Fischer Black and Myron Scholes published their famous article outlining a formula for the pricing of derivatives products, a mathematical and theoretical development that was to fundamentally transform the financial realm, and indeed the whole global economy (Bryan and Rafferty 2006). In brief, the Black-Scholes formula, along with advances in computing and network technology, took finance away from physical trading floors and conventional investment and into a vast world of algorithmic speculative gambles, dominated by a handful of technologically augmented corporations, investment banks, and hedge funds (MacKenzie 2006; Pasquale 2015). The Black-Scholes formula was thus a central part of the acceleration of transnational financial flows and increasing mobility of dematerialized capital, leading to the growth of global supply-chains, brands, corporations, and a suite of other forces associated with "globalization" (Li Puma and Lee 2004).

Martin (2015b) suggests that financialization emerged as a means by which capitalism adapted to respond to decolonization movements that by 1973 had largely succeeded in destabilizing the world system. This adaptation includes the replacement of direct colonialism, partly in response to anti-colonial struggles, by neocolonial politics of indirect debt domination, sabotaged "development," and covert "counterinsurgency." An amorphous financial apparatus, headquartered in former colonial capitals, along with transnational institutions like the International Monetary Fund and World Bank, replaced costly imperialist methods—offering (the illusion of) self-rule while enriching former colonizers and maintaining colonial relations of dependency. For Martin, financialization also offered a way to respond to the "decolonial" demands of youth and marginalized people within those colonizing countries, including those articulated by racial justice, feminism, student, queer, and counterculture movements—a means by which capitalism transformed to encompass, divide, and coopt these struggles by offering a more flexible, even personalized economic system, tolerant of various modalities of reproduction. Indeed, where real wages (adjusted for inflation) have fallen steadily since the early 1970s, personal debt has fueled the expansion of consumerism and the production of new financialized subjectivities (Lazzarato 2012).

This shift was enabled by and helped drive a transformation at the level of institutional reproduction towards the policies and ideologies associated with neoliberalism. 1973 provided a perfect opportunity for free-market advocates to test long-proposed theories on a controlled population when the US sponsored a military coup in Chile that installed the pro-market dictator Augusto Pinochet in power. Pinochet's US advisors "strongly suggested" he employ the students of University of Chicago free-market guru Milton Friedman. The resulting wave of deregulations, privatizations, and trade "liberalizations" offered the prototype of neoliberalism, which would become globally hegemonic over the next three decades (Harvey 2005; Klein 2007). In addition to this market-oriented policy package, neoliberalism also represented a restructuring of the values, measurements, and protocols of public and private institutions towards the ideals of market-driven efficiency, instrumentalism, outsourcing and streamlining and institutional risk management (see Springer, Birch, and MacLeavy 2016). More generally, neoliberalism has overseen the elevation of individual ambition, competition, and self-promotion to cardinal virtues and compulsory survival strategies (Giroux 2008; Hall, Massey and Rustin 2013).

Neoliberal financialization has also overseen shifts in the organization of work, reflected in new scholarly approaches to "cognitive capitalism" (Vercellone 2007; de Angelis and Harvie 2009) or capitalism's "new spirit" (Boltanski and Chiapello 2005). These shifts are also often dated to 1973 as the apex of a global cycle of struggles among workers, to which capitalism responded by adopting a more flexiblized, individualized, and diversified orientation (Hardt and Negri 2000; Katsiaficas 2006). In tandem with the global North's deindustrialization and new communication and production technologies, the notion and reality of the "masses" as the foundation of the working class gave way to an archipelago of sites of labor and consumption that are increasingly "precarious": short-term, part-time, contract-based (Berardi 2009). Reaching its apotheosis in today's platform-mediated "gig economy," the new model worker is not the blue-collar "lifer" but, ironically enough, the artist whose allergy to long-term fixed relationships allows them to design their own career based on talent and passion (Harvie 2013; McRobbie 2015).

The shift towards this new form of capitalism has equally demanded shifts on the level of social reproduction, subjectivity, and everyday life. Increases in consumerism are accompanied by the decay of social institutions, collective forms of insurance (such as those provided by community cohesion and the welfare state), and compulsory labor mobility (Federici 2012). As more and more tasks related to the reproduction of social life are privatized and made into commodities, the service sector becomes a generalizable model: even "productive" labor is seen as a "service" to be rented (Hansen 2015; Katsarova 2015). These transformations have required the cultivation of a new wardrobe of subjectivities that encourage each of us to address ourselves as competitive entrepreneurs who see all aspects of our lives, from friendships to hobbies to physical attractiveness to educational attainment, as a portfolio of assets to be leveraged for future payback (Holmes 2002; Martin 2002; Haiven 2014).

Even in the wake of the global financial crisis of 2008, these transformations have continued to accelerate. They represent not only shifts in the logics of the three spheres of reproduction under capitalism, but also the collapsing of those spheres into one another. Whereas in the later 1960s and early 1970s it may have seemed possible for artists to intervene in one or another of these arenas, in recent years it has become hard to imagine, for instance, a social institution that is not both structured by the global circulation of capital and transformative of social reproduction and subjectivity. Likewise, any such institution would also be dependent to some extent on the financialization of social reproduction and subjectivity and in turn be part of the reproduction of the global circulation of capital. Hardt and Negri (2000) adapt a classical Marxist term to describe this moment as the "real subsumption" (and opposed to the formal subsumption) of society to capitalism, wherein the system shifts away from the generation of surplus value and towards "biopolitical production," the production of life itself. In short, capitalism under neoliberal financialization is not satisfied to ensure the reproduction of capital's circulation by subordinating social institutions and social reproduction to this end while providing them with relative autonomy. Rather, today's capitalism blends and integrates all three spheres of reproduction in complex and shifting new ways. How artists respond to this situation is the topic of the final section of this chapter.

In what follows, I address another three artists in reverse order, beginning with artists focused on the sphere of social reproduction, then on the reproduction of institutions, and finally on circulation; as will become clear, part of my argument is that such distinctions have become less durable.

Geheimagentur, Schwartzbank (2012)

In 2012, the German art and theatre ensemble geheimagentur ("secret agency") placed a modified white shipping container in the center of the insolvent former coal-mining city of Oberhausen (Broll 2012; geheimagentur 2012; Jalsovec 2012). Stripped by global financial flows of its fossil-fuel livelihood, the city experienced a significant economic and social crisis. geheimagentur's shipping container was a grim monument to the forces of globalization that had denuded Oberhausen of its prosperity. But it also contained the Schwartzbank ("Black Bank," a pun on the identification of dubious financial institutions in the 2008 financial crisis) distributing the Kohl (or "Coal"), a new unit of local currency.

FIGURE 5.9: geheimagentur's "Schwartzbank" (2012). Fundus Theater Hamburg.

Citizens could earn Kohl by performing an hour of service for the community: for instance, taking care of children, cleaning the streets, or running errands for the elderly. geheimagentur negotiated with local businesses, social services, and other commercial and public institutions to accept Kohl at parity with Euros. This temporary parallel currency was aimed less at replacing fiat legal tender and more at opening a critical interval in an urban space otherwise seemingly destined to economic obsolescence.

The Schwartzbank's ambition was to reveal the play of other, non-commercial values at work within the terrain of urban social reproduction that, despite going unsung and unrewarded, are vital to the reproduction of cities and communities. By creating a functioning parallel currency, geheimagentur sought to revalidate forms of labor that are the bedrock of the reproduction of the capitalist order but that can usually find no value within it, especially in economically depressed zones.

Importantly, geheimagentur imported to the "first world" a suite of techniques from the "third," basing their currency on that of the Banco Palmas, a community bank established by social movements in Fortaleza, Brazil to prevent capital from fleeing precarious communities. Banco Palmas has been cited in international reports as a praiseworthy social enterprise and microcredit institution for its success at managing the accounts of local lenders and borrowers and providing capital and liquidity to grassroots businesses (Jayo et al. 2009). Despite the very real risks of such initiatives being vectors of grassroots neoliberal restructuring and the exploitation of the micro-financed (Bateman 2010), Banco Palmas' particular successes and challenges are secondary to their importance for Schwartzbank. Staging an opportunity for the notoriously fiscally prudent

Germans to learn "financial literacy" and financial acumen from the global South reversed a colonial narrative that elevated the German banking sector (notably Deutschebank) to global preeminence (Varoufakis 2016). Meanwhile, the lessons of Banco Palmas offered useful correctives to all-too-common narratives of economic rationality. Banco Palmas, for instance, expects and celebrates that customers will try to cheat their systems and reflexively designs its currencies to facilitate their diverse financial behaviors, including gifts, barter, and cooperating in the common interest (see www.schwarzbank.org/).

Here, geheimagentur picks up on questions of devalued and secret labor opened up by Lozano's work, not only taking seriously the value of reproductive labor by opening it up to remuneration, but crafting a public ritual for recognizing and rewarding its value. Further, the art collective draws upon and subverts the present-day enthusiasm for art as a vehicle for urban economic salvation. In the mid-2000s, following the rise of Florida's (2004, 2005) bestsellers on the value of the so-called "creative class," and thanks to a variety of urban planning and state policy orientations that saw "culture" as the key to economic growth in post-industrial landscapes, the arts were increasingly invoked as the catalyst for urban renewal (Yúdice 2003; Harvie 2013; Rosler 2013). Since the 1980s, accusations have circulated that artists seeking low rents and studio space represented the "shock troops of gentrification," displacing the inhabitants of less affluent and racialized neighborhoods before themselves being displaced by wealthier professionals. By the 2000s, this pattern had been incorporated into official government policy (Cameron and Coafee 2005; Lees, Slater, and Wiley 2008). While public arts budgets were slashed, it was hard to find a city in the global North (or, increasingly, in the global South) that was not investing in an "arts hub" or rebranding itself as "the next" hotspot on the global cultural frontier. geheimagentur's project reflected on this milieu, where a city like Oberhausen, having abandoned all hope of economic recovery using any conventional tools of economic development, would be keen to allow artists to try their hand.

Yet rather than promise that Schwartzbank would attract the creative class or national or foreign investment, geheimagentur's bank focused on celebrating and sharing the inherent wealth and abundance of the community itself. In this sense, as in Beuys' hijacking of legal tender, the Kohl acted as a vehicle for economic exchange as well as social meaning-making, opening onto the shared creative potential of existing economic actors.

At stake here are the politics of a moment Fraser (2016) characterizes as the crisis of care, wherein the reproduction of capitalism begins to endanger the reproduction of social life. Fraser generally supports the restoration of the welfare state as a means to provide equitable and reliable forms of (fairly remunerated) care labor. But there is another approach (e.g., Federici 2014) that, while not entirely abandoning anti-neoliberal struggles, understands reproductive labor as a terrain of activism and advocates for grassroots practices of social reproduction as a platform for radical social change. geheimagentur's field of action is the crisis of care as it affects the forgotten zones of global capitalism. But to what extent can art stimulate new forms of care and reproductive labor when the money runs out? Should this be art's task?

Zach Gough, Bourdieu: A Social Currency *(2014)*

Turning to the sphere of the reproduction of institutions, we once again examine a work at the cusp of radical participatory art and institutional critique, but this time one that intervenes at conferences and events dedicated to this very topic. On three occasions in 2014, Zach Gough, a Canadian social practice artist, orchestrated a demonstrative game played with the Bourdieux, an invented currency, at key gatherings of fellow social practice artists and researchers in New York, Melbourne, and Portland, Oregon. The rules were as follows:

> At the beginning, the currency is distributed in correlation with the hierarchies present at the conference: keynotes get the most, presenters and panelists get lots, artists get some, attendees get just a bit, and the general public get none at all.
>
> People are invited to exchange the currency for information and items of social value in whatever way they see fit. Email addresses, ideas, inspiration, influence, contact information, inside jokes, URL links, website coordinates, PDFs are bought, sold, and traded with Bourdieux.
>
> Participants are encouraged to discuss how they generate power in an art context, who accumulates social capital in socially engaged art works. At the end of the conference, participants use their accumulated wealth of Bourdieux to bid in an auction for prizes rich in social capital.

Like Lozano, Gough uses money (or its proxy) to create an artificial ritual that reveals the underlying rituals of value, commodification, and neoliberal subject formation germane to a financialized moment. Gough continues:

> The project aims to reveal the economy of social and cultural capital already present within the discipline and at conferences for socially engaged art. It also shows how our economies of power mimic or operate under similar rules to our financial economy. Further, the project presents currency as an abstracted representation of our social relationships and explores the danger of quantifying value.

Gough's intervention resonates with recent commentary from institutional-critique pioneer Fraser (2012) that calls even critical and radical art to task for its participation in financialization. In the face of the Occupy movement and

FIGURE 5.10: Zach Gough's "Bourdieu: A Social Currency" (2014). Zachary Gough.

FIGURE 5.11: Zach Gough's "Bourdieu: A Social Currency" (2014). Zachary Gough.

commitments of many critical artists to the struggle against the proverbial 1%, Fraser explores how the art world from which such work emerges and within which it circulates is saturated by the money and influence of the financial class. It is not simply that financiers (or those enriched by financial wealth) represent the lion's share of art collectors and continue to monopolize the boards of museums, galleries, and funding bodies (Taylor 2011). It is that this funding, and the entanglements of the art world with high finance, exert a gravitational pull on artistic institutions and initiatives, including those that avowedly (often hyperbolically) seek to reject and escape this influence.

The history of twentieth-century art shows us that yesterday's "outsiders" are today's art-world innovators and the creators of tomorrow's most desirable art-commodities (Rosler 1997). The commodification and marketization of feminist, performance, and conceptual art stands as evidence that the structure of the art market is a reflection of broader financial markets, which are constantly seeking out the new, the fringes, the frontier, the bleeding edge as an opportunity for future profitability (Malik and Phillips 2012). As with finance in the age of the derivative (Martin 2015a), in which financial techniques can be used to cultivate value based on conjectural gambles on not-immediately-commodifiable processes (the weather, for instance), the art market need not directly commodify artwork to derive value from it. Decommodified provocative performances and interventions are regularly commissioned by major galleries and dealers at transnational art fairs to generate buzz and attract attention to the art for sale, or simply to add to the prestige of the gallery. Performative and conceptual works can be cultivated in ways that increase the symbolic capital of funders, curators, museum directors, and even activists, who can then be lauded for their daring and foresight (Thompson 2008; Horowitz 2011).

To note this neoliberal turn, where even the non-commodified, dematerialized artwork and art workers are conscripted, is not, however, to suggest that it dissolves radical art's other values. Like Beuys, Gough's gesture is not merely cynical and derisive; it is compassionate and yearns for transformation. It does not call for the abolition of the genre but rather the refinement of strategies. As we have seen, part of art's enduring appeal to capital and capitalists stems from its promise to escape or transcend the forms of capitalism that are the conditions of its emergence. Yet the reality is that art and money have always been entangled, and these entanglements are becoming trickier and more contradictory as financialization transforms the nature of money and the nature of art. While Gough's game/ritual may feel uncomfortable and profane, it calls its participants to refine their strategic imagination and focus their political lens.

As Bishop (2012) has noted, the turn towards "participation" and interactivity in contemporary art since the 1970s (already exhibited in the work of Beuys, Haacke, and Lozano) is equally the product of artistic radicalism seeking to break down the hierarchies between artist and audience and a neoliberal tendency towards the consumption of experience and demands that art be "accessible" for the consumption of broad publics. For Bishop, "participation" is too often uncritically accepted as a political virtue in itself, in ways that render opaque the imperatives of cognitive capitalism, which demand each of us become "active" participants in our own self-management.

For "participatory" art to be politically expedient, it needs to be more cunning in the way it engages with a financialized moment in which money is no longer an alien power threatening art's virtuous chastity but rather an integral element of art's (even radical art's) conditions of emergence. Gough's piece, then, offers not a cynical trap but a collective exercise in the radical imagination (see Holmes 2012). It resonates with the broader corpus of his work, such as the Precarious Workers of the World Songbook, the Commoner's Almanac, or the Radical Imagination Gymnasium, each of which encourages artists to understand themselves also as workers and catalysts for non- or anti-capitalist transformation: yes, subjects of capital, but also bearing particular skills and potentials that might reveal radical opportunities to exit capitalist relations or generate resistance at their weakest points.

At stake in Gough's intervention is the curious proposition that, within financialized social institutions, the artist figures not as the unruly malcontent, but as the model worker. As McRobbie (2001) noted over a decade ago, the artist has come to signify the flexibilized, adaptable, passion-driven, and enthusiastically precarious subject of a neoliberal age where long-term, secure employment is replaced with a relentless "gig economy," even for manual and service-sector workers. The new romance of the artist as idealized worker goes beyond the exaltation of their creative freedom and devil-may-care lifestyle; it also encompasses their virtuosic quasi-anthropological vantage on the workplace, its codes of value, hierarchies, and customs—all the better to navigate an individualized path of self-maximization. Gough's work implicitly questions how such aptitudes might be used otherwise, towards the sabotage or subversion of such institutions in the name of other values.

Nuria Güell and Levi Orta, various interventions (2015–present)

How might the tools of financial circulation be appropriated to undermine or challenge that system? In 2015, the Catalan artist Nuria Güell, working with the Cuban artist Levi Orta, received a grant from a public arts institution, which they used to start a tax haven in Panama. The action took place amidst a tax avoidance scandal involving prominent political figures and members of the Spanish royal family, many of whom had supported the hyper-neoliberal regime of austerity forced upon Spain after the 2008 financial and subsequent Eurozone crisis. That regime led to unprecedented rates of home foreclosures, cuts to public services, skyrocketing rates of unemployment, funneling wealth to corporations, banks, and foreign investors, and draconian measures to silence and quash dissent. Güell and Orta approached a Madrid private business school whose neoliberal orientation was well known and whose faculty had been key advisors to the indicated politicians, requesting a consultation regarding how to secure legal services to establish a tax haven allowing them to embezzle public arts funding through a secret account. Güell and Orta then offered use of the account to a Catalonian network of cooperatives and anti-capitalist enterprises. They sought to exploit the legal impunity and anonymity of offshore accounts as a means of rejecting the policies of the Spanish state.

In a second, related project, Güell and Orta created a Troika Fiscal Disobedience Consultancy (disobedience.eu) to provide a platform for likewise studying and appropriating the techniques of transnational capital. The TFDC, for example, uses shell companies to offer fake invoices for services rendered to social movement-aligned organizations and individuals, allowing them to avoid paying taxes to the state. In a third project, Güell and Orta sent curators at two contemporary art institutions to secure €9,500 in corporate sponsorships to create a "Self-Sustaining Creative Economy Award." While Güell and Orta helped define the criteria, they did not sit on the jury, instead using their insider information to help their preferred candidate, the Freedom.Coop platform that facilitates cooperation between anti-capitalist initiatives, apply and win the prize—thus using art as a vehicle to transfer corporate wealth to activist hands. While Güell and Orta proudly announce such projects under their own names as art, they are careful to detach themselves from their administration so as to avoid criminal liability.

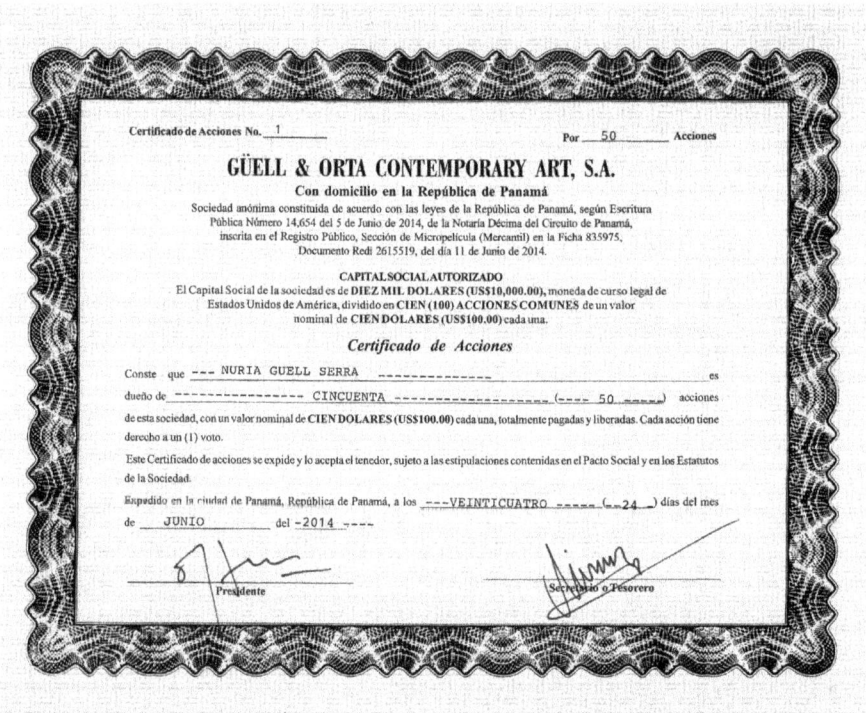

FIGURE 5.12: Núria Güell and Levi Orta's "Arte Político Degenerado" (2014). ADN Galeria.

Güell and Orta's work is part of a wider set of techniques at the cusp of art and activism that attempt to appropriate and expropriate a globally integrated financial system in the name of other, non- or anti-capitalist values. Such art exhibits a post-cynical pragmatism in a moment when the reproduction of the circulation of capital has been elevated globally, rendering it increasingly immune to democratic agency (often in ways that have corrupted allegedly democratic institutions). While this radical art may participate in traditions of "drawing attention," "revealing," and "problematizing" the excesses of power, it does not stake its success on a moment of revelation, as if upon seeing the art, we will have the scales fall from our eyes and become radicalized to participate in some revolutionary movement. Artists like Güell and Orta are skeptical of the potential of the nation-state and its legacy institutions to re-regulate global capitalism, in part because they see the agencies of global capitalism as too well entrenched to be curtailed by popular will, in part because—as students of 1973—they harbor no nostalgia for the Keynesian moment.

Rather, Güell and Orta and many other young artists are interested in using the strange semi-autonomy and institutional liquidity of "art" to kick open holes in the capillaries of global capital and redirect energies and funds to living anti-capitalist alternatives. A similar effort on the other side of the Atlantic is the Occupy Wall Street offshoot group Strike Debt's Rolling Jubilee platform, which crowdfunded money to play the secondary, discounted debt markets in order to buy and then forgive random people's medical debt (McKee 2016). It is these alternatives, such as the aforementioned network of cooperatives and anti-capitalist enterprises, that such artists see as true interventions in the imagination, not simply because they represent models for a different mode of human cooperation, but because they actually provide food, housing, information, ideas, and care within and against the crumbling system. Güell and Orta recognize that, under austerity, the reproduction of capitalist circulation has been sustained and accelerated at the expense of the social reproduction of citizens, with wealth and social resources claimed by transnational corporations, financial institutions, and elites while public services are cut, tax burdens are regressively redistributed, and civil rights are curtailed. They aim to reverse those flows, redirecting resources from the circulation of financial capital into grassroots efforts to reclaim the means of social reproduction. In this sense, Güell and Orta's work resonates less with contemporary art and more with social movements the world over that are seeking to appropriate and subvert global capitalism by creating new economic networks, livelihood methods, and parallel currencies.

It is significant that art becomes the vehicle for this work. Part of Güell and Orta's success, in terms of gaining resources for these actions and avoiding legal ramifications, stems from the residual prestige and ideological immunity afforded to art in a moment of austerity. Against all odds, "art" retains a cocoon—or, better, a cuckoo—of possibility. Perhaps this has to do with the enthusiasm for contemporary art among today's social elites, which in turn demands resources and indulgences offering radical artists some space to move and wealth to appropriate. Perhaps it has to do with the melancholia of the neoliberal nation-state, which, denied tools once used to assert sovereignty over fiscal matters, now turns to support "culture" as one of its only domains of action. Whatever the case, Güell and Orta are part of a generation of artist-activists who see art, the art world, and the art market as opportunities for expropriation and experimentation with alternatives. There is little hope here in the liberating or enlightening potential of art itself, but rather a post-cynical, utilitarian approach to art as a platform for other projects of grassroots creativity, militant imagination, and anti-capitalist economic cooperation.

CHAPTER SIX

Money and its Interpretation

The Future of Money in Speculative Fiction

SHERRYL VINT[*]

I well remember going to conferences in 2006 and 2007 where trendy social theorists presented papers arguing that these new forms of securitization, linked to new information technologies, heralded a looming transformation in the very nature of time, possibility—reality itself.

—David Graeber, (2011: 18)

Yet it seems to me that all social scientists, all journalists and commentators, all activists in the unions and in politics of whatever stripe, and especially all citizens should take a serious interest in money, its measurement, the facts surrounding it, and its history. Those who have a lot of it never fail to defend their interests.

—Thomas Piketty, (2014: 577)

Visions of the future of human social organization necessarily include future economic systems, and the role of money in human affairs has been an element of political speculation from at least as early as Plato's *Republic*. Plato viewed money as destructive, and Thomas More's *Utopia*, the volume that gave the genre its name, was similarly suspicious of money, seeing its elimination as necessary for justice. More recent speculative fiction (sf) generally sees money as inevitable, but it continues to focus attention on similar issues: shifts in economics are profound catalysts for other social change, from the disruptive effects market economies had on Ancient Greece, to the destruction of medieval European feudal systems facilitated by the rise of banking, to our context of global capital. This chapter focuses on how sf has responded to and extrapolated from the ways modern economic regimes have changed—and continue to change—patterns of daily life.

Representations of money in Western cultures have long been associated with the otherworldly, such as the equation of speculation with devilry in the eighteenth century by Jonathan Swift and Daniel Defoe. Concern that money is mystification intensified in the twentieth century, as it was detached from physical manifestations (a commodity such as gold; a marker such as banknotes) and became invisible, electronic data. Scott (2014) points out that increasingly in the twentieth century real banks functioned like those in gaming worlds, like a fiction: "if you have '£350 in the bank', it merely means the bank has recorded that for you in their data center." La Berge (2014: 84) argues that money in a financialized economy seems fictitious because it is temporally displaced, "a claim on future wealth," and that literature can represent this condition where political economy cannot. Crosthwaite (2014: 39) similarly argues that "supernatural depictions" of money "highlight the imaginary and ungrounded aspects of financial systems" and thus our potential to "reimagine those systems along alternative lines." Such pronouncements echo techniques in sf, making it ideal for depicting finance in an age in which money seems to be increasingly immaterial and oriented toward the future. Imagining how the world might be different, sf gives voice to anxieties and preoccupations about money and its role in social organization.

In *Capital in the Twenty-First Century* (2014), Piketty claims that money has disappeared from literature because shifts in capital and the rate of return on fixed assets destabilized what it signified. Nineteenth-century fiction almost never fails to mention capital, since the relationship between land and a fixed rate of return via rent can be taken for granted and used to convey information about characters' class (133, 207). Such concrete information about money could no longer ground fiction in the modern age, but critics such as Marsh and La Berge argue that twentieth- and twenty-first century literature found other modes. Examining British fiction, Marsh (2008: 2) argues that it countered "disabling mystification[s]" in financial rhetoric, while La Berge (2014: 4) finds in US texts a new aesthetic that emerged from the financial economy's "tension and possibility between present and future." Speculative fiction offers a particularly rich archive of texts: as the epigraph from Graeber suggests, money itself now seems almost a kind of sf. Dodd (2014: 6–7) argues that money is "a socially powerful—and socially necessary—illusion," and his interest in "the possibilities for improving society through the way we organize its money" is similarly evocative of sf in their shared aim of enacting change in the material world through representation.

FIGURE 6.1: Interior of the Hong Kong Stock Exchange, *c.* 1990s. Gary Cralle/ The Image Bank/Getty Images.

In the twenty-first century, speculative and other literatures converged. The idea that the world became more science fictional extended to money, not only the emergence of digital currencies but also ongoing financial crises in a system in which instruments such as derivatives and collateralized debt obligations make the economy itself both a fiction and a technology. While Golden Age sf of the 1930s and 1940s imagined marvelous improvements through technology, it often simply assumed that a capitalist market economy would continue, rewarding the innovators, even if this system imagined some new currency, often issued by a global government. More explicit attention to the economy as an engine of society can be found in Isaac Asimov's *Foundation* series (1942–1953; 1981), which projects thousands of years of future history of a galactic empire organized by mathematical governance, which entails a planned economy.[1]

The remainder of this chapter looks at examples of sf that interrogate three central questions that also occupy social theorists of money and shape public debate: What is the source of money's value, and what unit of value does it measure? What does it mean to understand money as a technology, and what changes might follow from the creation of new technologies for creating and distributing money? How can we understand money after the global financial crisis, given a new emphasis on money as debt rather than money as capital?

CURRENCY AND VALUE: WHAT DOES MONEY MEASURE?

A recurrent theme in sf that focuses on money is the relationship between currency and gold, which speaks to the frequent preoccupation with the meaning of gold in social theories of money. George Allan English's *The Golden Blight* (1916) is one of many transmutation stories that ask us to consider what might happen if a technology could turn something into gold or, in this case, gold into something worthless; for English, this frees humanity from enthrallment to capitalists. More innovative is Frank O'Rourke's *Instant Gold* (1964), extrapolated from Roosevelt's Executive Order 6102 (1933), which sought to prevent the hoarding of gold by outlawing its personal possession and suspending US citizens' capacity to exchange banknotes for gold. In O'Rourke's story, a firm markets a powder called "instant gold" that, when combined with water, produces an amount of gold worth $60 more than the purchase price of the powder, gold the government is compelled to buy. The book satirizes policy that deflates currency by creating more money without acquiring the equivalent in gold: in its future, the United States is freed from the specter of foreign-controlled debt, because it now has the gold to pay off these bonds. This crisis of the gold standard would eventually lead to our system of floating currencies, all measured against the dollar, after 1971 (see Beggs, this volume).

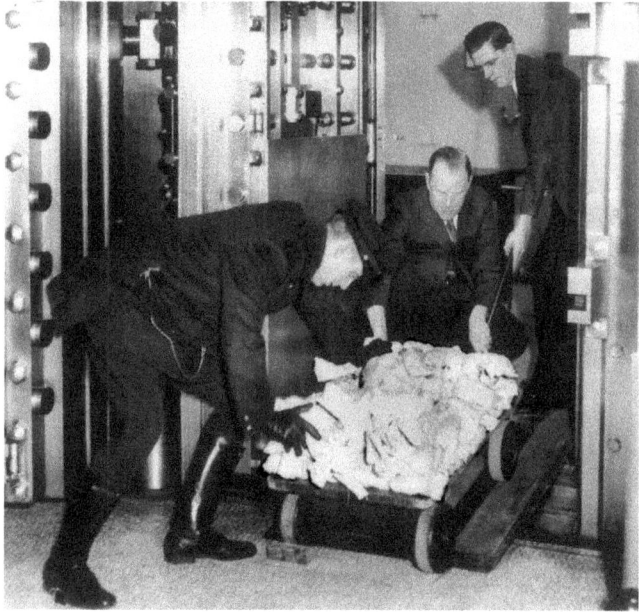

FIGURE 6.2: Sacks of gold exchanged against currency are stocked in the vaults of a New Jersey bank, 1993. Keystone-France/Gamma-Keystone/Getty Images.

These stories about gold reveal that one of the central difficulties in thinking about money in the future is confusion about what, precisely, money is. Most agree that money is composed of at least three elements: an abstract unit of value, a system of accounting indebtedness and credits, and a store of value. Yet it is not clear how these three interrelate. Is money the physical commodity, such as gold? Or is its essence more properly understood as a system of credits and debits, with gold coin serving as a token of these values? Since coinage was invented, we have tended to think of money as simultaneously a marker of value and a thing of inherent value: gold coins could always be melted down and sold—and might at times be worth more than their face value.[2] The faith that people have in the "inherent" value of gold continues to shape how we think of money even after 1971, Ferry (2016) notes; she argues that this confidence in the value of gold fuels both suspicion of paper currencies and a positive attitude toward the digital crytographic currency Bitcoin, whose semiotic allusions to gold mining transfer such attitudes to the technology (74).[3] Stories raise questions about whether gold has any "inherent" value, such as Edgar Allan Poe's "Von Kempelen and His Discovery" (1849), in which gold prices fall dramatically once a method of transforming brass into gold is invented. Yet many sf projections about future money technologies—including changes we have since lived through: from coins to paper to electronic information; new payment systems such as credit and debit cards—do not fundamentally shift the underlying thing they track.

Money is perhaps better understood as neither a commodity (like gold) nor a medium of exchange (like a system of accounts) but instead as "a social technology: a set of ideas and practices which organize what we produce and consume, and the way we live together" (Martin 2015: 33). This definition best reflects the way that sf treats money, focused more on the kinds of social orders it enables than the unit adopted to measure its value. Even when sf has delighted in imagining novel units of currency, the focus has been on the way such a currency structures other social interactions: from the "ob" currency of Eric Frank Russell's "And Then There Were None" (1951), a system of mutual aid in which people strive not to become over-obligated by providing as much as they take from the community; to the whuffie currency of social fame metrics in Cory Doctorow's *Down and Out in the Magic Kingdom* (2003), a post-scarcity world in which money as we know it is irrelevant;[4] to time itself as a currency in Andrew Niccol's film *In Time* (2011), used to make visible how unjust economic orders extend the lives of the wealthy as they simultaneously shorten those of the indebted. Real examples of local currencies reflect a similar understanding that the unit of economic exchange is always, at root, a measure of human interaction. Local adoption of currencies such as the Ithaca dollar or Brixton pound, for example, aim to keep exchange local. Often the design of "artisanal cash" reflects the values of the social order it seeks to reinforce (Crane 2015).

FIGURE 6.3: Brixton pound notes featuring British musician David Bowie, a local currency introduced for use in the south London borough of Brixton. CHRIS RATCLIFFE/AFP/Getty Images.

Martin (2015) argues that money is a social technology of transferable credit; looking at the same history from the opposite side, Graeber (2011) sees money primarily as a system of indebtedness, focusing especially on how what he calls "human economies" of social obligation and mutual aid become distorted by market economies that transform debt into abstract, measurable, and transferable monetary value. Both agree that money can do social harm if not balanced against other ethical considerations. Martin (2015: 149) argues that debates over "the extent to which money should really be the coordinating mechanism for social life" disappeared with the Enlightenment's mistaken understanding of the value of money as inherent in the physical commodity of gold, reducing once "vital questions of moral and political justice to the mechanical application of objective scientific truths." Similarly, Graeber (2011: 13) emphasizes that debt as a strict financial measure is "simple, cold, and impersonal." His book traces the origins of money in imperial expansion, arguing that a moral discourse around the repayment of debts has historically justified social relations founded on violence; he sees the invention of abstract economic value as key to the extension and worsening of slavery (155).

Speculative fiction is premised on the extrapolation of new social worlds, often propelled by a new science or technology. Its power is that it explores such innovations embedded within a social world of other relations, not as abstractions in a laboratory. If we understand economics as a science,[5] we can similarly see that wider implications for human culture are often not addressed within the discipline, but are extrapolated by sf. Graeber's work is motivated by the injustice he sees in a predatory economic system that destroys lives for the sake of profit, and many sf writers are similarly motivated to explore money as a social technology of alienation.

Samuel R. Delany's "The Tale of Old Venn" (1979) considers what happens when a tribal society encounters a market economy, using the voice of a woman, Old Venn, who lives in the tribal location but comes from a money-based, urban culture. Teaching some of the local children written notation, she warns them that the system was invented for "the control of slaves" (85). In Delany's fictional tribe, harmony exists between the genders, and women play a substantial role in an economy based on fulfilling material need. Echoing observations made by anthropologists who study the consequences of money's introduction via colonialism, in Delany's tribal society money is ceremonial and oriented to prestige rather than necessity, making it the province of men according to their social patterns. Yet the more money circulates, the more it distorts what is considered of value, as a barter system[6] of exchanging valued skills and goods is displaced by a prestige system of wealth accumulation: skilled women now

> had to go to someone with money, frequently a man, exchange her goods for money, and then exchange the money for what she needed. But if there was no money available, all her strength and skill and goods gave her no power at all—and she might as well not have had them.
>
> —Delaney 1979: 93

Money, Venn argues, mirrors and flattens things in concert,[7] changes social life and hides the depth of this change: "the values we live with now are a reversal of those we had before, even if the forms that express those values are not terribly far from what they were" (100).

Following the economic crisis of the 1970s and linked to the emergence of personal computers, cyberpunk centered on economics but did not focus on money per se. Projecting a future in which corporate governance displaced democratic systems, cyberpunk extrapolated the worst aspects of global capitalism, focusing on outsider figures who hack fortresses of accumulated wealth. In his novel *Neuromancer*, William Gibson describes life in the metropolis as

> a deranged experiment in social Darwinism, designed by a bored researcher who kept one thumb permanently on the fast-forward button. Stop hustling and you sank without a trace, but move a little too swiftly and you'd break the fragile surface tension of the black market; either way, you were gone.
>
> —Gibson 1984: 7

Gibson's work gave us the term cyberspace and catalyzed research communities to produce many of the social media and banking technologies we take for granted today. Money is everywhere in *Neuromancer*, in the sense that its pursuit drives the characters, and yet cyberpunk does little to revise our understanding of money.

Gibson's most recent book, *The Peripheral* (2014), connects control of economic systems with the production of the future. Building on his critique of advertising culture in the *Zero History* trilogy (2003–2010), this book imagines a future kleptocracy reliant on humanoid drone laborers (peripherals) and a complicated plot to forestall what they call "the jackpot," a series of environmental, economic, and social collapses that will kill most of humanity. From the post-jackpot 2098, individuals interact with people from the pre-jackpot 2028 via a technology that allows them to send information back in time, including financial information. These 2098 protagonists can send "money" back, in the sense that data sent to banks becomes access to financial resources for those in the 2028 timeline—an apt image of how financialization has rendered money invisible. La Berge and Crosthwaite notice the way that new technologies of money come to stand in for the social anxieties about money—from the mechanical clatter of the stock ticker tape representing an impersonal economic order (Crosthwaite 2014: 42) to the cool mystery of the ATM embodying the emergence of inhuman, financial society (La Berge 2014: 43)—and Gibson's time-traveling money symbolizes the way finance relies on a complex entanglement of present and future in its creation of value. The protagonists in the near-future refer to those in the far-future as "adventure

FIGURE 6.4: A stock ticker is introduced for the first time in New York, 1929. Bettmann/Getty.

FIGURE 6.5: The ATM is introduced in Paris, France, 1968. Keystone-France/Gamma-Keystone/Getty Images.

FIGURE 6.6: The company floor of Interactive Brokers, a leading electronic and online trading firm, 2014. Photograph by ☐, Wikimedia Commons, CC BY-SA 4.0.

capitalists," a term that should remind readers of venture capital and its own metaphorical time travel through speculative investment and derivatives trading.

Gibson draws our attention to parallels between the far future's open kleptocracy and the more hypocritical political and financial structures of the near future (and the reader's present). Two factions in the far future fight to control their past and thus the world that will survive, pitting rival "predatory trading algorithms" (271) against their opponents in a tale that reminds us how much the contemporary economy depends on speculative markets that seem precariously ephemeral. *The Peripheral* also speaks to ongoing anxieties—reflected as well in popular discourses—that as money's embodiment changes from coins or notes to digital data, it becomes more open to manipulative speculation by elites.

While Gibson sought to catalogue the corrosive effects of globalized capital, his contemporary Kim Stanley Robinson focuses on imagining futures that offer alternatives to capitalism and its uneven distribution of social goods. Robinson is best known for his environmental sf, but from the beginning, his vision contends that more ecologically sustainable societies will require a more equitable economic system. Although Robinson does not write about new kinds of money per se, he repeatedly demonstrates the centrality of economic systems to shaping the kinds of societies in which we might live. His first novels, known as the *Three Californias* trilogy, explore different visions of the future of Orange County, California projected from a mid-1980s vantage point of rapid technological development and recent deregulation. The first, *The Wild Shore* (1984), focuses on a small group of survivors after a limited nuclear war, part of an America that has been cordoned off from the rest of the world. The book shows the efforts of survivors to rebuild trade and civilization, but their efforts are hampered by external policing and internal suspicion, seemingly bred by a capitalist ethos of competition that they remember from the United States they lost.

The Wild Shore begins with a macabre scene of adolescent children digging up cemeteries, seeking the riches of silver they have been led to believe adorned the coffins of people from the decadent pre-war era. They want to be "kings of the swap meet" (4)—and queens, one belatedly adds—but all they find is plastic painted silver. This sense of disappointment sets the tone for all their aspirations of the bygone world of consumerist comfort. Near the end, Tom, an elderly man who was eighteen when the bombs when off in 1987, tries to make them see that while their ancestors had accumulated wealth as measured by consumer goods, the infrastructure required to sustain that level of consumption was not worth the cost. In a speech that echoes contemporary sentiment about the "rat race" of high finance, he tells them,

> It was a stupid life really, and that's why I can't see it when people talk about fighting to get back to that. People back then struggled at jobs in boxes so they could rent boxes and visit other boxes, and they spent their whole lives running in boxes like rats. I was doing it myself, and it made no sense.
>
> —222

The Wild Shore marks its difference from other works of post-nuclear rebuilding by this focus on critiquing the economic system of the lost world. Trying to explain to the younger generation why the United States remains in quarantine, Tom explains,

> The world was starving and we ate like pigs, people died of hunger and we ate their dead bodies and licked our chops. . . . we were a monster and we were eating up the world and they had reasons to do it to us.
>
> —296

The glimmer of hope in this harsh world is that a new, more equitable America might rise from these ashes.

The Gold Coast (1988) shows us what a future America might look like if nothing intervened to end the expansion of technology and capital. Set in the near-future of 2027, it extrapolates increased urban sprawl, and while this world is not post-apocalyptic, it is dystopian. Protagonist Jim McPherson is drifting through life, unable to find a job at twenty-seven, unable to commit to his art in a meaningful way, involved in only the most superficial of interpersonal relationships, and continually seeking new drugs to distract himself. Robinson makes clear that Jim's ennui is produced by the kind of profit-driven economic order in which he lives, one that emphasizes personal freedom over social responsibility. Jim argues with his mother over IMF lending policies that destroy local economies and force the production of export crops over subsistence farming (22) and is attracted to the socialist vision of his friend Arthur. Through him, Jim becomes involved in anti-weapons protests. The book intersperses chapters of this reality with ones about the past of Orange County, lovingly describing periods of sustainable agriculture, abundant fauna, and flourishing fruit tree groves. Jim is nourished by such visions of the past, recounted by Tom, who in this reality is dying in an impersonal hospital, plagued by dementia. A trip to Egypt in which Jim sees the most abject suffering due to poverty, only blocks away from the opulence of his Sheraton hotel room, prompts feelings of revulsion (231) and increased alienation. The novel ends with Jim's commitment toward leading a different kind of life, driven by his sense that economic injustice destroys sociality.

The most challenging of the novels is *Pacific Edge* (1990), set in El Moderna in 2065, with some portions of the narrative describing the experiences of another version of Tom trying to find his way from his alienating life in the 1980s into the sustainable and collective governance we see in El Moderna. The novel is careful not simply to posit an imaginary utopia that is cut off from the rest of social existence but instead to show how a better world could be built by repurposing the remains of this one. The central focus remains on ecologically sustainable lifestyles, but economics plays a prominent role. Tom recognizes during the 1980s that the economy is globalized and thus his American lifestyle, "on little islands of luxury," requires that the rest of the world remain "great oceans of abject misery, bitter war, endless hunger" (60). A first step in building El Moderna was finding ways to "convert the military parts of the economy" toward civilian needs without "causing a depression" (57), just as they have converted their homes from being sources of climate change into living structures that use solar energy and grow their own food, all managed through efficient computer systems. In the contrast between Robinson's extrapolation and Gibson's, we see how sf is not about technological determinism but rather about human choices regarding how to use technology, the computers used to sustain ecology or to speculate in high finance.

El Moderna is in political crisis, with rival factions of Greens and Federalists struggling over the last lot of undeveloped space. The Federalists wish to change its zoning to commercial so that a new biotech facility can be built, while the Greens are suspicious of rapid industrial expansion, remembering the political struggle to limit the power of corporations. This economy retains money, but it also has features such as the communal ownership of public land and utilities, a graduated income tax that most heavily taxes the wealthiest, and public labor service owed to the community by all who reside there. Corporations have been downsized to "companies" (187), with the requirement that they have local sites, employees, and social obligations. This new biotech enterprise requires larger capitalization that many see as a risk to their entire way of life, and the company in question seeks to hide some of its income from community taxation so that it can further invest in its own expansion. As Tom notes, the original aims may have been laudable, "this equipment . . . saves lives," but faulty logic extends this goal into an economic one: "Save more lives, make more money—the two are all mixed up in his business, and if you try to limit the latter in any way, it looks to him like you're limiting the former" (253). Economic growth too easily becomes its own justification, and they conclude that the risks of returning to the old infrastructure far outweigh any benefits the biotech might provide.

In Robinson's more recent *2312* (2012), about an interstellar civilization three hundred years hence, his concern for sustainability remains but the urgency of his critique of capitalism grows more vehement. He recounts the periodization of a fictional historian who explains how humanity managed to find its way out of the looming economic and ecological crises of the twenty-first century and into this twenty-fourth century of expansive human settlement.

The key elements are found in the Turnaround of 2130–2160 with its "mutation of values" (246) and, following this, the signing of the Mondragon Accords, which meant that space settlement was based on economic values of mutual aid rather than competition.[8] For Robinson, a revolution in economic values is as essential to human futures as any other kind of technological change.

MONEY AND/AS TECHNOLOGY

One of the ways that money frequently appears in sf is through visions of new kinds of technologies for payment in a future that has eliminated physical cash. The genre's period of wide emergence in the 1940s and 1950s coincides with a major shift in postwar economics toward the massive expansion of debt through guaranteed home loans, initially for veterans, as well as new forms of consumer debt in credit cards (Diners Card 1950, American Express 1958), which soon became profitable parts of banking (La Berge 2014: 40–41; Swartz and Stearns, this volume). Fiction from the 1960s and 1970s tends to refer to currency as "credits" rather than as dollars—for example, Philip K. Dick uses PosCred in his anti-consumerist *Ubik* (1966)—but for the most part, such sf does not fully work through the implications of paying for things via credit. Bátiz-Lazo et al. (2014: 104) note that the adoption of new technologies is based "as much on imagined futures as it was on existing realities," and they show how the financial industry drew on speculative techniques to project the utopian future of the "cashless society" as they promoted new instruments such as credit cards. Such innovations did not fundamentally change how money operated or how its value was derived, merely the "*mechanisms* that allow a society to *exchange* money" (Bátiz-Lazo et al. 2014: 108). As early as Edward Bellamy's *Looking Backward: 2000–1887* (1889), sf envisioned such a tool, in this case a debit card that automatically loaded each citizen's share of collectively produced wealth. Bellamy's vision thus involved cashless payment based on *deposits* while the credit card system that emerged grew out of consumer debt.

Along with newly available mortgages, credit cards transformed the social technology of money, and "within a generation, debt became not only the norm but the expected right of virtually the entire middle and working class" (Weatherford 1997: 224). This shift continued to have significant social consequences into the twenty-first century, most dramatically in the 2008 global financial crisis, which was precipitated by banks packaging "assets" of consumer mortgage debt owed to them into instruments of investment: an imaginary edifice of value that came crashing down as soon as it become clear that the underlying debts would never be paid and thus none of the money was "real."

An ongoing issue in social theories of money in the modern age is this question of what makes it "real," and this convergence of the speculative imagination with the speculative nature of value once again reinforces how we

FIGURE 6.7: A commuter pays her fare using a bank card and a chip-and-pin machine on the Moscow Underground, 2016. Dmitry Serebryakov/TASS/Getty Images.

might conceptualize the economy itself as a kind of sf, especially in the twenty-first century. The shift toward electronic forms of payment—credit and debit cards, bank transfers, new mobile forms of payments developed by Apple and Samsung—changed the place of cash and social relations rooted in cash exchange. These shifts have reinforced the role of financial institutions that mediate between consumers and creditors, increasing their power over daily life. Such changes inform a larger conversation about access to financial institutions as necessary for civic inclusion, inspiring experiments with digital currencies, further fusing sf and material invention.

Perhaps the most discussed of these experiments is Bitcoin, which has strong connections to sf, especially cypherpunks, a group of libertarian, computer-savvy individuals who advocate for personal privacy through cryptography. Their early embrace of Bitcoin in the immediate aftermath of the 2008 crisis rested in part on its reputation for being beyond government control. But as Scott (2014) points out, this view mistakenly implies that "privacy alone is what enables social empowerment"; as Scott argues, Bitcoin's individualist appeal "is essentially an ideology of the already-empowered, not the vulnerable." Neal Stephenson's *Cryptonomicon* (1999), a sweeping tale linking events in World War II to an IT start-up contemporary to the novel's publication, envisions how to create an electronic currency and why one might wish to do so. There are important differences between the e-currency Stephenson imagines and Bitcoin; centrally, Stephenson sees the currency as a tool for online spending money only.[9] Although he shares the libertarian ideals that advocates of Bitcoin proselytize, the novel does not extrapolate significant social change beyond avoiding taxes.

Cryptonomicon opens with a scene of the chaos in Shanghai in 1941 as the streets are clogged with the transit of stacks of paper currency among the city's many banks, taken to their issuing bank so that the requisite amount of silver can be paid to the bank holding the note. The ongoing faith in the materiality—hence, *reality*—of a metal currency shapes the novel, which includes detailed explanations of how both currency and cryptography work. Characters in World War II end up in possession of Japanese gold buried in the Philippines. The main protagonist in the 1990s setting, Randy Waterhouse, is an IT security specialist who establishes a secure data haven in the fictional Asian empire of Kinakuta, whose Sultan articulates the dream of cypherpunks everywhere: "total freedom of information. I hereby abdicate all government power over the flow of data across and within my borders" (319).

Randy and his partners also develop a real-time encryption and decryption tool, Novus Ordo Seclorum, "a new order for the ages," the motto of the Great Seal of the United States, printed on US dollar bills since 1933. *Cryptonomicon* links its concerns with privacy to a libertarian ethos associated with the founding of the United States as a new kind of political entity committed to individual freedom; the book represents the invention of anonymous and unmonitored e-currency as the next step toward a social order that will renew freedom. Randy's business partner, Avi, who is of Jewish descent and obsessed with preventing future holocausts, believes that internet privacy is necessary for freedom from dictators. The data haven and e-currency are a way to avoid taxes—a moral issue, they contend, because the government will only spend such money on military endeavors they do not support.[10] Democracy and social justice are ensured by maximum freedom, including a currency free from any state control. *Cryptonomicon* thus entwines privacy with private banking with the continuation of individual liberty. Fundamentally the vision of the novel is one that trusts individuals and distrusts corporate entities, especially the government, and thus fails to think through what kinds of human suffering might be facilitated by an anonymous and untraceable banking system.

In his analysis of Bitcoin, Scott (2014) comes to precisely the opposite conclusion. People attach a high value to its blockchain verification technology, because it allows parties on both sides of a transaction to trust in the each other's veracity without a context of personal contact or a third-party institution serving as guarantor. Far from being evidence of the inherent trustworthiness of individuals as compared to the corruption of institutions, he argues, it is a technological update to Hobbesian social contract theory that views humans as inherently untrustworthy individuals whose first instinct is to maximize their self-interest.

More substantive visions of how cryptocurrency might transform the underlying economic system are absent from Stephenson's work, although we can see hints of these values in Robinson's fiction discussed above—and in contemporary developments. The alternative cryptocurrency FairCoin, for example, is premised on ideals of anarchist collectivism and an economic policy that seeks "equality and redistribution" as higher ends than "rigid protection of historical property rights" (Scott 2016). Such values also shape the futures Robinson creates. This contrast underlines the fact that money is doubly a system for facilitating payments *and* an expression of the values structuring how material goods circulate. Robinson extrapolates the latter without reimagining currency, while Stephenson reinvents currency without reimagining standards for social distribution. *Cryptonomicon* also fails to take on many of the issues that have plagued Bitcoin, such as its role in markets for illegal trade or the consequences of private tax havens for the collective state—precisely the problem that Piketty diagnoses as central to the crisis of twenty-first-century economies.

Stephenson envisions e-currency working in a way that is consistent with the history of commodity currencies. Paper currency is a promise for redemption in gold, and for such a system to function, there must exist a gold reserve that could enable this exchange; the Japanese gold similarly secures Stephenson's e-currency.[11] His characters contend that the gold reserve was "old fashioned" only until "all of the unbacked currencies in Southeast Asia went down the toilet" (565), endorsing the fantasy that gold represents some kind of "real" value that transcends representative money. Maurer et al. (2013: 273) call this "digital metallism" and argue that Bitcoin, too, shares this fetish: although it is not based on a material repository like Stephenson's currency, its linguistic evocation of mining encourages us to think in these terms, and its features such as "the anti-inflationary economics of a hard cap on the money supply and the labor of a community of human miners and nonhuman hardware and software" replicate, conceptually and discursively, a metal standard. Yet, they also point out, Bitcoin is not a commodity currency, like gold: it is fundamentally a kind of credit money.

The vision of e-currency in *Cryptonomicon*, then, both changes and does not change money. Its virtual instantiation as digital certificates may seem revolutionary, but in fact this only anticipates the channels of e-commerce through which national currencies operate today. Its innovation is that it is "Anonymous. Untraceable. And untaxable" (728). Since this currency will circulate alongside national currencies, Stephenson does not address some of the problems that currencies such as Bitcoin may have to face, including how a currency might be stabilized in times of inflation or deflation (the role of the government monetary policy); and in their libertarian zeal to avoid taxation, its inventors give little thought to how government might continue to function in the absence of any tax base, should a digital currency become the dominant

FIGURE 6.8: A sign displaying "Bitcoins accepted" is seen on the front door of the Old Fitzroy Pub in Sydney, Australia, September 2013. Photo by Cameron Spencer/ Getty Images.

one.[12] Advocates of Bitcoin see utopian promise in both its anonymity and its capacity to reach those who cannot access banking financial services (e.g., women in patriarchal counties who cannot legally own property). In practice, however, the hardware requirements to mine, own, and exchange Bitcoin produce different exclusions, its anonymity has proven more utopian than actual, and the ecological impact of the energy needed to run the computer "rigs" to mine ever-waning stores militates against regarding it as an unambiguous social good.

Stephenson returned to the relationship between digital and national currencies in *Reamde* (2012), a novel about the entanglements of social and financial systems. It combines ransom-ware demands with the lucrative industry of massive multiplayer online role-playing games, like World of Warcraft. Such digital games have internal economies in the sense that characters gain attributes and objects based on the hours of play and achievements. The more one accumulates such objects and experiences, the more power one has and, generally, the more enjoyable the game. Stephenson envisions a system in which people with time and skill to play, but few other sources of income, transform their game activity into productive labor by selling their augmented characters.[13] These "gold farmers" are a real-world phenomenon as well, often based (as they are in Stephenson's novel) in China (Nardi and Kow 2010).

Speculative fiction often literalizes metaphor, allowing us more easily to see a feature of our social world. Stephenson makes visible how invested we remain in material ideas of value even as we imagine digital currency. His game T'Rain is designed using a complex algorithm to mimic the geological location of minerals, and it welcomes gold farmers as an anticipated part of play. Significant attention is paid to its internal economy, including mineral deposits based on earth science algorithms, a feudal structure that includes "bot" characters who accumulate wealth for their lords, and game-play that includes physical mining for gold in this scientifically accurate geology. T'Rain allows real-world currency to be extracted and paid to the player's credit account: normally games allow for real currency to enter through in-game purchases, but not this reverse. A realistic exchange rate between in-game and real-world currencies is maintained, and the same value cannot be in both places at once. Hackers exploit this system and demand ransom-ware payments in T'Rain currency.

Bitcoin, in contrast to Stephenson's gold-based monies, is based on the technology of the blockchain and takes its value from the collective belief that others will regard it as "real" money and treat it thus; without a community, Bitcoin is only code, as Maurer et al. (2013) argue. Bitcoin adds even more ambiguity to the question of what money is: it is an international currency that does not rely on either a national government or a reserve of gold for its value, relying on people's faith in a mathematical algorithm. Bitcoin as a technology creates a publicly verifiable blockchain ledger and thus a decentralized network of trust. Many of the utopian possibilities attached to this technology have less

FIGURE 6.9: Inside a Bitcoin "mine" near Kongyuxiang, Sichuan, China. Photo by Paul Ratje/For *The Washington Post* via Getty Images.

to do with its relationship to privacy and more to do with the elimination of fees for financial activities, part of a desire to detach society from commercial banks in whom people no longer have faith.[14] As a utopian technology, Bitcoin aimed to revise a financial system that had become predatory in the public mind (especially since 2008), but the more Bitcoin develops as a technology, the more various financial services—wallet apps, exchange markets, and the like—introduce structures that make Bitcoin more like existing currencies.

Blockchain technology drives a variety of new enterprises, and some hope decentralized peer-to-peer exchanges could turn the economy into the "public utility that it's supposed to be" (Vigna and Casey 2015: 330). Enthusiasts envision a future of "entities owned by multiple shareholders for which routine financial decisions—when to release funds to pay for expenses, how big a dividend to pay—are automated by the firm's guiding software and entrusted to a tamperproof system that's verified by the blockchain" (Vigna and Casey 2015: 230). This approaches the posthuman vision of Iain M. Banks' *Culture* series (1987–2012) and Charles Stross's *Accelerando* (2005). The former is a series of novels set in a distant future in which all necessary work is done by non-sentient machines and the economy is planned and managed by AIs, while the latter is about the implications of the technological singularity, whose posthuman inhabitants include financial instruments, such as derivatives, who have become a kind of AI. Similar fantasies fuel utopian speculations about the future made possible by blockchain technology. Cameron and Tyler Winklevoss, for example, imagine a future in which "a Trade Singularity will occur, whereby trade between machines, computers and things, will exceed trade between humans. Uncreative tasks will become primarily automated causing goods and services to become much cheaper and living standards to rise" (in Swartz 2017: 93). Echoing a technocratic note sounded throughout sf's history, such projects envision the future of the economy as "immune from human error or corruption, and therefore fair" (Swartz 2017: 94). Although current blockchain technologies cannot materialize such fantasies, Swartz (2017: 83) argues that—like s.f.— they are "meaningful as an inventory of desire" about economic futures.[15]

Stross turns more centrally to financial futures in *Halting State* (2007) and *Neptune's Brood* (2013). The first concerns the same mix of digital gaming culture and real-world money that Stephenson explores in *Reamde*, but Stross's novel was published first and engages more directly with how digital cryptocurrencies emerged. It starts with a bank robbery within game space. Confused police are asked to review the recording of role-playing gamers who enter the game's central vault and steal the items of value stored there. As the company's executives patiently explain, although in game-play this looks like a physical robbery, "stealing" items is really hacking and changing their property attributes. In-game treasure is then transformed into real-world currency by selling it to other gamers. More importantly, Stross imagines his game running on a distributed platform across multiple devices, with authentication of ownership working like the blockchain structure that validates Bitcoin.

The problem Stross confronts here—how to verify and validate digital transactions without a third party—is shared by Bitcoin itself, which requires that the blockchain be replicated by every node of the network.[16] Stross also works through the problem of how a digital currency might use monetary policy to control inflation. His digital gaming companies contract with a financial services team, Hayek Associates,[17] whose job is to manage the economy of gameplay. They note:

> Playing the game is inflationary because they keep burgling the tombs of dead gods, breaking into the governor of Jamaica's dungeon vaults, colonizing the Andromeda galaxy, and so on. And you know, you can't tax them or make the money decay, because that would be No Fun, and if the game stops being Fun, why play?
>
> —57

Thus in-game banks take value out of circulation, not using it for speculation (as do commercial banks), but the sale of in-game items to other players or to other gaming environments creates a complex system of "exchange rates between games—and not just game-to-game, I'm talking game-to-euro rates, game-to-yuan, game-to-rupee ... even US dollars. So there's currency speculation and an external market in gaming currency hedge funds" (57). Like real-world banks, these reduce the amount of circulating currency by charging service fees. Stross complicates the interaction between in-game and external-world economies further through the revelation that Hayek Associates is a front for MI5: one operation uses people who believe they are part of a live-action, role-playing game, Spooks, to conduct routine surveillance; another conducts online surveillance of "certain disorderly elements who like to meet up in one game space or another" (223). The theft of items from the vault leads the protagonists to uncover a conspiracy related to quantum computers and plans to hack the networked infrastructure, all in the name of economic hegemony. As a MI5 handler explains, this "is maintained by broadcasting your vision of how the global trade system should be structured" (240). The various candidates for economic hegemon include the EU, China, and India; Stross, a Scot, imagines a future in which Scotland is independent and has become a center for global banking, and he sardonically projects that the United States will be out of the running by the mid-twenty-first century: "the USA went post-industrial first. Their infrastructure is out-of-date and replacing it, now oil is no longer cheap, is costing them tens of trillions of euros to modernize. Plus, they've got all those rusty aircraft carriers to keep afloat" (240).

Control of quantum decryption will allow whoever possesses this device to make subtle changes, "footnotes inserted in government reports feeding into World Trade Organization negotiating positions" and the like: "You don't want to halt the state in its tracks, you simply want to divert it into a siding of your choice" (271).[18] The entire plot rests on a disgruntled investor, a Hayek employee who took a short position against his own company's success. Not among those aware of the real purpose of the firm, he read the market, expected them to fail, and was blindsided by the fact that "Hayek Associates were doomed to succeed: Michaels's friends in the shadowy machinery of state simply kept pouring liquidity into their Potemkin dot-com" (347). Beleaguered by his financial losses, he sells the authentication key that enables the digital theft. We might see a real-world parallel here with the mortgage crisis and the role of the ratings agencies who did not accurately evaluate these bonds, frustrating efforts to short them, as recounted by Michael Lewis in *The Big Short* (2011). Stross's novel was published before these revelations were made, and this similarity points us once more to the conflation of reality and sf in the speculative economy of the modern age.

MONEY AND/AS DEBT: THE FINANCIAL CRISIS

Stross's *Neptune's Brood* projects digital currencies further into the future and thinks through the economics required to underpin interstellar civilization; it was inspired by Stross's reading of Graeber (2011). This future is populated by metahumans, descendants of what we might call AI today, but with a range of affective capacities that make them much closer to organic life. The protagonist Krina Alizond-114 is "a scholar of the historiography of accountancy practices" (16), created by her matriarch Sondra Alizond-1, whose progenitors "were a credit union and a gambling cartel" (42). Stross imagines a future in which a digital currency verified by a blockchain is the common currency, but this decentralized structure has not resulted in greater freedom. Rather, communities and some individuals become their own banks, and the system of currency rests on debt that is continually projected into a future of promised repayment. Stross carefully shows us the kind of values that would be needed to found a society in which repayment of debt is the highest social value. Krina explains to us that she was born into child slavery, but then hastens to add that this should not unduly prejudice us against her matriarch, who thereby enabled her children to "repay the not-insubstantial debt of our creation as soon as possible, without falling victim to the full misery of compound interest" (15).

Playfully echoing Jane Austen, Krina begins the tale of her adventures by observing, "It is a truth universally acknowledged, that every interstellar colony in search of good fortune must be in need of a banker" (42). As Krina explains, building spaceships and founding colonies are capital-intensive projects that will show a profit only decades into the future. Colonies thus begin in substantial debt to those who funded the construction of interstellar ships:

> But many are unaware that if there is one thing that is vital to the long-term stability and prosperity of a colony, it is the creation of interstellar debt instruments by means of a new Slow Bank. Without a Slow Bank, it's not possible to trade across the gulfs of interstellar space-time. . . . So there is good reason to set up a beacon as soon as possible after arrival and to transmit the we-are-here tokens to the neighboring system banks that will prompt them to acknowledge the existence of a new issuer that can create currency and act as a guarantor of the new colony's debt.
>
> —45

Stross envisions three kinds of future money. The most common is cash, "fast money," needed for daily transactions. Medium money is an investment; "something you buy with cash; something durable, something that is not easily liquidated or valued in fast money. Cathedrals and asteroids and debts and durable real estate and bonds backed by the honorable reputation of traders in slow money" (110). Holdings in medium money add stability to the financial system since their value changes slowly over a long duration, and it takes weeks or years to buy and sell them. The "flexible exchange rate" between fast and medium money enables "modern economies [to] decouple transient demand from the bones and muscles that underpin survival" (110).

Slow money pays for interstellar civilization, a currency whose transactions occur over very long durations. Local currencies cannot become universal because, in the example Krina gives,

> Offering to pay in Hector dollars for a valuable shipment of terraforming specialists is all very well, but if ten light-years separate buyer and vendor, then it takes ten years each for the bid and offer to crawl across the gap—and by the time the vendor tries to spend those Hector dollars, thirty or more years have passed, the speculative housing bubble has burst, the money markets have collapsed, and hyperinflation ensued.
>
> —54

Slow money has a fixed exchange rate with other kinds of money, and this economy privileges holdings in slow money since one takes a huge loss—upwards of 90 percent of putative value—when converting slow money into fast. At the same time, however, given the exchange rate, a single slow dollar becomes thousands if not millions of fast dollars, even with these service fees. Slow money is slow because it is "a bitcoinage" (194), and each transaction must be verified by a bank orbiting a different star from that where the transaction is made: it takes years for a transaction to complete.

The plot is complex and involves Krina's investigation of what at first seems to be a Ponzi scheme and is eventually revealed to be the genocide of a colony to enable a banker to steal its slow money. The novel opens with an epigraph from Graeber that emphasizes the consequences of a historical shift from understanding money as material to understanding it as abstract financial instruments, ultimately advocating for a political structure of debt forgiveness, a Biblical Jubilee that Graeber argues was central to the earliest human cultures. Graeber argues that a new Jubilee for international and consumer debt can remind us

> that money is not ineffable, that paying one's debts is not the essence of morality, that all these things are human arrangements and that if democracy is to mean anything, it is the ability to all agree to arrange things in a different way.
>
> —390

Stross offers a similar vision as his novel concludes. A new kind of matter transmission technology destroys the slow money economy (and thus the debts accumulated in it) and a newly wealthy Krina—whose good fortune has been facilitated by metahumans who deemphasize material wealth—is advised to "create wealth rather than hoarding it. Live life" (273).

Other lessons can be found in twenty-first century sf. Lionel Shriver's *The Mandibles: A Family, 2029–2047* projects a future in which the US dollar ceases to be the international standard, seen through the eyes of a middle-class family whose way of life is thereby destroyed. This book has interesting parallels with Jack Womack's *Dryco* series (1987–2000), set in a dystopian future of corporate governance, massive homelessness, and violent public spectacle that literalizes boardroom conflict.[19] Most of Womack's work emphasizes the dystopian reality produced by neoliberal policy that emerged contemporary to his publications, but *Random Acts of Senseless Violence* (1993) begins closest to the present. Clearly imitating *The Diary of Anne Frank* (1947), it recounts Lola's experiences as she is transformed from a child of middle-class privilege; through the economic upheavals during which her parents lose their jobs, home, and lives; and into a present in which she is a member of a street gang. Less overtly sf, Shriver's novel follows four generations of the Mandible family as it declines from upper middle-class security based on investment income to struggling to get by after the 2008 global financial crisis and, in the novel, the global adoption of a new international currency, the bancor,[20] which isolates America and devastates its economy.

What is striking about the differences between Womack's and Shriver's work is the degree to which the economy itself is the focus of the latter narrative.

Both explore poverty, but in *The Mandibles* economic policy and changes to money take center stage. Early in the novel we are told that bibliophile patriarch Douglas, "never a science fiction fan," now "immersed himself in the more recently minted genre of apocalyptic economics, rehearsing debt-to-GDP ratios as he had once memorized Saul Bellow" (48). Later, one of the youngest generation tells his novelist aunt that he finds her books impenetrable because her characters are detached from reality: for him, her characters "live in an economic vacuum," by which he means

> They make decisions because they're in love, or they're angry, or they want adventure. You never know how they afford their houses. They never decide not to do something because it costs too much. The whole book—you never find out how much these characters pay in taxes.
>
> —318

Perhaps, Shriver implies, we are returning to literature like that of the nineteenth century in which money was omnipresent because it was foundational to all other possibilities.

The siblings of the second generation initially occupy distinct class positions, with psychologist Avery married to a tenured economist, Lowell, while her sister, Florence, and Florence's Latino partner Esteban struggle to pay rent on working-class salaries whose buying power continually shrinks with inflation. Their brother Jared drops out from mainstream society and spends his education fund on farm land, a decision that proves fortuitous. Avery's children, used to private schools and music lessons, struggle following the American collapse, while Florence's son, Willing, has prescient insight into the end of American hegemony and guides his less adaptable family through the transition. The gradual erosion of economic privilege turns into disaster with demands that the bancor be backed by "real commodities—corn, soy, oil, natural gas, deed to agricultural land. Rare earths . . . copper . . . Oh, fresh water sources! And gold, of course" (46, ellipses in original). The inclusion of gold speaks once again to the fantasy that it has intrinsic value, as much utility as food or water. The United States struggles to afford bancors, forbids their use by citizens, enacts the International Emergency Economic Powers Act of 1977, and seizes all domestic gold. When this proves insufficient, they renege on their international debt, making US Treasury Bonds worthless, thus wiping out the last asset of Mandible wealth.

The novel pursues two themes though a plot that includes long discussions of fiscal policy and inflation, the bankruptcy of debt-financed economics (Lowell is frequently satirized), and the unassailable importance of the two resources: gold and land. The first relates to the consequences for coming generations of the current precarious state of the US economy, with deficit-financed social services the target of satire. Exasperated by his idealist elders and their ongoing discourse of the American "experiment," Willing rejects the analogy that the country is run like a business: "you can't close a country like a business. . . . You can't throw up your hands and say, too bad, guess 'the experiment' didn't work. People my age have a long time left to live" (225).[21] The second theme is the evil, and I use this word advisedly, of taxes, mainly when used to support an "entitlement" society. Inflation is what destabilizes the value of currencies, and inflation is "Money for the government. A tax that people don't see as a tax" (111). Without demands for social programs, governments will need less money, working people will not lose buying power due to inflation, and society will nonetheless find ways to care for people who need help, more authentic ways, Shriver seems to suggest. The conclusion acknowledges that "the caprices of kindness were no reliable substitute for a welfare system," but nonetheless insists on the superiority of a model in which the recipient is "beholden, not militantly 'entitled'" and that "benevolence freely given was not begrudged" (401).

In the final section, set in 2047, the reviving US government moves to a digital currency (making unconverted cash or gold worthless), monitored by a chip installed in everyone's head, which instantly tracks income and purchases, sending the data to the IRS in real time, with penalties enacted not only for failure to pay taxes but also for saving rather than spending. Willing sees the mandatory installation of this chip as equivalent to "rape" and offers a long rationale to justify this deeply inappropriate comparison; in the end the entire family moves to Nevada (a border they are led to believe is militarized, but is not), which has seceded and has neither tax nor welfare. Nevada uses paper banknotes, backed by real gold (luckily the family proves to have a secret store), printed in sepia tones and meant to resemble the Continentals first used by the new US Republic. The conclusion repeats the libertarian conflation of economic freedom with democratic freedom with US exceptionalism that informs *Cryptonomicon*.

Yet eventually Nevada, too, finds it needs a tax system, and the very last line of the novel reads, "In 2064, Nevada's flat tax was raised to 11 percent. Of course" (402)—leaving one to wonder whether the true target of the satire is not, in fact, the libertarians themselves.

CONCLUSION

In its depictions of the future of money, sf repeatedly returns to the connection between social structure and economic policy. It explores the relationship between management of wealth and the possibilities for democracy, even as authors diverge in political orientation. These preoccupations and concerns parallel those of social theorists of money, who worry that democracy is threatened by our present bifurcation into a small group of privileged owners of capital, leaving the rest of the world encumbered by debt and in various degrees of economic hardship. These pressures bring the continuation of the Eurozone into question and inform the polarized and cantankerous debate in recent US politics. Thinking about the future of money is an urgent question for our time, a fact made chillingly clear by Piketty's detailed quantitative analyses and his conclusion that, left unchecked, the current system will drive "the concentration of capital [to] attain extremely high levels—levels potentially incompatible with the meritocratic values and principles of social justice fundamental to modern democratic societies" (Piketty 2014: 26).

As *Neptune's Brood* suggests, the real issue is perhaps less the future of money than the future of the banking system used to create, distribute, and stabilize it. Since the mid-twentieth century, the social technology of money has created structures of vast inequity and debilitating indebtedness for most. The recent television series *Mr. Robot* (2015–) targets this financial system and its social ethos as the central malady of our time. Drawing on contemporary events, especially the Occupy protests and the exploits of the hacktivist group Anonymous, whose use of face masks certain characters imitate, this series exemplifies the convergence of speculative and other fictions in the modern age. In the first season the hacker group Fsociety succeeds in wiping out all financial records of consumer and mortgage debt, but the second season shows that it is not so simple to transform the social order. The absence of electronic money creates hardships in conducting daily life, and it is the poor who have the most difficulty getting access to paper money. Moreover, the violent response of the FBI in its efforts to restore the status quo suggests that the future of money may require us to think first about social change in other areas of life, such that we might create a society wherein a more just economic order might thrive.

The future of money, then, is paramount to the future, but simply changing our currency will not be sufficient to enact transformative social change. Speculative fiction, with its focus on examining the social consequences of changes in technology, offers us a range of images of the future that require us to recognize how much money itself is a social technology. Nigel Dodd concludes *The Social Life of Money* (2014) by reviewing several proposals that have been made to revise or invent currencies, arguing that instead of seeing money as inherently alienating, we must understand that there are many forms of money, including those "that are actively created by their users, as part of the commons" (268). He concludes that the most utopian prospect is "a genuine monetary pluralism in which as full a range of monies is available, circulating in networks that are free to all, for individuals to use according to need and circumstance" (383). Speculative fiction is an ideal genre for beginning to posit and work through some of these options, not least because, as we have seen, the economy itself increasingly tended toward speculative fiction in an era of financialization. The real issue, then, is not what money will look like in the future, but rather what the future will look like because of how we theorize and use money.

CHAPTER SEVEN

Money and the Issues of the Age

The Nature of Money and Post-Crisis Proposals for Reform

YEVA NERSISYAN AND L. RANDALL WRAY

INTRODUCTION: THE EVOLUTION OF MONETARY REFORM SINCE THE 1920S

Financial crises have bookended the modern era of money. The most recent, whose effects began to surface forcefully in 2008, reopened foundational questions about the very nature of money while often evoking debates from the longer history of money. Indeed, in the aftermath of the recent global financial crisis, there has been no dearth of proposals for reforming the financial system. Some of these propose to tinker around the edges of the system, while leaving its structure unchanged (e.g., the Dodd-Frank legislation in the United States). Others aim to fundamentally rethink and reform it. Two proposals for "radical" reform stand out for their calls to return control of money to the public sphere: "narrow banking" (or 100 percent reserve banking) and "debt-free money" proposals. The first aims to restrict bank issuance of deposits to the amount of reserves banks hold—effectively eliminating bank lending (or banks' ability to issue deposits while making loans, depending on the proposal). "Debt-free" money proponents, on the other hand, would like the government to finance its spending by directly issuing currency, often referring to the use of "greenbacks" in the United States in the nineteenth century. Some proposals, such as the Positive Money movement in the United Kingdom, attempt to combine both.

The last time calls for radical reform of the financial system garnered so much attention was during the 1920s and 1930s. It is during this period that narrow banking proposals from the likes of Henry Simons and Irving Fisher emerged (later embraced by a pre-monetarist Milton Friedman). At the same time, John Maynard Keynes was working to revolutionize economic theory. His *Treatise on Money* (1930) provided an alternative view of the *nature* of money based on his study of ancient monies after he came across a remarkable

FIGURE 7.1: John Maynard Keynes, "unofficial economic adviser to Great Britain," in his study in Bloomsbury, London, 1940. Tim Gidal/Picture Post/Getty Images.

article by A. Mitchell Innes, published in 1913. The *General Theory* (1936) introduced the revolutionary theory of a *monetary economy*. Unfortunately, his approach to the nature of money was ultimately ignored, and his theory of a monetary economy was reduced to a simplistic theory of aggregate demand management in recessions.

The US Great Depression of the 1930s provided a setting in which Keynes's theory of effective demand, and the positive role government could play in such a situation, would gain wide acceptance. At the same time, it was obvious—especially in the United States, where the government had to rescue the banks—that the financial system had played the key role in bringing on the economic disaster of the depression. This, inevitably, led to calls to "fix" the banks. The Roosevelt administration adopted a strategy of tight regulation and segregation of investment and commercial banking rather than the Chicago Plan of narrow banking. It kept the payments system safe through the creation of deposit insurance.

These New Deal reforms proved to be effective for several decades after World War II. However, financial innovations increasingly subverted constraints. As Hyman P. Minsky had predicted in the late 1950s, financial crises began to reappear; over time, these became increasingly frequent as well as more difficult to resolve. At the same time, claims that greater reliance on "free markets" to discipline banks would provide greater stability, as well as pressures on the government to deregulate, increased.

Over this period, "Keynesian" policy also fell out of favor. Monetary theory returned to the ideas that had been popular in the 1920s—in particular, the quantity theory of money, as revived by Friedman. If anything, academic economists adopted even more simplistic theories of money than those Keynes had attacked. Money and finance became essentially irrelevant in modern economic theory. When the British Queen asked why her economic advisors had not seen the 2007–08 global financial crisis (GFC) coming, the answer was obvious: the theories they used to model the economy had no room for money.

As had been the case in the 1930s, there was a popular reaction against banking excesses. National governments tried to rein in financial institutions, yet many in the early twenty-first century remained worried that the actions taken were insufficient. There is no question that they fell far short of what Roosevelt's New Deal had done. As a result, there were popular reform movements that strove for more radical action, including renewed calls for narrow banking. In addition, there was a return to attempts to stimulate sluggish recoveries through "Keynesian" stimulus. The problem, however, was a widespread perception that governments were already too heavily indebted and that spending more would only increase debt burdens. This, in turn, encouraged investigation of alternative methods of financing government spending, including relying on public banks or simply by "printing money."

This chapter will critically assess the narrow banking and debt-free money (greenbacker) reform proposals in light of modern monetary operations, including coordination among the central bank, treasury, and private banks as well as the rise of the shadow banking system. Our main goal, however, is not the critique of these proposals *per se*. Rather, we use our critique as an opening to discuss the nature of money, both private and public, as well as what implications this has for macroeconomic policy. We argue that these proposals are not really "radical," because theoretically they do not depart from the mainstream view of money. We will use the framework of a relatively new approach, Modern Money Theory (or MMT), to present an alternative view of money and policy.

In the next section, we begin by providing an overview of the dominant approach to money that Keynes faced in the 1920s, with a brief summary of his development of an alternative. In the third section, we examine two twenty-first century radical reform proposals and their origins. The fourth section addresses the confusion surrounding the nature of government money, demonstrating that currency issued by the state is not "debt-free" money. While currency does not promise to pay interest or conversion into something else, it is still the government's liability—and *is* redeemed through taxation. Furthermore, as we discuss in the fifth section, if the goal is to prevent the government from paying interest to the private sector, it can be accomplished within the current monetary framework as long as the central bank adopts a zero interest-rate policy.

In the sixth section, we turn to the proposals for eliminating banks' ability to issue deposits, arguing that the narrow focus on banks ignores other sources of instability, such as that arising from shadow and parallel banks. Banks are not the only entities that create money, and eliminating banks' ability to create demand deposits out of "thin air" will not eliminate private money creation. Indeed, we believe imposing such restrictions on banks will simply shift the weight of the financial system further away from regulated banks and toward shadow banking. We conclude by offering some solutions to the excesses of the financial system.

THE 1920s ORTHODOXY AND KEYNES'S ALTERNATIVE

During the past two centuries money has often been at the center of important economic debates. Whether the issue has been inflation or exchange rate depreciation, unemployment or financial crises, money has been a convenient culprit. Attempts to reform the economy have, therefore, also been attempts to rethink and reform the monetary system.

In very broad terms, the debate has always been between two camps: those who believe that money is (or should be) a commodity that acts as a medium of exchange and those who view it as a credit–debt relationship. These two radically different perspectives on the nature of money have crystallized during the modern era, leading to disagreements about what constitutes money and who issues it, as well as on policy questions about who should issue it and how much. The commodity theory has had difficulty explaining the widespread acceptance of paper money that is not backed, supposedly, by anything "real." Nevertheless, its proponents have been vocal in advocating for either tying the value of paper money to some precious metal (e.g., the gold standard) or for limiting its quantity by other means (such as central bank control of the quantity of money).

The dominant approach to money in the 1920s, both in the United States and the United Kingdom, was the quantity theory of money. In this theory, money is first and foremost a medium of exchange, created to reduce the transaction costs associated with barter. Money, itself, is viewed as a special commodity, chosen for inherent characteristics that make it an efficient medium of exchange: high market value, easily transportable, divisible, and relatively resistant to wastage (and thus low storage costs). Early coined money was probably refined gold or silver, eventually stamped and milled to certify fineness and weight. Its value as money (nominal value) is linked to its relative (or real) value as a commodity. Warehouse receipts for precious metals could serve money's function as a medium of exchange, retaining value so long as sufficient reserves of the real stuff were held to redeem the receipts for metal. Fractional "reserve" banking developed out of this practice, allowing a given stock of metal to support circulation of a greater quantity of redeemable notes (Innes 1913; Wray 1990, 1998, 2004).

The problem with fractional reserves is that note issue can become excessive, causing money's real value to fall (stated differently, the money prices of other commodities could rise). While the notion that excessive money supply can lead to inflation goes back at least as far as Aristotle, this worry, framed in this way, became central to modern understandings of money. It was the so-called Currency School, active in the United Kingdom in the 1830s–1840s, that pushed for regulation of the quantity of "money" to maintain the "external" value of the currency and the Gold Standard (Cramp 1962: 7–8; Wray 1990). But regulating the quantity of "money" required defining money, which according to the Currency School was limited to bank notes. By the time of the debate between the adherents of the Currency School and the opposing Banking School, central bank notes and coins of the realm had replaced precious metal reserves. Therefore, constraining the issuance of central bank notes would also constrain the amount of country bank notes in the economy (Cramp 1962: 8–9). "The Currency School's case for a strict gold standard was also based on the consideration that it would remove the currency from the control by particular economic interests" (Ingham 2004b: 43), a point proponents of narrow banking and debt-free money also make, as we will see.

At the time, the Banking School argued that such a constraint was not necessary, because excessive note issue was inconceivable so long as banks promised to redeem notes on demand. Any excessive notes would be withdrawn from circulation in redemption; hence, they could not play any role in fueling inflation. They also insisted that financial instruments, such as bills of exchange and bank deposits, were also money (Cramp 1962: 10–11). Therefore, limiting the quantity of central bank notes wouldn't necessarily restrict the amount of money in the economy.

While the Banking School lost the policy debate, the argument that private bank creation of money would not be excessive so long as banks followed prudent practice was revived early in the twentieth century as the Real Bills Doctrine. If commercial banks only create deposits to finance the production process, the money would be removed from circulation automatically: banks create money to finance wages and other production costs, but when the incomes generated during production are spent on final output, the producing firms retire their loans, cancelling the deposits that had been created to allow the production process to begin. Critics argued, however, that real world banks do not limit themselves to financing real production; hence, the Real Bills Doctrine does not hold. Too much money creation by banks can cause prices to rise. And again, proponents of narrow banking make a similar argument: banks' excessive lending to finance purchases of existing assets pushed up their prices (e.g., van Lerven et al. 2015).

The discovery of the impact of central bank open-market operations on bank reserves (central bank purchases of treasury debt increase reserves, bank deposits at the central bank plus currency in the bank's vault; central bank sales reduce them) added impetus to the proposal that the central bank ought to limit the quantity of reserves in order to control private bank creation of money, thus, inflation.[1] By this time, the British "political economy" based on neoclassical theory—already long dominant in the United Kingdom—had spread to the United States and was gradually replacing the so-called Institutionalism that had dominated US theory and policy since the last quarter of the nineteenth century. Neoclassical theory was based on "real" analysis, with all real variables (employment, real output, interest rates, relative prices) determined without reference to money—which was said to be "neutral," only important in determining nominal values. Since money serves simply as a medium of exchange, an increase in its quantity should not affect production. Rather, an imbalance between the medium of exchange and the quantity of real stuff would only affect prices. We would have a situation of "too much money chasing too few goods."

To be sure, it would be misleading to claim that neoclassical theory was either fully coherent or universally adopted, even in the United Kingdom, by the 1920s. In an important sense, it was Keynes who provided the first complete explication of the neoclassical theory, as he had to clarify the theory that he intended to destroy with his revolutionary *General Theory* (*GT*). He had already begun developing an alternative in 1914 with his review in the *Economic Journal* of an article by Innes. Keynes commented positively on Innes's departure from the orthodox perspective that claimed that a "sound" monetary system must either be based on a commodity or "mimic" a commodity money system by strictly controlling the quantity of money. In his review, Keynes notably states,

> Not only has it been held that only intrinsic-value money is "sound," but an appeal to the history of currency has often been supposed to show that intrinsic-value money is the ancient and primitive ideal, from which only the wicked have fallen away. Mr. Innes has gone some way towards showing that such a history is quite mythical.
>
> —Keynes 1914: 421

This then seemed to spur what Keynes called his period of "Babylonian Madness" as he investigated the origins of money (Ingham 2000). Much of this remained unpublished for decades after his death. However, it heavily influenced his *Treatise on Money*, which was completed in 1930. By that time, Georg Friedrich Knapp's *State Theory of Money* had been translated into English and was endorsed by Keynes in the *Treatise* (see Wray 1990, 1998, 2004).

Keynes was dissatisfied with the *Treatise* even before it came out, and announced he was already working on a new book—which would become the *GT*. There were two problems with the *Treatise*. First, it took the aggregate quantity of output and employment as given; Keynes had not yet developed his theory of effective demand. Second, Keynes claimed that he still held the quantity theory of money at the time of its writing. The *GT* would resolve both of those problems. In some respects, the early drafts of the *GT* provided a clearer rejection of the quantity theory than did the final version, as he explicitly formulated a "monetary theory of production" that was quite similar to Marx's M-C-M' exposition (and to Thorstein Veblen's theory of business enterprise): not only is money not neutral, it is fundamental to the production process. All capitalist production begins with money in the expectation of ending up with more money later. Money is the purpose of production; hence, it can never be neutral. Further, the direct consequence of "too much money" is not rising prices but rather falling interest rates. While that could indirectly influence prices, Keynes (1962: 173) argued that there are "several slips between the cup and the lip." He abandoned the quantity theory's focus on central bank control over the money supply in favor of greater emphasis on fiscal policy.

Keynes let most of the monetary details fall into the background in the *GT*, as he had already dealt with them in the two volumes of the *Treatise*, which not only addressed monetary theory but also the practice of money creation and management through detailed institutional analysis. It is a shame that the discussion of "money supply and money demand" is so abbreviated in chapters 13 and 15 of the *GT*, as this provided an opening for the resurgence of simplistic treatment both by Keynes's purported followers who adopted Hicks's IS-LM analysis (which replaces Keynes's complex argument with a simplistic model in which a point of equilibrium is defined by a combination of interest rate and income that clears the money and goods markets), as well as by Keynes's monetarist critics who revived the quantity theory. Both groups assumed an "exogenous" money supply fixed by the central bank. This was clearly not the case in Keynes's *Treatise*, nor is it consistent with much of the *GT*—especially chapter 17, which offers an integration of his alternative view of money's importance with his theory of effective demand. Nor does Keynes reprise the *Treatise*'s endorsement of Knapp's *State Theory of Money* (and the article of Innes that he had reviewed), although one could argue that it lies behind his policy prescriptions outlined in the *GT*'s final chapter (euthanasia of the rentier by driving interest rate policy to zero, eliminating the scarcity of capital, and socializing investment). In all these respects, the *Treatise* is superior to the *GT*.

Post-Keynesian economists have continued Keynes's program of breaking away from mainstream theory. Post-Keynesian endogenous money theory (discussed below), embraced at the end of the modern era even by some in the mainstream, long held that the quantity of money in the economy cannot be controlled by the central bank. Instead, the supply of bank money (bank deposits) depends on the demand for bank loans. The endogeneity of money also implies that money is not separate from the production process and therefore cannot be neutral. Furthermore, post-Keynesians agree with the Banking School's insistence that there cannot be too much money in the economy because money enters the economy when there is demand for loans. Any perceived "excess" would be used to pay off bank loans, thus destroying bank money.

Moreover, post-Keynesian theory, by adopting the view that money is credit/debt, lends itself to a broader conception of money, which includes liabilities of nonbank financial institutions (Nersisyan and Dantas 2017). In this view, what determines whether money is "sound" is not the quantity of monetary assets or its relation to a quantity of another asset, such as reserves. Instead, what matters is the quality of the debt, or the IOUs that back the creation of liquid money-like liabilities.

The Keynes/post-Keynesian view provides an alternative to the orthodox view that dominated in the early twentieth century and which still dominated at the end of the modern era: that money was invented to facilitate exchange, that money's value originally derived from its commodity value, that money is first and foremost a medium of exchange, that money is largely neutral (at least in the long run), that excessive money causes inflation, and—therefore—that policy ought to constrain the quantity of money to prevent inflation (whether of goods or asset prices). The "radical" reforms that we examine next largely accepted this view of money, even after the twenty-first century global financial crisis.

DEBT-FREE MONEY AND NARROW BANKING

Many critics of the behavior of the biggest global financial institutions that brought us the global financial crisis coalesced in the early twenty-first century around two fundamental proposals: narrow banking, which would severely limit "private money" creation, and a return to "government money" creation to finance public spending. This would reduce the destabilizing role of private finance while relieving government of constraints on using its fiscal power to encourage growth and employment. In the United States, there were "greenbacker" as well as "public bank" initiatives (e.g., Brown 2013; www.publicbankinginstitute.org), proposed as alternatives to relying on private bankers to fund both government spending as well as at least some private spending. In the United Kingdom, there was a growing "Positive Money" movement (e.g., Dyson et al. 2016) pursuing similar aims, which obtained at least some support from luminaries like the journalist Martin Wolf (2014).

FIGURE 7.2: People rally in front of the New York Stock Exchange in New York City to protest the proposed government buyout of financial firms, September 25, 2008. Spencer Platt/Getty Images.

These efforts could be synthesized as in Milton Friedman's long-forgotten, pre-monetarist proposal, which combined narrow banking with currency-financed government spending. In his 1948 article, "A Monetary and Fiscal Framework for Economic Stability," Friedman proposed that all government spending be "money financed" (by new currency issue)—with all taxes paid using the government's currency—so that the government would run a balanced budget only at full employment, with deficits in recession (increasing the money supply) and surpluses in economic booms (reducing the money supply). There was nothing too controversial about this view of the proper fiscal stance, as it was incorporated into postwar orthodox "Keynesian" thought. What was unusual was Friedman's "proposal" to finance budget deficits through net money creation. He thus proposed to combine monetary policy and fiscal policy, using the budget to control monetary emission in a countercyclical manner.

Friedman also proposed to eliminate private money creation by banks through a 100 percent reserve requirement, the "Chicago Plan" proposal he had adopted from Fisher and Simons in the 1930s. Hence, there would be no "net" money creation by private banks—they would expand the supply of bank money only as they accumulated reserves of government-issued money.

It is this second element of the Friedman proposal that seems to have motivated the return of the 100 percent money proposal advocated by the "Positive Money" movement. They were rightly concerned that "run-away" finance brought on the GFC and that there had, to that point, been no significant attempt to restrain it. Likewise, the original narrow banking proposal originated in the 1930s during another major crisis driven by Wall Street's excesses. The perception at that time was, rightly, that banks had overextended their lending in the late 1920s and had financed speculative rather than productive activities. The resulting boom and bust in the stock market depressed investment and marked the beginning of the Great Depression. The proponents of the Chicago Plan believed that the system's flaw was allowing banks to issue "private" currency, in the form of deposits. Narrow banks, on the other hand, would issue deposits but could not make loans. Rather, they would hold only safe assets, such as government currency, treasury bonds, and central bank reserves, ensuring that depositors' money was never at risk—making the payments system safe.

Twenty-first-century "greenbackers" wanted the government to issue its own currency—i.e., "debt-free" money—to finance its spending. They approached the issue from a moral perspective: it was wrong to let private bankers profit from money creation to finance government spending. Why not cut out the middleman, reducing government's costs as it directly spends currency, rather than borrowing "private money" and paying interest to the bankers? These arguments echoed those of original greenbackers, who believed that "money was a social product, and [. . .] its identification with gold masked the bankers' private control of the public good that should be under popular control" (Ingham 2004b: 45).

As we will explain in the following sections, these modern proposals to eliminate "private money creation" and return money to the public domain misunderstand the *nature* of money, the way modern government spends, and how modern financial institutions operate. While these were presented as "radical" proposals, theoretically they did not depart from the mainstream view on money, as Keynes and post-Keynesians do. Both mainstream economists and narrow banking proponents were motivated by two main concerns. The first was the fear of excessive "money" creation, which might either compromise the soundness of the currency (e.g., inflation) or lead to speculative bubbles. Paper money is not intrinsically valuable, yet it is the ultimate embodiment of abstract value and can be used to acquire real things (Ingham 2004a). It can also be issued in seemingly unlimited quantities, leading to an imbalance between the amount of goods and the amount of money.

Narrow banking proposals, therefore, were an attempt to make money "sound" again, even if that was not their explicit goal. Instead of backing money with gold, as the proponents of "sound money" proposed, they advocated backing private money with public money (i.e., banks maintain 100 percent reserves for their deposits). Some proponents understood that mainstream claims that the central bank can control the money supply were wrong. What they were trying to do was reform the system to make it possible for the central bank to control it. Hence, they departed from mainstream economics not based on a fundamentally different understanding of money, but rather in terms of their focus on private banks and on the role money can play in speculation (rather than simply on inflation).

Second, since money was ostensibly no longer made of anything "real," it was feared that those entities with the privilege of issuing money were getting something (specifically, seigniorage income, the difference between the nominal value of the money and the cost of "producing" it) for nothing—a free lunch, so to speak. Narrow banking proponents wanted to prevent the private sector from getting something for free.

This concern was shared by the mainstream of the economics profession, although the latter were more worried about abuse by the public sector, because they believed that the central bank already controled inflation and indirectly the quantity of bank money by controlling the interest rates. Their concern, therefore, was not the abuse of money creation by the private sector but by the public sector. Hence the motivation for a strict separation between the fiscal and monetary authorities, through rules that prohibit the central bank from directly buying government securities, for instance.

Central bank independence is a code phrase for keeping fiscal policy constrained to prevent excessive issuance of currency and a "free lunch" for the government. The following statement by former US Federal Reserve Chairman Paul Volcker (2008: 12) best summarizes this anxiety of mainstream economists over paper money: "The dollar, after all, is a fiat currency, backed only by the word and policies of our government, exemplified by an independent central bank committed to a price stability."

MONEY IS ALWAYS AND EVERYWHERE DEBT

For reasons we explore in this section, we take the position that all money represents a liability of its issuer. We therefore depart both from mainstream economics and the "radical" reform proposals, which suggest that money is or was a commodity, that the monetary system should mimic a commodity-money system, or that money can be debt-free.

Exactly where we draw the dividing line between "money" and "credit" or "debt" is not important in that respect. Demand deposits and savings deposits are the debt of the issuing bank. Shares in a money market mutual fund (MMMF) are the liabilities of the fund. Reserves and central bank paper notes are the debt of the central bank. Treasury notes and coins are the treasury's debt. Government bills and bonds are treasury liabilities. Corporate bonds are the debts of the corporate issuers. Some of these liabilities pay interest (bills, bonds, MMMF shares), while others do not (treasury and central bank notes, coins). Some have paid interest under some institutional arrangements, but not under others. (In the United States, for example, demand deposit rates were fixed at zero under Regulation Q—which regulated banks' capital reserve requirements beginning in 1933—and until recently, reserves at the Federal Reserve paid zero.)

The analogy of the cloakroom token, put forth by Knapp, is useful in understanding money as an IOU:

> When we give up our coats in the cloak-room of a theatre, we receive a tin disc of a given size bearing a sign, perhaps a number. There is nothing more on it, but this ticket or mark has legal significance; it is a proof that I am entitled to demand the return of my coat.
>
> —Knapp 1924: 31

To pick up your coat, you simply present the token. The attendant then "redeems" herself from the debt by returning your coat. Once the attendant gets the token back, the debt is eliminated, while the token is simply warehoused, waiting to be used again. When the token is in the cloakroom, it is not a debt, but a circular piece of plastic or cardboard. It makes no difference what form the token takes; it is simply evidence of a debt, a "coat debt" that is redeemed by return of the coat.

Both the proponents of debt-free money and, to a lesser degree, of narrow banking seemed to misunderstand this nature of money. The authors of an International Monetary Fund report argued, for instance, that

FIGURE 7.3: A sign at the entrance to the payments industry conference Money 20/20 in Las Vegas, Nevada exhorts attendees to "treat your badge like cash," October 2016. Courtesy of Lana Swartz.

> the stock of reserves, or money, newly issued by the government is not a debt of the government. The reason is that fiat money is not redeemable, in that holders of money cannot claim repayment in something other than money. Money is therefore properly treated as government equity rather than government debt, which is exactly how treasury coin is currently treated under US accounting conventions.
>
> —Benes and Kumhoff 2012: 6[2]

There seems to be an inconsistency, for if the government's central bank issues notes, these are counted as "debt money," but if the treasury issues coins—and presumably notes (as many treasuries have done in the past)—these are "equity," not "debt."[3] This seems to be based on the belief that the central bank (in at least some countries) is "independent" of government—a point to which we will return.

Greenbackers, on the other hand, wanted the government to finance its spending not by issuing bonds, which they see as debt, but with currency, which is seen as debt-free. So when the US Treasury issues treasury bills, the US government goes into debt, but if it were to issue its own currency—e.g., "greenbacks"—it would not accrue debt. This demarcation between bonds and currency betrays a misunderstanding of money—which, as we will argue, is always debt—and of government debt (bonds), which are incorrectly viewed on the same footing as private debt.

It appears that the distinction between "debt-free" money and "debt" money rests on two criteria: the promise to pay interest and the promise (or lack thereof) to convert an asset into something else (or to redeem it for something else). We first deal with the issue of the "redeemability" of government currency and then address the payment of interest by the government on its "debt". At the same time, we demonstrate that, despite conventional wisdom, a sovereign government is not financially constrained under modern monetary arrangements, something that greenbackers (and some narrow bankers) were trying to accomplish by halting government "borrowing" to be replaced with "printing money."

How modern governments spend

The conventional wisdom in the modern age was that the government must either tax or borrow to be able to spend. While it could also finance its spending by "printing money," this was generally not seen as desirable, as it might compromise the "soundness" of money. Mainstream economists, therefore, made a big deal out of the separation between monetary and fiscal authorities and central bank independence; if the treasury could not sell its bonds directly to the central bank then it had to rely on markets to borrow.

Post-Keynesian economists who developed Modern Money Theory long argued that sovereign governments with nonconvertible fiat currencies are not financially constrained; they do not and cannot spend tax and bond revenue. That taxes are not needed for revenue purposes was easier to see in the past, when states directly spent their metallic coins, paper notes, and tally sticks into existence and then collected them in payment. In the twenty-first century few treasuries issue their own notes (which "greenbackers" want) and in any case do not make direct payments; the central bank stands between the treasury and recipients of government spending, as well as between the treasury and taxpayers making payments to government.

While on the surface it may seem that this makes governments dependent on tax and bond sales revenue, a closer examination shows that nothing of substance has changed (e.g., Tymoigne and Wray 2013; Bell 2000). The modern central bank is the treasury's bank, making and receiving payments on behalf of the treasury. Spending by government involves a central bank credit to a private bank's reserves and a credit by the bank to the recipient's demand deposit. The tax "return" is handled electronically as the taxpayer's deposit account is debited and the reserves of the bank of the taxpayer are also debited by the central bank. The term "return" is, in fact, revealing, reflecting its Latin and French origins (*revenue*): the taxpayer "returns" the sovereign's liability in payment. When government spends, bank reserves (the liability of the government's central bank) rise; when taxes are paid, bank reserves decline. The spending by modern government takes place in central bank liabilities, not (usually) through issuing treasury liabilities. The central bank liabilities are "redeemed" (debited) when taxes are paid.

All of this was recognized by Beardsley Ruml, a New Dealer who chaired the Federal Reserve Bank in the 1940s and who was the "father" of income tax withholding. Ruml (1946b: 84) argued that with the creation of "a modern central bank" and suspension of convertibility of the dollar into precious metals, "our federal government has final freedom from the money market in meeting its financial requirements [. . .]. National states no longer need taxes to get the wherewithal to meet their expenses."

While many would see taxes as a means to "pay for" government spending, Ruml rejects that view. He counts four reasons for national government taxes:

> (1) as an instrument of fiscal policy to help stabilize the purchasing power of the dollar; (2) to express public policy in the distribution of wealth and of income as in the case of the progressive income and estate taxes; (3) to express public policy in subsidizing or in penalizing various industries and economic groups; and (4) to isolate and assess directly the costs of certain national benefits, such as highways and social security.
>
> —Ruml 1946a, 36

The first of these is related to the issue of inflation: taxes can be raised to deflate aggregate demand should it become excessive. The second purpose is to use taxes to change the distribution of income and wealth. The third purpose is to discourage bad behavior, however that is defined politically: pollution of air and water, use of tobacco and alcohol, or purchasing imports—to make imports more expensive through tariffs (essentially a tax to raise import costs and thereby encourage purchase of domestic output). The fourth is to allocate the costs of specific public programs to the beneficiaries. What is important is that he claimed taxes are "obsolete" for "revenue" purposes—government doesn't need "income" to finance its spending.

Sovereign government IOUs are "redeemed," not "converted"

Ruml, however, leaves out one important function of taxes—that of redeeming government (nonconvertible) currency. Modern "greenbackers" drew a strict line between government bonds as debt and currency as debt-free money, because the former promises conversion to currency at maturity, while the latter does not promise conversion to anything. However, currency issued by a sovereign government operating on a floating exchange rate (rather than a peg to gold or a foreign currency), while not convertible on demand at a fixed rate into anything else, is still redeemable. Like any issuer of debt, the national government promises to accept its own debt—the currency and central bank reserves—in payment to itself for all payments due. Hence, even though US Federal Reserve notes and reserves and Treasury coins are not convertible into anything else, they are "redeemable by the mechanism of taxation" (Innes 1914: 152); they are still IOUs.

This becomes clear if one studies the history of coinage and of the issue of paper money from before the modern era. Grubb (2017), for example, demonstrates the principle of imposing taxes for redemption of paper notes in his examination of colonial Virginia's use of paper currency. The American colonies were prohibited by England from issuing coin, so as to protect the king's monopoly of coinage. To increase fiscal capacity, the colonial governments began to issue paper money. Virginia's colonial government passed a series of acts to authorize the issue of treasury notes. Each law would include the total value of notes to be issued (denominated in Virginia pounds) and would set a date for final "redemption" (the term used by Grubb, as well as the lawmakers themselves). Interestingly, the law also would impose a new set of taxes at the time of the note issue:

> Every paper money act included additional new taxes, typically a land tax and a poll tax, that were operative for a number of years. The number of years over which these new additional taxes were operative was chosen so as to generate enough funds to fully redeem the notes authorized by each respective paper money act. The date in each paper money act set for the final redemption of the notes authorized by that act closely matched the end to the taxing period set by that act.
>
> —Grubb 2015: 98

What did the treasury do with the notes it received in tax payment? Grubb (2015: 103) reports that the notes were "removed and burned"—not spent. This runs counter to the common belief in the modern age that government needed tax revenue in order to spend. The US colonial case shows that government first had to spend before it got tax revenue, and once it received the revenue, the government destroyed it rather than spending it. The problem with spending notes in excess of redemption would not be government insolvency but rather inflation. Removing the notes from circulation was thus intended to protect the value of the government's paper currency—not to provide "revenue" that government could spend.

The role of taxes to redeem the currency was a central focus of Innes (1913, 1914). He insisted that any issuer of an IOU is obligated to accept it in payment: "the right of the holder of credit (the creditor) to hand back to the issuer of the debt (the debtor) the latter's acknowledgment or obligation" and thus to "redeem" himself/herself was the most important attribute of credit (Innes 1914: 161).[4] The treasury, as issuer of currency, must accept it in payment of taxes and other obligations due to the government. Likewise, the bank that issues notes or deposits must accept them in payments due to the bank (e.g., loan payments). Both the government that issues debt and the private bank that issues debt must accept it in "redemption." This is, according to Innes, the fundamental driver of demand for both currency and bank notes and deposits: The taxpayers need currency to pay taxes, and the bank's borrowers need notes or deposits to repay their loans.

Again, when treasuries issued liabilities directly, the process of redemption was easier to understand. Innes's discussion of medieval tallies sheds further light on the issue (see also Desan 2014; Graeber 2017). He notes, "the principal instrument of commerce" in Western Europe for hundreds of years was the tally, issued by kings, as well as by the private sector as records of debt (Innes 1913: 394).[5] The sticks were split into two parts, stock and stub, which together formed "a complete record of the credit and debt" (ibid.: 394). At the time of redemption two ends were matched and then destroyed. In the case of the king's tallies, Redemption Day was tax day, when the king's representative (the exchequer) arrived in the village, spread cloth on the ground, and matched stock and stub. The tally stick had value because it could be used to "redeem" oneself on tax day. You owed the king his taxes, and he owed you the right to deliver evidence of his debt (recorded on the stick) to pay your taxes.

Modern interpretations of "redemption" often associated it with conversion of one's own IOUs to third-party IOUs (or perhaps to precious metals). They were based on a narrow definition that applies when the issuer of a currency promises to "redeem" that currency for either gold (in the case of a gold standard) or a foreign currency (fixed exchange rate) at a promised exchange rate. As such, they related back to a particular, and somewhat brief, historical context during which conversion to something else was common (see also Helleiner 2002).

Of course, there were issuers even in the twenty-first century who made conversion promises (i.e., states on currency boards).[6] What we are arguing is that the more common (and more fundamental) promise is that of accepting one's own liabilities in payments due—such as taxes owed to the issuer of a

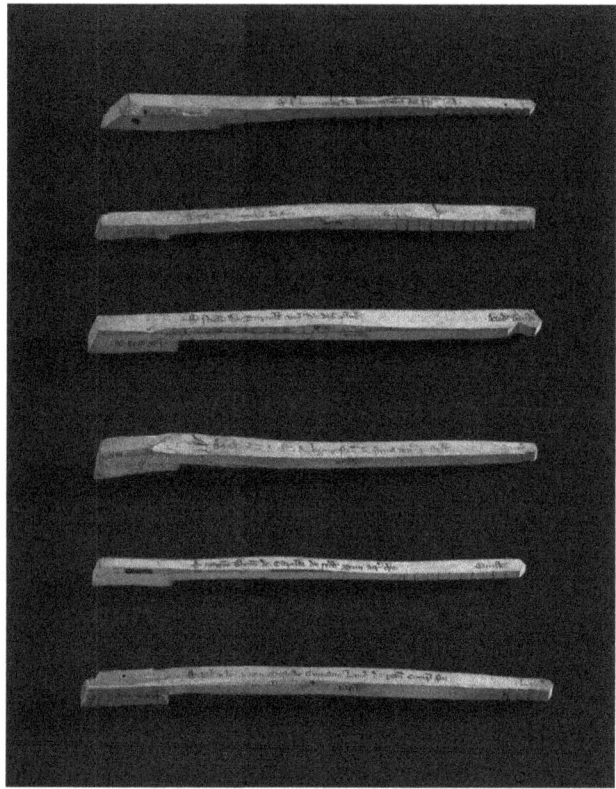

FIGURE 7.4: Tally sticks from the British Exchequer, c. 1440. SSPL/Getty Images.

sovereign currency. Redemption in this case thus refers to the ability of a debtor to "wipe the slate clean" and emerge debt-free by returning to the creditor—whether public or private—the creditor's own IOU. Even in this case, the sovereign can also promise to "redeem" the currency for gold or foreign currency (as the Virginia colony promised redemption in English coin). We see this as an additional promise that applies in many cases, but a promise that was rare in the global North as of the early twenty-first century; the members of the European Union who shared the euro were exceptions, as we discuss below. The promise to accept the issuer's own liability in payment is the more fundamental promise of "redemption."

To recap this section, if the state's currency is not pegged to another currency or metal, then it is *the* means of final settlement in an economy. This allows the government to make payments in its own IOUs without needing to accumulate credits on others (technically, the imposition of taxes grants the government credit against the entities who owe taxes). The ability to spend by emitting tokens of indebtedness permits the government to move resources from the private to the public sector—an ability that it can use to achieve the public purpose. The government's token money is then redeemed through taxation (Wray 1998; Wray 2015).

GOVERNMENT BONDS AND INTEREST ON RESERVES

It should be clear that issuing bonds by a sovereign government is ultimately a matter of choice. It cannot become insolvent in its own currency; it can always make all payments as they come due in its own currency. Indeed, if the government spends currency into existence (similar to how banks create deposits when they lend, as we will explain below), it clearly does not need tax revenue before it can spend (Nersisyan and Wray 2016; Wray 1998; Wray 2015). Further, if taxpayers pay their taxes using currency, then the government must first spend before taxes can be paid. Since money is an IOU, it must be issued first and returned later. Once it is returned to the issuer, this cancels the issuer's debt.

These IOUs can be converted to other government IOUs, such as treasury coins or central bank notes.[7] More importantly for the question at hand, they can also be converted to treasury bills and bonds, or treasury liabilities that pay interest. When the government issues a bond, it promises to pay interest and (eventually) to retire it. This is what "greenbackers" see as a problem: the government pays interest to private financial institutions to "borrow" money to finance its spending and then must pay off the debt at retirement.

But what does the government pay the bondholders when these mature? When a non-sovereign entity (firm, household, state or local government) issues debt, it promises to service the debt by paying interest and eventually to retire the debt. Payment is made using liabilities of a third party, generally those of financial institutions or the government. A sovereign government, on the other hand, usually only promises to make payments *in its own debts,* including currency, but mostly central bank reserves—in other words, swapping one liability for another.

Note, however, that in the twenty-first-century United States, the Federal Reserve paid interest on bank reserves at a rate determined by the Federal Open Market Committee and basically identical to the US Treasury's rate paid on bills. As the Treasury's bill rate closely tracked the Fed's target federal funds rate, there was no longer any functional difference between bills and bank reserves—both were liabilities that pay a policy-determined interest rate. In other words, even if the government spent by issuing reserves and leaving them in the system, its central bank would still pay interest to private banks.

Proponents of "debt-free" money might respond that even if government debt payments were swapping one government liability for another, they allowed the private sector to charge the government interest so that banks could earn income for holding safe, default-free securities. However, if the goal is for the government to stop paying interest on its liabilities, this can be achieved within the current monetary system if the central bank maintains a zero interest-rate policy indefinitely.[8] With its interest rate target at zero, the central bank does not have to worry about excess reserves putting downward pressure on interest rates. It can stop draining reserves through treasury sales.[9]

Alternatively, the treasury can simply stop issuing bills or bonds to banks and the nonbank public.[10] Instead, the central bank would provide overdrafts to the treasury (obtaining a claim on the treasury). Central bank payments for the treasury would lead to a credit to banking system reserves, offset on the central bank's balance sheet by a treasury overdraft. This would allow the central bank to keep its target rate above zero without entailing interest payments by the treasury to the banks; instead, the central bank would simply pay the target interest rate on reserve holdings (as the Fed currently does).

In both cases, we would achieve what "debt-free money" advocates proposed—elimination of interest payments by the treasury—within the current system. Yet the currency spent by government and accumulated as net financial assets by the private sector would not be "debt-free money," but liabilities of the central bank (central bank notes and reserves) and perhaps some small amount of treasury coins.

Non-sovereign currencies

While our discussion so far has focused on countries with their own currency, there are exceptions to this norm. Until the late modern era, such cases were largely limited to small states or former colonies (see Nelms and Guyer, this volume). The glaring recent exception, however, was the European Monetary Union (EMU), in which member states gave up their own currencies and adopted the euro. Although perceived by each member state as its currency, the euro was more akin to "foreign currency." None of the individual euro states had control over the issuance of the euro, which was relinquished to the supranational European Central Bank. From the perspective of the framework adopted in this chapter, the euro is not a sovereign currency.

While European integration was not simply an economic project, one of the motivations for the single currency was to create a real (rather than imaginary) separation between monetary and fiscal authorities. It should be clear from the discussion so far that the single currency had its roots in the mainstream view of money; it was an attempt to tie the hands of profligate governments and establish a "sound" currency. As a result, member states lost control not only of their monetary policy (a problem often recognized by mainstream economists), but also of their fiscal policy (something that was welcomed by many economists, although its significance was overlooked by almost all of them until after the global financial crisis). The fiscal policy space of EMU member states was

FIGURE 7.5: The original design for the new Euro banknotes are displayed at the European Central Bank in Frankfurt, Germany in August 2001. The architecture featured on the bills are stylized representations of European monuments that do not actually exist, but are instead designed to evoke a shared European cultural heritage. DANIEL ROLAND/AFP/Getty Images.

constrained by financial markets and the independent central bank's willingness to buy sovereign government debt. If markets refuse to buy sovereign bonds, their price will decrease and rates will increase. All else being equal, governments have to increase their borrowing to be able to cover the higher interest payments, leading to further borrowing and further increase in rates, and so on. In sum, the separation between the monetary and fiscal authorities was largely the source of troubles in Eurozone economies that emerged in the first decades of the twenty-first century (Kelton and Wray 2009; Papadimitriou et al. 2010).

More generally, any country with a pegged exchange rate must constrain domestic policy to ensure it can maintain the peg. While it could still run fiscal deficits and control its interest rate, it could lose foreign reserves. A peg, therefore, skews policy in the direction of higher interest rates and lower government deficits to constrain the outflow of foreign currency reserves.

PRIVATE MONEY CREATION: BANKS AND SHADOW BANKS

So far our discussion has focused on government money creation and its relation to spending and taxation. As we have demonstrated, what "debt-free" money proponents wanted to accomplish was either already happening within the current system, in the late modern era, or it could happen with relatively minor changes to monetary arrangements. In this section, we turn to proposals that aimed to eliminate private money creation by restricting banks' ability to make loans.

The idea that banks create money when they grant loans was not new, but it received renewed interest since the GFC exposed Wall Street's excesses. While mainstream economists maintained that the banking system could create money through the deposit multiplication process, their argument rested on the belief that banks need reserves to make loans and issue deposits (creating money). If that was true, then bank lending could be constrained by raising the required reserve ratio (i.e., to 100 percent, under the narrow banking proposal), or by tight constraints over reserves (the monetarist proposal). Post-Keynesian economists, on the other hand, long argued that banks create money when they make loans without needing reserves first—a view increasingly shared in the twenty-first century by policymakers and central bank followers alike (McLeay et al. 2014; Sheard 2014; on post-Keynesian endogenous money theory, see also Moore 1988; Lavoie 1984; Wray 1990). It was the latter idea that caught on after the GFC, with commentators like Wolf (2014) lamenting the ills of "*ex nihilo*" money creation, its production "out of thin air."

Even if not explicitly stated, thinking of bank money creation as happening "out of thin air" seems to imply the possibility of a different form of money, a proper one, perhaps money that is made of something with intrinsic value. (Note that even government fiat money is "thin-air" money; hence, eliminating banks' ability to issue money does not eliminate the *ex nihilo* creation of money *per se*.) In that sense, the modern monetary system is seen as an aberration from historical experience, causing much anxiety over excessive money issuance and hyperinflation, as we mentioned above.

But is money—which is an acknowledgment of debt—really as ephemeral as "thin air"? As Ingham (2002: 141) argues, "the promise to pay is not *ex nihilo*— it is a social relation." When banks grant loans and issue IOUs, such as demand deposits, they do so as they accept the IOUs of the borrowers. Hence, there *is* "something" behind the bank's creation of deposits—the borrower's promise to pay. The bank accepts the borrower's promissory note and in exchange gives its own IOUs: deposits. If banks did diligent underwriting, they would only accept the IOUs that were "backed" by useful economic activity, however we want to measure it, including, for example, prospective income from employment of the borrower or the business income of a firm.

While banks also *issue* deposits when they take in deposits of coin and currency—IOUs of the state—this was not seen as problematic by advocates for narrow banking, who did not want to restrict banks' ability to take in deposits of government money. We should note, however, that this action is similar to the one described above, except that the issuance of deposits in this case is backed by the state's IOUs rather than those of firms and households. In both instances, we have liabilities "backing up" the issuance of bank IOUs—the only difference being that the government's IOUs are net private sector assets and free of default risk.

The proponents of narrow banking and debt-free money often talked in moral terms: it is not "right" to allow banks to issue money and to earn seigniorage revenue that "rightly" belongs to the state. However, as we already explained, governments with their own currency not pegged to another currency or metal have not given up their ability to issue currency. Moreover, banks do not earn seigniorage revenue when they lend. Rather, they earn the difference between what they pay on their liabilities and what they earn on their assets, similar to nonbank financial institutions. Lastly, banks' ability to issue money is not unlimited but constrained by bank capital (Nersisyan and Wray 2017).

Shadow banks

While banks have access to the government safety net, they are not unique in their ability to issue "money." Those who single out banks do so based on a narrow definition of money as the assets that serve as medium of exchange and means of payment.[11] If money is debt denominated in the prevailing money of account, however, then "everyone can create money" by issuing an IOU and getting it accepted, as Minsky (1986) maintained. While we may want to draw lines between assets for analytical purposes, where we draw them depends on what we are trying to accomplish (and who the "we" are in a particular political context). There is no single definition of money that is appropriate for all purposes (Chick 1973: 60). Indeed, if the goal is to prevent instability, limiting our analysis to a narrow set of liabilities and the institutions that issue them constrains our understanding of the sources of instability.

Once we adopt a broader definition of money, we can see that shadow banks and parallel banks also create money. Pozsar (2014: 9), for instance, defines money as those financial claims that "trade at par on demand" against the state's own IOUs.[12] In other words, it is the "proximity to the government" that defines the "moneyness" of various financial instruments, rather than their function as a means of payment. This "proximity to the government," in turn, depends on the "strength of their [financial claims'] promise of par on demand and par at maturity," which in turn depends on the "mix of liquidity and credit puts backing them" (Pozsar 2014: 10). For instance, bank demand deposits are financial claims that promise on par conversion on demand. These claims are backed by liquidity (lender of last resort) and credit "puts" (deposit insurance) by the government, making demand deposits the private liabilities with the closest proximity to the government.

Note that in the run-up to the GFC, the biggest financial institutions increasingly relied on overnight commercial paper—not demand deposits—to finance their positions in assets. When times were good, this commercial paper was perceived as safe as a bank deposit. It was bought by money market mutual funds (MMMFs), which issued deposit-like shares that, until the crisis, never "broke the buck"—that is, dropped in value below US$1 per share. And yet, the trigger for the crisis was the failure of the commercial paper market, which then forced the US government to extend deposit insurance-like guarantees to MMMFs.[13] In sum, eliminating banks' ability to issue deposits when granting loans will not eliminate the financial system's ability to create money-denominated liabilities—or be a source of instability. Further restrictions on banks will simply move more of the money creation into the "shadow" and "parallel" banking universe, as other institutions step in to fill the void left by banks (as Beggs, this volume, also notes). This will make the financial system more—not less—unstable.

CONCLUSION

While we share the view of reformers on the dangerous practices of Wall Street, we are skeptical that the solution is to prohibit regulated banks from making loans and issuing deposits. From World War II until the early 1980s, we had private banks and private money creation, but we did not have systemic financial crises on the level of the recent GFC (but see Beggs, this volume, and Nelms and Guyer, this volume, on recurring instability). Hence, it is not banking *per se* that is the problem, but rather how banks are managed and regulated.

Traditional commercial banking—in which banks do good underwriting and hold loans to maturity—reduces systemic risk in comparison to the still-growing practice of originating loans to securitize them. It is difficult to see how the "greenbacker" and "narrow banking" proposals would be an improvement over traditional commercial and savings-and-loan banking, as these proposals would accelerate trends of recent decades that fuel movement of activity off the balance sheets of the most closely regulated part of the system.

Following the critics of private banks, we have referred to banks' ability to create money as private money creation. We should note, however, that commercial banks with access to the government safety net should really be viewed as private–public partnerships (Mosler 2009; Wray 2010; Nersisyan 2013). We need to ensure that banks serve a public purpose by performing good underwriting and holding loans to maturity. Bringing banks under tighter control by the government is the right solution, as it allows for greater public control over private money creation. Risky practices cannot be permanently eliminated—but they can be constrained and pushed to the peripheries of finance by appropriate regulations.

Finally, the proposal to finance government deficit with currency seems to us to be unnecessary. As it stands, current procedures already ensure that governments can spend up to budgeted amounts—with one important caveat. In the United States, Congress imposes debt limits that must be raised as they are approached, or the Treasury has to engage in extraordinary procedures to continue to meet payments as they come due. The solution is simple: legislation to eliminate these debt limits. To be sure, even in the absence of formal debt limits, government spending is constrained by the fear of deficits held by elected representatives. This is a difficult barrier to remove, as deficit hysteria serves a useful political function. However, we doubt that politicians will be mollified by the solution offered by "debt-free" money proponents, who propose to simply print money to pay for government spending. This would actually add to the fear of deficit spending the fear of runaway hyperinflation—a fear that is somewhat better grounded and perhaps more deeply held. While both of these fears are, in our opinion, largely ill-informed, we believe the best strategy is to increase understanding of how government spending is actually financed. The debt-free and "greenbacker" arguments do more to confuse matters than to add clarity to the discussion.

The general understanding of money, banking, and government finance in the late modern age is, unfortunately, as faulty as it was in Keynes's day. And the policy response to the global financial crisis was far less effective than the response in the 1930s. In large part this was because both conventional and "radical" reformers misunderstood the nature of money. Relatively large government budget deficits in the United States, the United Kingdom, Japan, and throughout the EU stifled the fiscal policy response. Faith in the efficiency of private financial markets (as well as substantial lobbying power by the bankers of Wall Street, London, and Frankfurt) defeated attempts to deal with runaway financial innovation. While we welcome the efforts of the reformers to deal with both of these problems, we fear that their understanding of the issues led them back to Friedmanian proposals that are not up to the task. We advocate, instead, policy reform based on the understanding of money developed by Keynes, Knapp, Innes, and later by Ruml, Minsky, and Lerner,[14] among many others whose work has been ignored or forgotten.

NOTES

Introduction

1. In 2017, for example, the *New York Times Magazine* opened a special issue on money with a reference, like ours, to the notion that money "makes the world go round" (Wasik 2017).
2. As evidenced in the growing influence of behavioral economics, development economics, and heterodox stances on money from post-Keynesian, Austrian, and the so-called "market monetarist" perspectives.
3. In this, we echo Dick Bryan and Michael Rafferty (2016: 30), who write about the need to "refocus the concept of money away from propositions of social harmony that give money its popular, conventional condition of functionality and universal acceptance" and instead emphasize the "contradictions and disjuncture" in understandings of money, putting "conflict and change at their center."
4. Of course, high finance does not belong exclusively to the twentieth and twenty-first century. Marx, for example, wrote extensively about the political power of bankers and the "finance aristocracy" in the nineteenth century (e.g., in France after the revolution of 1830; see Marx 1895: 33). At the same time, financialization assumed new forms in the latter half of the modern age, and insofar as money seemed, post-1973, to reference only itself—"a tautological void" (Rotman 1987: 89)—it became identified with *post*-modernity. The discursive and epistemological centrality of finance to the postmodern critique of modernity and modernism by artists, novelists, and scholars like David Harvey (1990) and Fredric Jameson (1991) cannot be overemphasized (see La Berge 2015).
5. On the politics of post-crisis financial reform, see also Coombs 2017.
6. We do not adjudicate MMT's practical policy benefits and drawbacks here. See Wray 2014 for an intellectual history and overview, Matthews 2012 for a journalistic account of MMT's history.
7. These are not exactly the same thing. Liquidity is a general concept referring to the ease of money's exchangeability or usability in circulation (see Rogers 2005; Ho

2009; Desan 2010). Fungibility refers to money's "substitutability and exchangeability for itself, with one dollar the same as the next" (Cattelino 2009: 190). Negotiability is a technical legal term indicating the transferability of a financial instrument—that is, the legal capacity for ownership to be detached from one person and reassigned to another (Nyquist 1995). Each points to the capacity of value forms to circulate at par (Poszar 2014) and the "option" to convert between them (Bryan and Rafferty 2016). J.P. Koning (e.g., Koning 2013, 2014) has written insightfully about a moneyness approach, and we are also inspired by his work (see also Koddenbrock 2019).

Chapter 1

1. See, for example, Greenblatt (2010), Clifford (1997), and Appadurai (1996).
2. In many English-speaking countries, this payment instrument is known as a "cheque," but we will use the American English spelling of "check" throughout this chapter.
3. For more details on the "cashless society" vision, see Bátiz-Lazo, Haigh, and Stearns (2013).
4. This editorial, along with a description of the cashless publicity stunt Diners Club that accompanied it, is reprinted in Simmons (1991).
5. For exceptions and exclusions, particularly racial, see Swartz (2017).
6. For more on Diners Club and gender, see Swartz (2014).
7. For more on the origins of the BankAmericard system and its successor VISA, see Stearns (2011). For VISA's official corporate biography, see Chutkow (2001).
8. Although the electronic processing reduced fraud at the point of sale, they did little to stem fraud in other context, such as telephone and mail ordering. See chapter 7 of Stearns (2011).
9. For details on the struggles between the bank's EFTS plans and VISA's early debit card, see chapter 8 of Stearns (2011).
10. For more on the cultural politics of Silicon Valley, see Turner (2008).

Chapter 2

1. White and Schuler (2007) track the probable origin of Keynes' line to an anonymous report of an interview with Lenin appearing in London's *Daily Chronicle* in April 1919.
2. For example, an enormous wool price spike fed a wave of inflation in early 1950s Australia, leaving its cost structure elevated so that it suffered balance-of-payments problems for a decade after export prices receded.
3. Beggs (2015: 62–63) discusses the debate around depreciation in Australia in the 1950s, when the country faced recurrent balance-of-payments problems but declined to devalue.
4. In striking contrast to later attitudes, in the 1960s economists and businesspeople lamented the undermining of centralized control by market forces and began to hint that, as one put it, "the earnings-drift is therefore an important reason for believing that the widely processed goals of stable prices and full employment are irreconcilable" (Hancock 1966: 155). If a "trade-off" argument was being made, it was a conservative one in favor of higher unemployment as labor discipline.

5. The rise in the estimated NAIRU in the United States between the 1950s and late 1970s is less dramatic than elsewhere: American unemployment was substantially higher during the postwar long boom (US Congressional Budget Office 2016).
6. It also highlights the difference between monetarism and monetary *laissez-faire*. Friedman was against government intervention in just about every area except money, where a powerful central bank was essential to guarantee stability. True, the power of that central bank was to be disciplined by following a rule, keeping money supply growth steady, but history showed that this was not nearly as simple as controlling the base and leaving the rest to a passive banking system.
7. In the wake of the report, the *Banker's Magazine* published a Socratic dialogue in which the philosopher asks for a definition of "'the liquidity position as a whole', on which I understand the Committee places great emphasis." His economist interlocutor ruefully responds: "Well, the Committee doesn't actually define liquidity anywhere, Socrates" (Newlyn 1960).
8. By the 2000s, they were a bigger source of US bank funding than the federal funds market (Stigum and Crescenzi 2007: 209).
9. As he told an Australian television audience, while "trade unions—in your country and mine—do a great deal of harm [. . .] the harm which trade unions do is not in producing inflation" (Friedman 1975: 12).
10. John Nevile, an Australian economist who chaired one of Friedman's public talks in Sydney, later reported his annoyance that Friedman used simplistic graphs and arguments quite different from those in his academic work (Courvisanos and Millmow 2006: 125).
11. Monetary targeting called for stricter banking controls in some areas, and deregulation in others. For example, in Australia, meeting the targets involved an intensified use of bank lending controls but also a loosening of interest rate controls, enabling the banks to recapture business lost to the non-bank intermediaries who were less subject to official control (Beggs 2015: 234–246).
12. The recent rapid development of a "shadow banking" system in the highly regulated environment of China, including a lively repo market and the spread of asset securitization, is further striking evidence that financial *laissez-faire* is not a necessary condition. China's "shadow banking" is very different from that in the US and Europe—more directly operated by banks themselves. But it follows the same logic of regulatory arbitrage, exploiting market opportunities set up by regulation. The past few years have seen a familiar back-and-forth between new regulation and new practices. For overviews, see Sheng and Soon (2015); Elliot et al. (2015); Yan and Li (2016).

Chapter 3

1. See Black, 2010.
2. See Synan 1997: 93. Most likely it was Jim Crow laws. Parham's racism, which was no doubt extant, is probably given outsized importance due to his later vehement rejection of Seymour's Los Angeles efforts (see Wacker 2003: 232).
3. It should be noted that the devastating 1906 San Francisco earthquake happened during early days of the Azusa Street revival, giving these prognostications perhaps that much more weight.

4. This, of course, is not particular to Pentecostalism in any way; several forms of religious charity not only involve interest but also produce a kind of intimacy and continuity (see, e.g., Perry 1986).
5. Given this, it is interesting to note that at least some African Prosperity Gospel believers feel that their religion in some ways actually decelerates money; reporting on Tanzanian Pentecostals, Lindhardt (2009) has observed that believers hypothesize about the origins and effects of money based on its apparent speed; rapidly accumulated, or "fast" wealth, is thought to be of satanic origin and unstable in its capacity to be held onto, while "slow wealth," is thought to be divine.

Chapter 4

1. For overviews, see Gilbert 2005; Maurer 2006; Carruthers and Ariovich 2010; Dodd 2014.
2. Anthropologists and sociologists have made this argument forcefully (e.g., Zelizer 1994; Foster 1999; Keane 2001; Strassler 2009; Heslop 2016).
3. International political economy has made this point clearly (e.g., Strange 1971). But see also Blanc 2017; Kuroda 2008a, 2008b; Peebles 2011.
4. On everyday life under inflation, see, e.g., Dominguez 1990; Neiburg 2010; Muir 2015.
5. E.g., Lemon 1998; Pedersen 2002; Kwon 2007; Whitfield 2007; Truitt 2013; Roig 2016.
6. Early twenty-first-century Zimbabwe, which dollarized after a period of hyperinflation in the early 2000s, offers a compelling example, as prices for the same goods varied according to method of payment, and debit cards (transferring dollar-denominated deposits) and "bond notes" (low-value dollar-denominated bills issued by the government to supplement the circulation of US dollars) were accepted by merchants at a discount.
7. The literature on remittances is expansive; for overviews, see Hernandez and Coutin 2006; Cohen 2011; Sirkeci et al. 2012.
8. Embedded in debates about the morality of markets (Fourcade and Healy 2007), what Hochschild (2003: 30) called "the commodity frontier"—the morally and politically charged fence drawn between the alienable and inalienable—is a perennial topic of study, especially when it impinges on intimate relations (e.g., Singh 1997; Cole 2004; Hoang 2015; Kim 2018).
9. E.g., on windfall earnings such as lottery winnings (Hedenus 2014). In behavioral economics, earmarking is typically talked about in terms of "mental accounting" (Thaler 1999).
10. Other examples: in Canada, one-dollar coins are widely called "loonies" (because of the bird on the face); two-dollar coins are called, punningly, "toonies." In Australia, a colorful vocabulary has developed around notes of different denominations, from "red lobsters" to "pineapples."
11. See, e.g., Taussig 1977; Belk and Wallendorf 1990; Carsten 1989.
12. That is, nineteen pounds, nineteen shillings, and sixpence.
13. In the modern era, people's commitment to redistribution through public and collective life eroded in favor of taxation as legal obligation. On the cultures of

taxation, framed in terms of fiscal responsibility or as the non-optional transfer of personal savings to the state, see, e.g., Martin 2008 on mid-twentieth-century tax revolts in the US vs. Abelin 2012 on the class tensions of taxation in Argentina, or Larsen 2017 on the embrace of taxation in Sweden vs. Roitman 2005 on fiscal regulation and disobedience in colonial and postcolonial Central Africa.
14. Ardener and Burman 1995 provides a cross-cultural overview; see also Bähre 2007; Kear 2016.
15. This lobby includes the industries and organizations that manage cash-handling (like armored car companies and ATM manufacturers) and banknote production (like companies that supply paper, inks, and anti-counterfeiting technologies for banknotes).
16. Patterns of cash use around the world are mixed, although it is still the most widely used payment instrument by a large margin, and as we write, its use may be rising (Jobst and Stix 2017; Bech et al. 2018). In the postcolonial world, cash dominates, but even in areas where access to cards and other non-cash payment technologies is high, like Germany and Japan, cash remains more common. Demand for US dollars also remains strong (Judson 2017; O'Brien 2017; Wang 2017).

Chapter 6

* I would like to thank editors Taylor Nelms and David Pedersen for many helpful suggestions that guided me through the discourse on the sociology of money. This chapter is greatly improved by their input.
1. Paul Krugman, winner of the 2008 Nobel Prize for economics, credits the series as inspiring him, although he acknowledges that Asimov's psychohistory is different from economics.
2. In the seventeenth century, English coinage was reissued in response to the problem of clipping coins. Neal Stephenson explores this history, as well as the concurrent invention of bills of credit and, eventually, bank notes, alongside an imagined invention of a precursor to computers, in his *Baroque Cycle—Quicksilver* (2003), *The Confusion* (2004), and *The System of the World* (2004).
3. Following Vigna and Casey (2015), I use Bitcoin to refer to the technology and bitcoin to refer to the units of value created by it.
4. Doctorow's title is an allusion to George Orwell's *Down and Out in Paris and London* (1933), a semi-autobiographical exploration of contemporary poverty.
5. This is how the discipline understands itself. Piketty (2014: 573–575) pointedly critiques the narrowness that comes from an exclusive focus on mathematics, overlooking the social and political consequences of how economics creates the world in its models, especially the failure to think through how historical inequalities are perpetuated.
6. Graeber, joined by all recent historians of money, notes that the ideal of a primitive barter system that preceded money is unsupported by any scholarship in anthropology. Nonetheless, this mistaken concept of the origin of economics continues to be influential because it was embraced by Adam Smith and Smith's ideas continue to have power today.
7. Although he rejects this model, Dodd (2014: 7) notes that it is consistent with Georg Simmel's influential account of money: "as our social relations are increasingly

mediated by money, they become more abstract and featureless, and our inner lives are rendered ever more devoid of inner meaning and subjective value."

8. The name alludes to Mondragon, in Basque territory, and its experiments with worker cooperatives.
9. The novel was published before a secure method for online purchase was developed: PayPal was then emerging to fill this need, appearing under this name only in 2001.
10. Scenes set in the 1940s show the tremendous human suffering it cost to bury the stolen gold, and when Randy and his partners use it as the basis for their new bank, there is great solemnity attached to its recovery. All commit to using the money only for socially productive purposes, defined by economic growth, individual flourishing, and keeping money from governments and their militaries. Similar rationales are offered by some Bitcoin enthusiasts (Vigna and Casey 2015: 285). Scott (2014) notes that Bitcoin may undermine these ideals by becoming mainstream, thus requiring intermediaries like banks. Further, he suggests turning to Bitcoin might weaken the fragile institutions of a vulnerable country just at a point when they need to be strengthened (Scott 2016).
11. Contemporary to the novel's publication, a digital currency called e-gold was in circulation, which denominated its users' accounts in grams of gold as its currency measure. The world's first successful micro-payment system, it ended due to changes to financial regulations under the US Patriot Act.
12. The US Internal Revenue Service ruled that Bitcoin is property, a holding that may gain or lose value, and taxes it accordingly.
13. PlayerAuctions.com, for example, facilitates such trades and purchases, including in-game currency exchanges.
14. As Martin (2015: 250) explains, "global banking's current structure generates an unjust distribution of risks, where losses are socialized—taxpayers are on the hook for bail-outs—while gains are private—the banks and their investors alone reap any profits."
15. Swartz (2017: 88) worries that we are insufficiently attentive to the gap between "radical" blockchain visions, which would transform economic structures, and incorporative ones, which perpetuate the status quo in new guise. This tension mirrors the gap between how Robinson and Stephenson project economic futures.
16. Blockchain also needed protocols regarding which branch of a chain proved to be the "real" one when rival claims of ownership are simultaneously put forward, adopting a standard of community validation (building on one branch to reinforce its length and hence "real-ness") to adjudicate such overlaps.
17. The name alludes to economist Friedrich Hayek, whose work is widely understood as a leading inspiration of neoliberal policy.
18. There are real-world parallels with how the US dollar became the international standard following the Bretton Woods agreements. Early drafts referred to a currency exchangeable for gold, and a request for clarification led to "US dollar" being given as an example. The final document used the example *as* the standard, giving us our existing system of floating currencies. See episode 533, "The Dollar at the Center of the World," of *Planet Money* on NPR: www.npr.org/sections/money/2014/07/16/331743569/episode-552-the-dollar-at-the-center-of-the-world.

19. Womack's vision was inspired by Norman Jewison's *Rollerball* (1975); a character in *Ambient* (1987) says, "Everyone wore skates, and was armored, and outfitted. I believe Mister Dryden lifted the concept from an old movie he'd once seen, undoubtedly while kite-high" (30). This use of physical violence to stand in for corporate violence also structures Bret Easton Ellis's *American Psycho* (1991), which La Berge (2014) sees as the exemplar of a new financial aesthetic.
20. This is the name of the unit of currency proposed for international exchange by John Maynard Keynes, rather than using the US dollar as was adopted at Bretton Woods.
21. Graeber argues that there is a relationship between US militarism and the fact that most of the US economy is deficit financed. The system relies, he argues, on the fact that the US military can bomb any part of the world that it chooses:

> no other government has ever had anything remotely like this sort of capability. In fact, a case could well be made that it is this very power that holds the entire world monetary system, organized around the dollar, together.
> —2011: 366

Chapter 7

1. This was discovered as a result of central bank assistance in financing treasury spending during World War I.
2. Yet note that reserves at the Fed are counted as liabilities—and these are not "redeemable" per their definition either.
3. At the same time, Kumhoff seems to treat notes issued by the Federal Reserve as "debt money" (see, e.g., Kumhoff 2013, when he shows a dollar bill and claims it is "debt money"). It is not clear what criteria he uses to distinguish between "debt money" and "debt-free money."
4. Many of the words associated with money and debt were borrowed from religion—reflecting the commonality of debt to both the creditor and the gods (see Bialecki, this volume).
5. These tallies were used up to the beginning of the modern era. The cover of Wray (2004) shows a photo of tallies used on private estates in Agrigento, Sicily in 1905.
6. Promises to convert to foreign currencies were common in the developing world in the latter half of the modern age. This may be deemed necessary to increase external acceptability of a nation's currency. However, a nation's IOUs will be accepted internally without such promises, at least in payment to a functioning state that can enforce taxes and other obligations. We do not address the problems faced by nations in ensuring external acceptability, which is quite a different matter.
7. In the past, treasuries also issued other types of liabilities, such as notes and tax credits (securities that could be used to make tax payments).
8. Keynes favored a low-interest-rate policy in his call to euthanize the rentier class by eliminating a reward to those who hold riskless assets.
9. Bonds are functionally a monetary policy tool rather than a borrowing operation. The purchase of a government bond is completed when the central bank debits the reserves of a private bank (and the bank debits the deposits of the buyer unless the

bank is itself buying the bonds). The operational purpose of bond sales is, therefore, to reduce bank reserves; alternatively, from the point of view of private banks, it offers them a higher earning asset since bonds pay higher interest rates than reserves (Wray 1998, 2015).

10. Admittedly this would require a change of current US procedures, although it has been permitted in the past (and there has been and continues to be discussion at the Fed of permitting this in case of an emergency). See Garbade (2014) for examination of reinstituting procedures for selling US Treasury debt to the Fed.

11. Note that in the US bank deposits have not been proclaimed "legal tender" by the government. Even if they were, "legal tender" does not mean private sector participants cannot refuse to accept the particular IOU in payment (see www.treasury.gov/resource-center/faqs/Currency/Pages/legal-tender.aspx). In fact, businesses regularly exclude deposits or even the government's own IOUs—cash—from the list of acceptable means of payment.

12. Pozsar's definition, while narrower than Minsky's, is useful for focusing attention on monetary liabilities that are issued by banks as well as shadow banks and that played an important role in the GFC.

13. Despite a crisis of historic proportions, the US banking system faced almost no runs during the GFC; the current deposit insurance system clearly works. At the same time, we did have a run on the so-called shadow banking system.

14. Here we refer to Lerner's (1943) principle of "functional finance," according to which the government should spend and tax with the goal of achieving full employment and price stability, rather than balancing the budget. Lerner thought that leaving "such matters to the market would be like driving a car without using the steering wheel" (Forstater 1999: 476).

BIBLIOGRAPHY

Abelin, Mireille. 2012. "'Entrenched in the BMW': Argentine Elites and the Terror of Fiscal Obligation." *Public Culture*, 24(2): 329–356.
Adkins, Lisa. 2015. "What Are Post-Fordist Wages? Simmel, Labor Money, and the Problem of Value." *South Atlantic Quarterly*, 114(2): 331–353.
Aitken, Rob. 2015. *Fringe Finance: Crossing and Contesting the Borders of Global Capital*. New York: Routledge.
Akin, D. and Robbins, J. (eds.). 1999. *Money and Modernity: State and Local Currencies in Melanesia*. Pittsburgh: University of Pittsburgh Press.
Allen, John, and Michael Pryke. 1999. "Money Cultures After Simmel: Mobility, Movement, and Identity." *Environment and Planning D: Society and Space*, 17(1): 51–68.
Allon, Fiona. 2010. "Speculating on Everyday Life: The Cultural Economy of the Quotidian." *Journal of Communication Inquiry*, 34(4): 366–381.
Althusser, Louis. 2014. *On the Reproduction of Capitalism: Ideology and Ideological State Apparatuses*. New York: Verso.
Anderson, R.M. 1979. *Vision of the Disinherited: The Making of American Pentecostalism*. Peabody, MA: Hendrickson.
Anderson, Benedict. [1983] 2006. *Imagined Communities*. New York: Verso.
Ansell, Aaron. 2010. "Auctioning Patronage in Northeast Brazil: The Political Value of Money in a Ritual Market." *American Anthropologist*, 112(2): 283–294.
Appadurai, Arjun. 1996. *Modernity at Large: Cultural Dimensions of Globalization*. Minneapolis, MN: University of Minnesota Press.
Ardener, Shirley, and Sandra Burman (eds.). 1995. *Money-Go-Rounds: The Importance of ROSCAs for Women*. Washington, DC: Berg.
Armstrong, Philip, Andrew Glyn, and John Harrison. 1991. *Capitalism Since 1945*. Oxford: Blackwell.
Asimov, Isaac. 2004a. *Foundation*. New York: Bantam.
Asimov, Isaac. 2004b. *Foundation and Empire*. New York: Bantam.
Asimov, Isaac. 2004c. *Second Foundation*. New York: Bantam.
Atkins, Ralph. 2018. "Radical Reform: Switzerland to Vote on Banking Overhaul." *Financial Times*, May 28. Available online: www.ft.com/content/13b92d86-5810-11e8-bdb7-f6677d2e1ce8.

Bagnall, John, David Bounie, Kim P. Huynh, Anneke Kosse, Tobias Schmidt, Scott Schuh, and Helmut Stix. 2016. "Consumer Cash Usage: A Cross-Country Comparison with Payment Diary Survey Data." *International Journal of Central Banking*, 12(4): 1–61.

Bähre, Erik. 2007. *Money and Violence: Financial Self-Help Organizations in a South African Township*. Leiden: Brill.

Bandelj, Nina, Frederick F. Wherry, and Viviana A. Zelizer (eds.). 2017. *Money Talks: Explaining How Money Really Works*. Princeton: Princeton University Press.

Bandelj, Nina, Paul James Morgan, and Elizabeth Sowers. 2015. "Hostile Worlds or Connected Lives? Research on the Interplay Between Intimacy and Economy." *Sociology Compass*, 9(2): 115–127.

Bannerjee, Abhijit V., and Esther Duflo. 2011. *Poor Economics: A Radical Rethinking of the Way to Fight Global Poverty*. New York: Public Affairs.

Baradaran, Mehrsa. 2015. *How the Other Half Banks: Exclusion, Exploitation, and the Threat to Democracy*. Cambridge: Harvard University Press.

Bateman, Milford. 2010. *Why Doesn't Microfinance Work? The Destructive Rise of Local Neoliberalism*. London: Zed.

Bátiz-Lazo, Bernardo and Leonidas Efthymiou (eds.). 2016. *The Book of Payments: History and Contemporary Views on the Cashless Society*. London: Palgrave Macmillan.

Bátiz-Lazo, Bernardo, Thomas Haigh and David L. Stearns. 2014. "How the Future Shaped the Past: The Case of the Cashless Society." *Enterprise and Society*, 15(1): 103–131.

Baudrillard, Jean. 1981. *For a Critique of the Political Economy of the Sign*. St. Louis: Telos.

Bayley, Stephen. 2011. "Decimalisation Day: Forty Years Ago, We Lost the Rich and Beautiful Poetry in Our Pockets." *The Telegraph*, February 11. Available online: www.telegraph.co.uk/comment/personal-view/8317759/Decimalisation-Day-Forty-years-ago-we-lost-the-rich-and-beautiful-poetry-in-our-pockets.html.

Bayoumi, Tamim, and Barry Eichengreen. 1996. "The Stability of the Gold Standard and the Evolution of the International Monetary System." In Tamim Bayoumi, Barry Eichengreen, and Mark Taylor (eds.), *Modern Perspectives on the Classical Gold Standard*. Cambridge: Cambridge University Press, 165–188.

Bear, Laura, Karen Ho, Anna Tsing, and Sylvia Yanagisako. 2015. "Gens: A Feminist Manifesto for the Study of Capitalism. Theorizing the Contemporary," *Cultural Anthropology* website, March 30. Available online: https://culanth.org/fieldsights/652-gens-a-feminist-manifesto-for-the-study-of-capitalism.

Beasley-Murray, Jon. 2000. "Value and Capital in Bourdieu and Marx." In Nicholas Brown and Imre Szeman (eds.), *Pierre Bourdieu: A Fieldwork in Culture*. Lanham, MD: Rowman and Littlefield, 100–121.

Bech, Morten, Umar Faruqui, Frederik Ougaard, and Cristina Picillo. 2018. "Payments are A-Changin' but Cash Still Rules." *BIS Quarterly Review* (March): 67–80.

Beggs, Michael. 2015. *Inflation and the Making of Australian Macroeconomic Policy, 1945–85*. Basingstoke: Palgrave Macmillan.

Beggs, Michael. 2017. "The State as a Creature of Money." *New Political Economy*, 22(5): 463–477.

Belk, Russell W. and Melanie Wallendorf. 1990. "The Sacred Meanings of Money." *Journal of Economic Psychology*, 11(1): 35–67.

Bell, Stephanie. 2001. "The Role of the State and the Hierarchy of Money." *Cambridge Journal of Economics*, 25(2): 149–163.

Bellamy, Edward. 1889. *Looking Backward: 2000–1887*. New York: Houghton Mifflin. Available at www.gutenberg.org/ebooks/624?msg=welcome_stranger.
Benes, Jaromir, and Kumhof, Michael. 2012. *The Chicago Plan Revisited*. Washington, DC: International Monetary Fund.
Berardi, Franco "Bifo." 2009. *Precarious Rhapsody: Semiocapitalism and the Pathologies of the Post-Alpha Generation*. New York: Autonomedia.
Bernanke, Ben S. 2012. "The Great Moderation." In Evan F. Koenig, Robert Leeson, and George A. Kahn (eds.), *The Taylor Rule and the Transformation of Monetary Policy*. Stanford: Hoover Institution Press, 145–162.
Better Than Cash Alliance. 2018. "About the Better Than Cash Alliance." Available online: www.betterthancash.org/about.
Beuys, Joseph. 2010. *What Is Money? A Discussion*. West Hoathly: Clairview.
Bialecki, J., 2017. *A Diagram for Fire: Miracles and Variation in an American Charismatic Movement*. Berkeley: University of California Press.
Bialecki, J., 2018. "Deleuze." In *The Cambridge Encyclopedia of Anthropology*. Available online: www.anthroencyclopedia.com/entry/deleuze.
Binde, Per. 2005. "Gambling Across Cultures: Mapping Worldwide Occurrence and Learning from Ethnographic Comparison." *International Gambling Studies*, 5(1): 1–27.
Bishop, Claire. 2012. *Artificial Hells: Participatory Art and the Politics of Spectatorship*. New York: Verso.
Björkman, Lisa. 2014. "'You Can't Buy a Vote: Meanings of Money in a Mumbai Election." *American Ethnologist*, 41(4): 617–634.
Black, N., 2010. "Million Dollar Bill Gospel Tracts are Legal, Judge Rules." *The Christian Post*. Available online: www.christianpost.com/news/million-dollar-bill-gospel-tracts-are-legal-judge-rules-44580/.
Blanc, Jérôme. 2010. "Community and Complementary Currencies." In Keith Hart, Jean-Louis Laville, and Antonio David Cattani (eds.), *The Human Economy*. Cambridge: Polity, 303–312.
Blanc, Jérôme. 2017. "Unpacking Monetary Complementarity and Competition: A Conceptual Framework." *Cambridge Journal of Economics*, 41(1): 239–257.
Blanton, A., 2015. *Hittin' the Prayer Bones: Materiality of Spirit in the Pentecostal South*. Chapel Hill: University of North Carolina Press.
Bleaney, Michael. 1985. *The Rise and Fall of Keynesian Economics: An Investigation of its Contribution to Capitalist Development*. London: Macmillan.
Blinder, Alan S. 1998. *Central Banking in Theory and Practice*. Cambridge: MIT Press.
Bloch, Maurice, and Jonathan Parry. 1989. "Introduction: Money and the Morality of Exchange." In Jonathan Parry and Maurice Bloch (eds.), *Money and the Morality of Exchange*. Cambridge: Cambridge University Press, 1–32.
Blumhofer, E.W. 1993. *Restoring the Faith: The Assemblies of God, Pentecostalism, and American Culture*. Urbana: University of Illinois Press.
Bohannan, Paul. 1959. "The Impact of Money on an African Subsistence Economy." *The Journal of Economic History*, 19(4): 491–503.
Bolt, Maxim. 2014. "The Sociality of the Wage: Money Rhythms, Wealth Circulation, and the Problem with Cash on the Zimbabwean-South African Border." *Journal of the Royal Anthropological Institute*, 20(1): 113–130.
Boltanski, Luc, and Eve Chiapello. 2005. *The New Spirit of Capitalism*. Gregory Elliot (trans). New York: Verso.
Bornstein, Erica. 2009. "The Impulse of Philanthropy." *Cultural Anthropology*, 24(4): 622–651.

Bourdieu, Pierre, and Hans Haacke. 1994. *Free Exchange*. Stanford: Stanford University Press.

Bourdieu, Pierre. 1984. *Distinction: A Social Critique of the Judgement of Taste*. Richard Nice (trans.). Cambridge: Harvard University Press.

Bourdieu, Pierre. 1990. *The Logic of Practice*. Richard Nice (trans.). Stanford: Stanford University Press.

Bourdieu, Pierre. 1993. *The Field of Cultural Production: Essays on Art and Literature*. Randal Johnson (ed.). New York: Columbia University Press.

Bourdieu, Pierre. 2005. *The Social Structures of the Economy*. Chris Turner (trans.). Cambridge: Polity.

Bourgeron, Théo. 2018. "Optimising 'Cash Flows': Converting Corporate Finance to Hard Currency." *Journal of Cultural Economy*, 11(3): 193–208.

Bowler, K., 2013. *Blessed: A History of the American Prosperity Gospel*. New York: Oxford.

Bradford, Tonya Williams. 2015. "Beyond Fungible: Transforming Money into Moral and Social Resources." *Journal of Marketing*, 79(2): 79–97.

Braun, Benjamin. 2016. "Speaking to the People? Money, Trust, and Central Bank Legitimacy in the Age of Quantitative Easing." *Review of International Political Economy*, 23(6): 1064–1092.

Brightman, R., 1995. "Forget Culture: Replacement, Transcendence, Relexification." *Cultural Anthropology*, 10(4): 509–546.

Broll, Simon. 2012. "Theaterprojekt 'Schwarzbank': Mäuse, Piepen, Kröten." *Spiegel Online* (March 14). Available online: www.spiegel.de/kultur/gesellschaft/theaterprojekt-schwarzbank-a-820850.html.

Brown, Ellen Hodgson. 2013. *The Public Bank Solution: From Austerity to Prosperity*. Baton Rouge: Third Millennium Press.

Bryan, Dick, and Michael Rafferty. 2006. *Capitalism With Derivatives: A Political Economy of Financial Derivatives, Capital, and Class*. Basingstoke/New York: Palgrave Macmillan.

Bryan, Dick, and Michael Rafferty. 2013. "Fundamental Value: A Category in Transformation." *Economy and Society*, 42(1): 130–153.

Bryan, Dick, and Michael Rafferty. 2016. "Decomposing Money: Ontological Options and Spreads." *Journal of Cultural Economy*, 9(1): 27–42.

Bryan-Wilson, Julia. 2009. *Art Workers: Radical Practices in the Vietnam War Era*. Berkeley: University of California Press.

Bürger, Peter. 1984. *Theory of the Avant-Garde*. Minneapolis: University of Minnesota Press.

Burkett, Paul and Richard C.K. Burdekin. 1996. *Distributional Conflict and Inflation: Theoretical and Historical Perspectives*. Basingstoke: Macmillan.

Caffentzis, George. 1999. "On the Notion of a Crisis of Social Reproduction: A Theoretical Review." In Giovanna Franca Dalla Costa and Mariarosa Dalla Costa (eds.), *Women, Development, and Labor of Reproduction: Struggles and Movements*. Tronton, NJ and Asmara, Eritrea: Africa World Press, 153–188.

Caffentzis, George. 2013. *In Letters of Blood and Fire: Work, Machines, and the Crisis of Capitalism*. Oakland: PM Press.

Cameron, Stuart, and Jon Coaffee. 2005. "Art, Gentrification and Regeneration—From Artist as Pioneer to Public Arts." *International Journal of Housing Policy*, 5(1): 39–58.

Campbell, J.K., A.W. Coates, R.G. Halkerston, R.G. McCrossin, J.S. Mallyon, and F. Argy. 1981. *Final Report of the Committee of Inquiry into the Australian Financial System*. Canberra: Australian Government Publishing Service.

Capie, Forrest, and Geoffrey Wood. 2012. *Money Over Two Centuries: Selected Topics in British Monetary History*. Oxford: Oxford University Press.
Carruthers, Bruce G. 2010. "The Meanings of Money: A Sociological Perspective." *Theoretical Inquiries in Law*, 11(1): 51–74.
Carruthers, Bruce G., and Laura Ariovich. 2010. *Money and Credit: A Sociological Approach*. Cambridge: Polity.
Carruthers, Bruce G., and Wendy Nelson Espeland. 1998. "Money, Meaning, and Morality." *American Behavioral Scientist*, 41(10): 1384–1408.
Carsten, Janet. 1989. "Cooking Money: Gender and the Symbolic Transformation of Means of Exchange in a Malay Fishing Community." In Jonathan Parry and Maurice Bloch (eds.), *Money and the Morality of Exchange*. Cambridge: Cambridge University Press, 117–141.
Castoriadis, Cornelius. 1997. *The Castoriadis Reader*. David Ames Curtis (trans.). Oxford: Blackwell, 1997.
Cattelino, Jessica R. 2009. "Fungibility: Florida Seminole Casino Dividends and the Fiscal Politics of Indigeneity." *American Anthropologist*, 111(2): 190–200.
Cattelino, Jessica R. 2018. "From Locke to Slots: Money and the Politics of Indigeneity." *Comparative Studies in Society and History*, 60(3): 274–307.
Champ, Bruce. 2008. "Stamp Scrip: Money People Paid to Use." *Economic Commentary* (April). Federal Reserve Board of Cleveland. Available online: www.clevelandfed.org/newsroom-and-events/publications/economic-commentary/economic-commentary-archives/2008-economic-commentaries/ec-20080401-stamp-scrip-money-people-paid-to-use.aspx.
Changing Times. 1952. "Traveling? Put it on the Cuff: a new, all-purpose credit card lets you do just that" (February 24).
Chaum, David. 1985. "Security Without Identification: Transaction Systems to Make Big Brother Obsolete." *Communications of the ACM*, 28(10): 1030–1044.
Chick, Victoria. 1973. *The Theory of Monetary Policy*. London: Gray-Mills.
Christophers, Brett, Andrew Leyshon, and Geoff Mann (2017). "Money and Finance After the Crisis: Taking Stock." In Brett Christophers, Andrew Leyshon, and Geoff Mann (eds.) *Money and Finance After the Crisis: Critical Thinking for Uncertain Times*. Oxford: Wiley Blackwell, 1–40.
Chutkow, Paul. 2001. *Visa: The Power of an Idea*. Chicago: Harcourt.
Clark, T.J. 1999. *The Absolute Bourgeois: Artists and Politics in France, 1848–1851*. Berkeley: University of California Press.
Clay, Henry. 1929. "The Public Regulation of Wages in Great Britain." *Economic Journal*, 39(155): 323–343.
Cleaver, Harry. 2000. *Reading Capital Politically*. San Francisco: AK Press.
Cleaver, Harry. 2005. "Work, Value and Domination: On the Continuing Relevance of the Marxian Labour Theory of Value in the Crisis of the Keynesian Planner State." *The Commoner* 10. Available online: www.commoner.org.uk/10cleaver.pdf.
Clifford, James. 1997. *Routes: Travel and Translation in the Late Twentieth Century*. Cambridge: Harvard University Press.
Codere, Helen. 1968. "Money-Exchange Systems and a Theory of Money." *Man*, 3(4): 557–577.
Cohen, Benjamin J. 1998. *The Geography of Money*. Ithaca: Cornell University Press.
Cohen, Benjamin J. 2004. *The Future of Money*. Princeton: Princeton University Press.
Cohen, Jeffrey H. 2011. "Migration, Remittances, and Household Strategies." *Annual Review of Anthropology*, 40: 103–114.

Cole, Jennifer. 2004. "Fresh Contact in Tamatave, Madagascar: Sex, Money, and Intergenerational Transformation." *American Ethnologist*, 31(4): 573–588.
Coleman, S., 2000. *The Globalisation of Charismatic Christianity*. Cambridge: Cambridge University Press.
Coleman, S., 2004. "The Charismatic Gift." *Journal of the Royal Anthropological Institute*, 10(2): 421–442.
Coleman, S., 2006. "Materializing the Self: Words and Gifts in the Construction of Charismatic Protestant Identity." In Fenella Cannell (ed.), *The Anthropology of Christianity*. Durham: Duke University Press, 163–184.
Coleman, S., 2011. "Prosperity unbound? Debating the 'Sacrificial Economy.'" In Lionel Obadia, Donald C. Wood (eds.) *The Economics of Religion: Anthropological Approaches*, 23–45. Bingley: Emerald Group Publishing.
Coleman, S., 2017. "Morality, Markets, and the Gospel of Prosperity." In Rudnyckyj, D. and Osella, F. (eds.), *Religion and the Morality of the Market*. Cambridge: Cambridge University Press, p. 50.
Collins, Daryl, Jonathan Morduch, Stuart Rutherford, and Orlanda Ruthven. 2009. *Portfolios of the Poor: How the World's Poor Live on $2 a Day*. Princeton: Princeton University Press.
Comaroff, J. and Comaroff, J.L. 1999. "Occult Economies and the Violence of Abstraction: Notes from the South African Postcolony." *American Ethnologist*, 26(2): 279–303.
Coombs, Nathan. 2017. "Macroprudential Versus Monetary Blueprints for Financial Reform." *Journal of Cultural Economy*, 10(2): 207–216.
Cooper, Melinda, and Angela Mitropoulos. 2009. "In Praise of Usura." *Mute* 2(13). Available online: www.metamute.org/editorial/articles/praise-usura.
Cooper, Melinda, and Martijn Konings. 2016. "Pragmatics of Money and Finance: Beyond Performativity and Fundamental Value." *Journal of Cultural Economy*, 9(1): 1–4.
Cooper, Melinda. 2015. "Shadow Money and the Shadow Workforce: Rethinking Labor and Liquidity." *South Atlantic Quarterly* 114(2): 395–423.
Cooper, Melinda. 2017. *Family Values: Between Neoliberalism and the New Social Conservatism*. Cambridge: MIT Press.
Copestake, James, Susan Johnson, Mateo Cabello, Ruth Goodwin-Groen, Robin Gravesteijn, Julie Humberstone, Max Nino-Zarazua, and Matthew Titus. "Towards a Plural History of Microfinance." *Canadian Journal of Development Studies*, 37(3): 279–297.
Courvisanos, Jerry and Alex Millmow. 2006. "How Milton Friedman came to Australia: A Case Study of Class-Based Political Business Cycles." *Journal of Australian Political Economy*, (57): 112–136.
Cox, John. 2018. *Fast Money Schemes: Hope and Deception in Papua New Guinea*. Bloomington: Indiana University Press.
Cramp, A.B. 1962. "Two Views on Money." *Lloyds Bank Review*, 65 (July): 1–15.
Crane, Dan. 2015. "Do You Have Change for a Bowie?" *New York Times*, August 9, 2015. Online.
Creswell, Timothy. 2006. *On the Move: Mobility in The Modern Western World*. New York: Routledge.
Crisp, L.F. 1961. "The Commonwealth Treasury's Changed Role and Its Organisational Consequences." *Australian Journal of Public Administration*, 20(4): 315–330.

Crosthwaite, Paul, Peter Knight, and Nicky Marsh (eds.). 2014. *Show Me the Money: The Image of Finance, 1700 to the Present*. Manchester: Manchester University Press.

Csordas, T.J., 1997a. *The Sacred Self: A Cultural Phenomenology of Charismatic Healing*. Berkeley: University of California Press.

Csordas, T.J., 1997b. *Language, Charisma, and Creativity: The Ritual Life of a Religious Movement*. Berkeley: University of California Press.

Currid, Elizabeth. 2007. *The Warhol Economy: How Fashion, Art, and Music Drive New York City*. Princeton: Princeton University Press.

Cushing, Marshall H. 1893. *The Story of Our Post Office: The Greatest Government Department in All Its Phases*. Boston: A.M Thayer Company.

Dai, Wei. 1998. "Bmoney." Available online: www.weidai.com/bmoney.txt.

Dalinghaus, Ursula. 2017. "Keeping Cash: Assessing the Arguments about Cash and Crime." *Cash Matters*. Available online: www.imtfi.uci.edu/files/images/2017/Keeping_Cash_Whitepaper_download_PDF_US_Letter_Size.pdf.

Dalla Costa, Giovanna Franca. 2008. *The Work of Love: Unpaid Housework, Poverty and Sexual Violence at the Dawn of the 21st Century*. Enda Brophy (trans.). New York: Autonomedia.

Dalton, George. 1965. "Primitive Money." *American Anthropologist*, 67(1): 44–65.

Dalziel, Paul. 2002. "The Triumph of Keynes: What Now for Monetary Policy Research?" *Journal of Post Keynesian Economics*, 24(4): 511–527.

Davies, William. 2018. "Introduction to Economic Science Fictions." In William Davies (ed.) *Economic Science Fictions*. London: Goldsmiths Press, 1–28.

Davis, Ben. 2016. "'Panama Papers' Show Art's Role In Tax Dodge." *ArtNet News* (April 4). Available online: https://news.artnet.com/opinion/panama-papers-tax-dodging-superrich-465305.

Day, Richard. 2005. *Gramsci Is Dead: Anarchist Currents in the Newest Social Movements*. London: Pluto.

De Angelis, Massimo, and David Harvie. 2009. "'Cognitive Capitalism' and the Rat-Race: How Capital Measures Immaterial Labour in British Universities." *Historical Materialism*, 17(3): 3–30.

De Certeau, Michel. 1984. *The Practice of Everyday Life*. Steven Rendall (trans.). Berkeley: University of California Press.

De Long, J. Bradford. 2000. "The Triumph of Monetarism?" *Journal of Economic Perspectives*, 14(1): 83–94.

de Paiva Abreu, M. 2006. "The External Context." In V. Bulmer-Thomas, J. Coatsworth, and R. Cortes-Conde (eds.), *Cambridge Economic History of Latin America*. Volume 2. Cambridge: Cambridge University Press, 101–134.

de Vries, Margaret Garrison. 1987. *Balance of Payments Adjustment, 1945 to 1986: The IMF Experience*. Washington, DC: International Monetary Fund.

Debord, Guy. 1962. "Perspectives for Conscious Changes in Everyday Life." Ken Knabb (trans.). *Internationale Situationniste*, 6. Available online: www.cddc.vt.edu/sionline/si/everyday.html.

Delany, Samuel R. 2014. "The Tale of Old Venn." *Tales of Nevèrÿon*. Amazon Digital: Open Road, 80–139.

Deleuze, G. and F. Guattari. 1983. *Anti-Oedipus: Capitalism and Schizophrenia*. Minneapolis: University of Minnesota Press.

Deleuze, G. and F. Guattari 1999. *A Thousand Plateaus: Capitalism and Schizophrenia*. Minneapolis: University of Minnesota Press.

Desan, Christine. 2010. "Coin Reconsidered: The Political Alchemy of Commodity Money." *Theoretical Inquiries in Law*, 11(1): 361–409.
Desan, Christine. 2014. *Making Money: Coin, Currency, and the Coming of Capitalism*. Oxford: Oxford University Press.
Desan, Christine. 2016. "Money as a Legal Institution." In David Fox and Wolfgang Ernst (eds.) *Money in the Western Legal Tradition: Middle Ages to Bretton Woods*. Oxford: Oxford University Press, 18–35.
Dharia, Namita, and Nishita Trisal (eds.) 2017. "Demonetization: Critical Responses to India's Cash(/less) Experiment." *Cultural Anthropology*, Hot Spots (September 27). Available online: https://culanth.org/fieldsights/1222-demonetization-critical-responses-to-india-s-cash-less-experiment.
Dick, Philip K. 2012. *Ubik*. New York: Mariner.
Doctorow, Cory. 2003. *Down and Out in the Magic Kingdom*. New York: TOR.
Dodd, Nigel. 2005. "Reinventing Monies in Europe." *Economy and Society*, 34(4): 558–583.
Dodd, Nigel. 2014. *The Social Life of Money*. Princeton: Princeton University Press.
Dominguez, Virginia R. 1990. "Representing Value and the Value of Representation: A Different Look at Money." *Cultural Anthropology*, 5(1): 16–44.
Donovan, Kevin. 2015. "Mobile Money." In *The International Encyclopedia of Digital Communication and Society*. Volume 1. Oxford: Wiley-Blackwell, 619–626.
Dooley, M.P., D. Folkerts-Landau, and P. Garber. 2003. "An Essay on the Revived Bretton Woods System." NBER Working Paper Series 9971. Available online: www.nber.org/papers/w9971.
Dyson, Ben, Graham Hodgson, and Frank van Lerven. 2016. "A Response to Critiques of 'Full Reserve Banking.'" *Cambridge Journal of Economics*, 40(5): 1351–1361.
Dzokoto, Vivian Afi Abui, Jessica Young, and Edwin Clifford. 2010. "A Tale of Two Cedis: Making Sense of a New Currency in Ghana." *Journal of Economic Psychology*, 31(4): 520–526.
Edin, Kathryn J., and H. Luke Schaefer. 2015. *$2.00 a Day: Living on Almost Nothing in America*. New York: Houghton Mifflin Harcourt.
Edwards, Paul. 2010. *A Vast Machine: Computer Models, Climate Data, and the Politics of Global Warming*. Cambridge: MIT Press.
Edwards, Sebastian, and Santaella, Julio A. 1992. "Devaluation Controversies in the Developing Countries: Lessons from the Bretton Woods Era." NBER Working Paper 4047. Available online: www.nber.org/papers/w4047.
Ehrenreich, Barbara. 2001. *Nickel and Dimed: On (Not) Getting By in America*. New York: Holt.
Eichengreen, Barry J. 2008. *Globalizing Capital: A History of the International Monetary System*. 2nd edition. Princeton: Princeton University Press.
Eichengreen, Barry. 2010. *Exorbitant Privilege: The Rise and Fall of the Dollar and the Future of the International Monetary System*. Oxford: Oxford University Press.
Eijkman, Frederik, Jake Kendall, and Ignacio Mas. 2010. "Bridges to Cash: The Retail End of M-Pesa." *Savings & Development* 34(2): 219–252.
Elliott, D., A. Kroeber, and Y. Qiao. 2015. "Shadow Banking in China: A Primer." Washington, DC: Brookings Institution. Available online: www.brookings.edu/wp-content/uploads/2016/06/shadow_banking_china_elliott_kroeber_yu.pdf.
Elyachar, Julia. 2012. "Next Practices: Knowledge, Infrastructure, and Public Goods at the Bottom of the Pyramid." *Public Culture*, 24(1): 109–129.
Engels, Friedrich. [1845] 1993. *The Condition of the Working Class in England*. Oxford: Oxford University Press.

England, George Allan. 1916. *The Golden Blight*. New York: H.K. Fly Co. Available online: https://archive.org/details/thegoldenblight00englrich.

Eriksen, A., 2012. "The Pastor and the Prophetess: An Analysis of Gender and Christianity in Vanuatu." *Journal of the Royal Anthropological Institute*, 18(1): 103–122.

Eriksen, A., 2014. "Sarah's Sinfulness: Egalitarianism, Denied Difference, and Gender in Pentecostal Christianity." *Current Anthropology*, 55(S10): S262–S270.

Evans, David S. and Richard Schmalensee. 2005. *Paying with Plastic: The Digital Revolution in Buying and Borrowing*. Cambridge: MIT Press.

Fanon, Frantz. 1963. "On National Culture." In *The Wretched of the Earth*. New York: Grove, 206–248.

Federici, Silvia. 2005. *Caliban and the Witch: Women, Capitalism and Primitive Accumulation*. New York: Autonomedia.

Federici, Silvia. 2012. *Revolution at Point Zero: Housework, Reproduction, and Feminist Struggle*. Oakland: PM Press.

Feingold, Ellen R. 2015. *The Value of Money*. Washington, DC: Smithsonian.

Ferguson, J., 1999. *Expectations of Modernity: Myths and Meanings of Urban Life on the Zambian Copperbelt*. Berkeley: University of California Press.

Ferguson, James. 2015. *Give a Man a Fish: Reflections on the New Politics of Distribution*. Durham: Duke University Press.

Ferguson, Sue, and David McNally. 2015. "Social Reproduction Beyond Intersectionality: An Interview." *Viewpoint 5*. Available online: https://viewpointmag.com/2015/10/31/social-reproduction-beyond-intersectionality-an-interview-with-sue-ferguson-and-david-mcnally/.

Fernelius, Leonard W. and David Fettig. 1992. "The Dichotomy Becomes Reality: Ten Years of the Federal Reserve as Regulator and Competitor." *Federal Reserve Bank of Minneapolis*.

Ferry, Elizabeth. 2016. "On Not Being a Sign: Gold's Semiotic Claims." *Signs and Society*, 4(1): 57–79.

Field, Michele, and Timothy Millett. 1998. *Convict Love Tokens: The Leaden Hearts the Convicts Left Behind*. Adelaide: Wakefield.

Finke, R. and Stark, R., 1988. "Religious Economies and Sacred Canopies: Religious Mobilization in American Cities, 1906." *American Sociological Review*: 41–49.

Firestone, Shulamith. 2003. *The Dialectic of Sex: The Case for Feminist Revolution*. New York: Farrar, Straus and Giroux.

Firth, Raymond. 1929. "Currency, Primitive." In *Encyclopaedia Britannica*. 14th edition, Volume 6. London: The Encyclopaedia Britannica Company: 880–881.

Fisher, Irving. 1933. *Stamp Scrip*. New York: Adelphi.

Fisher, Irving. 1935. *100% Money*. New York: Adelphi.

Fisher, Mark. 2018. "Forward." In William Davies (ed.) *Economic Science Fictions*. London: Goldsmiths Press, xi–xiv.

Flohr, Udo. 1996. "Electric Money." *Byte* (June).

Florida, Richard L. 2004. *The Rise of the Creative Class: And How It's Transforming Work, Leisure, Community and Everyday Life*. New York: Basic Books.

Florida, Richard L. 2005. *The Flight of the Creative Class: The New Global Competition for Talent*. New York: HarperBusiness.

Foley, Duncan. 2004. "Marx's Theory of Money in Historical Perspective." In Fred Moseley (ed.), *Marx's Theory of Money: Modern Appraisals*, 36–49. Basingstoke/New York: Palgrave Macmillan.

Forder, James. 2014. *Macroeconomics and the Phillips Curve Myth*. Oxford: Oxford University Press.

Forrest, Adam. 2017. "The Rise of the Cashless City." *The Guardian*, January 9. Available online: www.theguardian.com/cities/2017/jan/09/rise-cashless-city-contactless-payments-exclusion-cashfree-society.

Forstater, Matthew. 1999. "Functional Finance and Full Employment: Lessons from Lerner for Today." *Journal of Economic Issues*, 33(2): 475–482.

Fortunati, Leopoldina. 1995. *The Arcane of Reproduction: Housework, Prostitution, Labor and Capital*. New York: Autonomedia.

Foster, Gladys Parker. 1986. "The Endogeneity of Money and Keynes's General Theory." *Journal of Economic Issues*, 20(4): 953–968.

Foster, Robert J. 1998. "Your Money, Our Money, the Government's Money: Finance and Fetishism in Melanesia." In Patricia Spyer (ed.), *Border Fetishisms: Material Objects in Unstable Spaces*. London: Routledge, 60–90.

Foster, Robert J. 1999. "In God We Trust? The Legitimacy of Melanesian Currencies." In David Akins & Joel Robbins (eds.), *Money and Modernity: State and Local Currencies in Melanesia*, 214–231. Pittsburgh: University of Pittsburgh Press.

Foucault, Michel. 1978a. *Discipline and Punish: The Birth of the Prison*. Alan Sheridan (trans.). New York: Pantheon.

Foucault, Michel. 1978b. *The History of Sexuality: An Introduction*. Robert Hurley (trans.). New York: Pantheon.

Fourçade, Marion, and Kieran Healy. 2007. "Moral Views of Market Society." *Annual Review of Sociology*, 33: 285–311.

Fourçade, Marion, and Sarah L. Babb. 2002. "The Rebirth of the Liberal Creed: Paths to Neoliberalism in Four Countries." *American Journal of Sociology*, 108(3): 533–579.

Fradkin, Phillip L. 2002. *Stagecoach: Wells Fargo and the American West*. New York: Free Press.

Fraser, Andrea. 2012. "There's No Place Like Home / L'1% C'est Moi." *Continent*, 2(3): 186–201.

Fraser, Nancy. 2013. *Fortunes of Feminism: From State-Managed Capitalism to Neoliberal Crisis*. New York: Verso.

Fraser, Nancy. 2016. "Contradictions of Capital and Care." *New Left Review*, 100: 99–117.

Friedman, Milton, and Anna Jacobson Schwartz. 1963. *A Monetary History of the United States, 1867–1960*. Princeton: Princeton University Press.

Friedman, Milton. 1948. "A Monetary and Fiscal Framework for Economic Stability." *American Economic Review*, 38(3): 245–264.

Friedman, Milton. 1956. "The Quantity Theory of Money: A Restatement." In Milton Friedman (ed.), *Studies in the Quantity Theory of Money*. Chicago: University of Chicago Press.

Friedman, Milton. 1963. *Inflation: Causes and Consequences*. New York: Asia Publishing House.

Friedman, Milton. 1968. "The Role of Monetary Policy." *American Economic Review*, 58(1): 1–17.

Friedman, Milton. 1975. Transcript of televised appearance (April 14). *Monday Conference*. Sydney: Australian Broadcasting Commission.

Gabor, Daniela, and Jakob Vestergaard. 2016. "Towards a Shadow Theory of Money." INET Working Paper. Available online: www.ineteconomics.org/research/research-papers/towards-a-theory-of-shadow-money.

Gabor, Daniela, and Sally Brooks. 2017. "The Digital Revolution in Financial Inclusion: International Development in the Fintech Era." *New Political Economy*, 22(4): 423–436.
Garbade, Kenneth D. 2014. "Direct Purchases of US Treasury Securities by Federal Reserve Banks." *Liberty Street Economics* (September 29). Available online: http://libertystreeteconomics.newyorkfed.org/2014/09/direct-purchases-of-us-treasury-securities-by-federal-reserve-banks.html.
Gardiner, Geoffrey W. 2004. "The Primacy of Trade Debts in the Development of Money." In L. Randall Wray (ed.), *Credit and State Theories of Money*. Cheltenham: Edward Elgar, 128–172.
Geheimagentur. 2012. "Black Bank—Coal for All!" Available online: www.geheimagentur.net/projekte/schwarzbank-kohle-fur-alle/.
Gibson, William. 1981. *Necromancer*. New York: Ace.
Gibson, William. 2003. *Pattern Recognition*. New York: Putnam.
Gibson, William. 2007. *Spook Country*. New York: Putnam.
Gibson, William. 2010. *Zero History*. New York: Putnam.
Gibson, William. 2014. *The Peripheral*. New York: Berkeley.
Gil, Isabel Capeloa, and Helena Gonçalves da Silva (eds.). 2015. *The Cultural Life of Money*. Berlin: De Gruyter.
Gilbert, Emily, and Eric Helleiner. 1999. *Nation-States and Money: The Past, Present, and Future of National Currencies*. London: Routledge.
Gilbert, Emily. 1999. "Forging a National Currency." In Emily Gilbert and Eric Helleiner (eds.), *Nation-States and Money: The Past, Present and Future of National Currencies*. New York: Routledge.
Gilbert, Emily. 2005. "Common Cents: Situating Money in Time and Place." *Economy and Society*, 34(3): 357–388.
Giroux, Henry A. 2001. *Theory and Resistance in Education: Towards a Pedagogy of the Opposition*. 2nd edition. Westport, CT: Bergin & Garvey.
Giroux, Henry A. 2008. *Against the Terror of Neoliberalism: Politics beyond the Age of Greed*. Boulder, CO: Paradigm.
Goodhart, Charles. 1989. *Money, Information, and Uncertainty*. 2nd edition. Basingstoke: Macmillan.
Goodhart, Charles. 2007. "Whatever Became of the Monetary Aggregates?" *National Institute Economic Review*, 200: 56–61.
Goodwyn, Lawrence. 1978. *The Populist Moment: A Short History of the Agrarian Revolt in America*. Oxford: Oxford University Press.
Gordon, Robert J. 1982. "Why US Wage and Employment Behaviour Differs from that in Britain and Japan." *Economic Journal*, 92(365): 13–44.
Gordon, Robert J. 1997. "The Time-Varying NAIRU and Its Implications for Economic Policy." *Journal of Economic Perspectives*, 11(1): 11–32.
Graeber, David. 2001. *Toward an Anthropological Theory of Value: The False Coin of Our Own Dreams*. New York: Palgrave.
Graeber, David. 2011. *Debt: The First 5,000 Years*. New York: Melville House.
Graeber, David. 2017. "Tallies." In Bill Maurer and Lana Swartz (eds.), *Paid: Tales of Dongles, Checks, and Other Money Stuff*. Cambridge: MIT Press, 133–144.
Greenblatt, Stephen. 2010. *Cultural Mobility: A Manifesto*. New York: Cambridge University Press.
Gregory, C.A. 1996. "Cowries and Conquest: Towards a Subalternate Quality Theory of Money." *Comparative Studies in Society and History*, 38(2): 195–217.

Greider, William. 1987. *Secrets of the Temple: How the Federal Reserve Runs the Country*. New York: Simon & Schuster.

Grierson, Philip. 1977. *The Origins of Money*. London: Athlone.

Grossman, Peter Z. 1987. *American Express: The Unofficial History of the People Who Built the Great Financial Empire*. New York: Crown.

Grubb, Farley. 2017. "Colonial Virginia's Paper Money Regime, 1755–74: A Forensic Accounting Reconstruction of the Data." *Historical Methods*, 50(2): 96–112.

Grutzner, Charles. 1956. "Living High Without Money: All the Traveler Needs Is a Thing Called the Credit Card." *New York Times* (December 2).

Guérin, Isabelle, Youna Lanos, Sébastien Michiels, Christophe Jalil Nordman, and Govindan Venkatasubramanian. 2017. "Insights on Demonetisation from Rural Tamil Nadu." *Economic & Political Weekly*, 52(52): 44–53.

Guyer, Jane I. (ed.) 1995. *Money Matters: Instability, Values, and Social Payments in the Modern History of West African Communities*. Portsmouth: Heinemann/James Currey.

Guyer, Jane I. 2004. *Marginal Gains: Monetary Transactions in Atlantic Africa*. Chicago: University of Chicago Press.

Guyer, Jane I. 2011. "Soft Currencies, Cash Economies, New Monies: Past and Present." *PNAS*, 109(7): 2214–2221.

Haacke, Hans. 2009. "Lessons Learned." *Tate Papers* 12. Available online: www.tate.org.uk/download/file/fid/7265.

Haacke, Hans. 2016. *Working Conditions: The Writings of Hans Haacke*. Alexander Alberro (ed.). Cambridge: MIT Press.

Haider, Asad, and Salar Mohandesi (eds.). 2015. "Social Reproduction." *Viewpoint 5*. Available online: https://viewpointmag.com/2015/11/02/issue-5-social-reproduction/.

Haiven, Max, and Alex Khasnabish. 2014. *The Radical Imagination: Social Movement Research in the Age of Austerity*. London: Zed.

Haiven, Max. 2011. "Finance as Capital's Imagination?: Reimagining Value and Culture in an Age of Fictitious Capital and Crisis." *Social Text*, 29(3): 93–124.

Haiven, Max. 2014. *Cultures of Financialization: Fictitious Capital in Popular Culture and Everyday Life*. New York: Palgrave Macmillan.

Haiven, Max. 2015a. "Art and Money: Three Aesthetic Strategies in an Age of Financialisation." *Finance and Society*, 1(1): 38–60.

Haiven, Max. 2015b. "Money as a Medium of the Imagination: Art and the Currencies of Cooperation." In Geert Lovink, Nathaniel Tkacz, and Patricia De Vries (eds.), *MoneyLab Reader: An Intervention in Digital Economy*. Amsterdam: Institute for Network Cultures, 173–188. Available online: http://networkcultures.org/blog/publication/moneylab-reader-an-intervention-in-digital-economy/.

Hall, Stuart, Doreen Massey, and Michael Rustin (eds.). 2015. *After Neoliberalism? The Kilburn Manifesto*. London: Lawrence and Wishart. Available online: www.lwbooks.co.uk/journals/soundings/manifesto.html.

Hall, Stuart. 1996a. "Cultural Studies and Its Theoretical Legacies." In David Morely and Kuan-Hsing Chen (eds.), *Stuart Hall: Critical Dialogues in Cultural Studies*. New York: Routledge, 262–275.

Hall, Stuart. 1996b. "The Problem of Ideology: Marxism without Guarantees." In David Morely and Kuan-Hsing Chen (eds.), *Stuart Hall: Critical Dialogues in Cultural Studies*. New York: Routledge, 25–46.

Halpern-Meekin, Sarah, Kathryn Edin, Laura Tach, and Jennifer Sykes. 2015. *It's Not Like I'm Poor: How Working Families Make Ends Meet in a Post-Welfare World*. Berkeley: University of California Press.

Han, Clara. 2012. *Life in Debt: Times of Care and Violence in Neoliberal Chile*. Berkeley: University of California Press.
Hancock, Keith. 1966. "Earnings Drift in Australia." *Journal of Industrial Relations*, 8(2): 128–157.
Handman, C., 2015. *Critical Christianity: Translation and Denominational Conflict in Papua New Guinea*. Berkeley: University of California Press.
Hansen, Bue Rübner. 2015. "Surplus Population, Social Reproduction, and the Problem of Class Formation." *Viewpoint* 5. Available online: https://viewpointmag.com/2015/10/31/surplus-population-social-reproduction-and-the-problem-of-class-formation/.
Hardt, Michael, and Antonio Negri. 2000. *Empire*. Cambridge: Harvard University Press.
Hart, Keith. 1986. "Heads or Tails? Two Sides of the Same Coin." *Man* (N.S.), 21(4): 637–656.
Hart, Keith. 2009. "Money in the Making of World Society." In Chris Hann and Keith Hart (eds.), *Market and Society: The Great Transformation Today*. Cambridge: Cambridge University Press, 91–105.
Harvey, David. 2006. *The Limits to Capital*. 2nd edition. New York: Verso.
Harvey, David. 1990. *The Condition of Postmodernity*. Oxford: Blackwell.
Harvey, David. 2003. *The New Imperialism*. Oxford: Oxford University Press.
Harvey, David. 2005. *A Brief History of Neoliberalism*. Oxford: Oxford University Press.
Harvie, Jen. 2013. *Fair Play: Art, Performance and Neoliberalism*. Basingstoke: Palgrave Macmillan.
Haynes, N., 2017. *Moving by the Spirit: Pentecostal Social Life on the Zambian Copperbelt*. Berkeley: University of California Press.
Hedenus, Anna. 2014. "Pennies from Heaven? Conceptions and Earmarking of Lottery Prize Money." *British Journal of Sociology*, 65(2): 225–244.
Helleiner, Eric. 1998. "National Currencies and National Identities." *American Behavioral Scientist*, 41(10): 1409–1436.
Helleiner, Eric. 2002. *The Making of National Money: Territorial Currencies in Historical Perspective*. Ithaca: Cornell University Press.
Henkin, David. 1998. *City Reading: Written Words and Public Spaces in Antebellum New York*. New York: Columbia University Press.
Henley, Jon. 2016. "Sweden Leads the Race to Become Cashless Society." *The Guardian*, June 4. Available online: www.theguardian.com/business/2016/jun/04/sweden-cashless-society-cards-phone-apps-leading-europe.
Hernandez, Ester, and Coutin Susan Bibler. 2006. "Remitting Subjects: Migrants, Money, and States." *Economy and Society*, 35(2): 185–208.
Heslop, Luke. 2016. "Catching the Pulse: Money and Circulation in a Sri Lankan Marketplace." *Journal of the Royal Anthropological Institute*, 22(3): 534–551.
High, Mette. 2013. "Polluted Money, Polluted Wealth: Emerging Regimes of Value in a Mongolian Gold Rush." *American Ethnologist*, 40(4): 676–688.
Hines, Tom M. and Terence T. Velk. 2009. "The United States Post Office Domestic Postal Money Order System in the 19th Century: A Nascent Banking System." Departmental Working Papers from McGill University, Department of Economics.
Ho, Karen. 2009. *Liquidated: An Ethnography of Wall Street*. Durham: Duke University Press.
Hoang, Kimberly Kay. 2015. *Dealing in Desire: Asian Ascendancy, Western Decline, and the Hidden Currencies of Global Sex Work*. Berkeley: University of California Press.

Hochschild, Arlie Russell. 2003. *The Commercialization of Intimate Life: Notes from Home and Work*. Berkeley: University of California Press.
Hoggart, Richard. 1998. *The Uses of Literacy*. New Brunswick: Transaction.
Holmes, Brian. 2002. "The Flexible Personality." *EIPCP*. Available online: http://eipcp.net/transversal/1106/holmes/en/base_edit.
Holmes, Brian. 2012. "Eventwork: The Fourfold Matrix of Contemporary Social Movements." In *Living As Form: Socially Engaged Art from 1991–2011*. Cambridge: MIT Press, 72–85.
Holmes, Douglas. 2013. *Economy of Words: Communicative Imperatives in Central Banks*. Chicago: University of Chicago Press.
Horowitz, Noah. 2011. *Art of the Deal: Contemporary Art in a Global Financial Market*. Princeton: Princeton University Press.
Humphrey, Caroline. 2002. *The Unmaking of Soviet Life: Everyday Economies after Socialism*. Ithaca: Cornell University Press.
Hutchinson, Sharon. 1992. "The Cattle of Money and the Cattle of Girls Among the Nuer, 1930–83." *American Ethnologist*, 19(2): 294–316.
Hymans, Jacques. 2004. "The Changing Color of Money: European Currency Iconography and Collective Identity." *European Journal of International Relations*, 10(1): 5–31.
Hymans, Jacques. 2010. "East Is East, and West Is West? Currency Iconography as Nation-Branding in the Wider Europe." *Political Geography*, 29(2): 97–108.
Ingham, Geoffrey. 2000. "'Babylonian Madness': On the Historical and Sociological Origins of Money." In John Smithin (ed.), *What is Money?* New York: Routledge, 16–41.
Ingham, Geoffrey. 2002. "New Monetary Spaces?" In *The Future of Money*. Paris: Organisation for Economic Co-operation and Development, 123–145. Available online: www.oecd.org/futures/35391062.pdf.
Ingham, Geoffrey. 2004a. "The Emergence of Capitalist Credit Money." In L. Randall Wray (ed.), *Credit and State Theories of Money*. Cheltenham: Edward Elgar, 173–222.
Ingham, Geoffrey. 2004b. *The Nature of Money*. Cambridge: Polity.
Innes, A. Mitchell. 1913. "What Is Money?" *Banking Law Journal*, 30(5): 377–408.
Innes, A. Mitchell. 1914. "The Credit Theory of Money." *Banking Law Journal* 31(2): 151–168.
Itoh, Makoto, and Costas Lapavitsas. 1999. *Political Economy of Money and Finance*. Basingstoke: Palgrave Macmillan.
Jackson, Eric M. 2004. *The PayPal Wars: Battles with eBay, the Media, the Mafia, and the Rest of Planet Earth*. New York: WND.
Jalsovec, By Andreas. 2012. "Oberhausen bezahlt mit einer Regionalwährung: Kohle von der Schwarzbank." *Süddeutsche Zeitung* (March 20). Available online: www.sueddeutsche.de/wirtschaft/oberhausen-bezahlt-mit-einer-regionalwaehrung-kohle-von-der-schwarzbank-1.1313925.
James, Deborah. 2015. *Money from Nothing: Indebtedness and Aspiration in South Africa*. Stanford: Stanford University Press.
James, Selma, and Mariarosa Dalla Costa. 1979. *The Power of Women and the Subversion of Community*. Bristol: Falling Wall.
James, Selma. 2012. *Sex, Race, and Class: The Perspective of Winning*. Oakland: PM Press.
Jameson, Fredric. 1981. *The Political Unconscious*. Ithaca: Cornell University Press.
Jameson, Fredric. 1991. *Postmodernism, or the Cultural Logic of Late Capitalism*. Durham: Duke University Press.

Jayo, Martin, Marlei Pozzebon, and Eduardo Diniz. 2009. "Microcredit and Innovative Local Development in Fortaleza, Brazil: The Case of Banco Palmas." *Canadian Journal of Regional Science* 32(1): 115–128.

Jevons, William Stanley. 1898. *Money and the Mechanism of Exchange*. New York: D. Appleton.

Jobst, Clemens, and Helmut Stix. 2017. "Is Cash Back? Assessing the Recent Increase in Cash Demand." *SUERF Policy Note*, 19 (October): 1–12. Available online: www.suerf.org/docx/f_fc528592c3858f90196fbfacc814f235_1623_suerf.pdf.

John, Richard. 1998. *Spreading the News: The American Postal System from Franklin to Morse*. Cambridge: Harvard University Press.

Judson, Ruth. 2017. "The Death of Cash? Not So Fast: Demand for US Currency at Home and Abroad, 1990–2016." Presentation at the International Cash Conference. Available online: https://econpapers.repec.org/paper/zbwiccp17/162910.htm.

Kalecki, Michał. 1943. "Political Aspects of Full Employment." *Political Quarterly*, 14(4): 322–330.

Karim, Lamia. 2011. *Microfinance and Its Discontents: Women in Debt in Bangladesh*. Minneapolis: University of Minnesota Press.

Katsarova, Rada. 2015. "Repression and Resistance on the Terrain of Social Reproduction: Historical Trajectories, Contemporary Openings." *Viewpoint 5*. Available online: https://viewpointmag.com/2015/10/31/repression-and-resistance-on-the-terrain-of-social-reproduction-historical-trajectories-contemporary-openings/.

Katsiaficas, George. 1987. *The Imagination of the New Left: A Global Analysis of 1968*. Boston: South End Press.

Katsiaficas, George. 2006. *The Subversion of Politics: European Autonomous Social Movements and the Decolonization of Everyday Life*. Oakland: AK Press, 2006.

Keane, W., 2007. *Christian Moderns: Freedom and Fetish in the Mission Encounter*. Oakland: University of California Press.

Keane, Webb. 2001. "Money is No Object: Materiality, Desire, and Modernity in an Indonesian Society." In Fred Myers (ed.), *The Empire of Things: Regimes of Value and Material Culture*. Santa Fe: SAR Press: 65–90.

Kear, Mark. 2016. "Peer Lending and the Subsumption of the Informal." *Journal of Cultural Economy*, 9(3): 261–276.

Kelton, Stephanie A., and L. Randall Wray. 2009. "Can Euroland Survive?" Levy Economics Institute Public Policy Brief No. 106. Available online: www.levyinstitute.org/publications/can-euroland-survive.

Kenny, Erin. 2016. "'Phones Mean Lies': Secrets, Sexuality, and the Subjectivity of Mobile Phones in Tanzania." *Economic Anthropology*, 3(2): 254–265.

Keynes, J.M. [1930] 1976. *A Treatise on Money*. Volumes I and II. New York: Harcourt, Brace & Company.

Keynes, J.M. [1936] 1962. *The General Theory of Employment, Interest and Money*. New York: Harcourt, Brace & World.

Keynes, J.M. [1943] 1969. "Proposals for an International Clearing Union." In K. Horsefield (ed.), *The International Monetary Fund, 1945–65: Twenty Years of International Monetary Cooperation*. Washington, DC: International Monetary Fund: 19–36.

Keynes, J.M. 1914. "*What is Money?* By A. Mitchell Innes." *The Economic Journal* 24(95): 419–421.

Keynes, J.M. 1919. *The Economic Consequences of the Peace*. London: Macmillan.
Keynes, J.M. 1923. *A Tract on Monetary Reform*. London: Macmillan.
Keynes, John Maynard. 1930. *A Treatise on Money*. Vol. 1. London: Macmillan & Co.
Kim, Jennifer. 2018. "Payments and Intimate Ties in Transnationally Brokered Marriages." *Socio-Economic Review*. Available online: https://doi.org/10.1093/ser/mwx061.
Kindleberger, Charles P. 1984. *A Financial History of Western Europe*. London: Allen & Unwin.
King, Mervyn A. 2002. "No Money, No Inflation—The Role of Money in the Economy." *Bank of England Quarterly Bulletin*, Summer: 162–177.
Klebaner, Benjamin J. 1974. *Commercial Banking in the United States: A History*. Hinsdale, IL: Dryden Press.
Klein, Naomi. *The Shock Doctrine: The Rise and Fall of Disaster Capitalism*. Toronto: Knopf, 2007.
Klima, Alan. 2006. "Spirits of 'Dark Finance' in Thailand: A Local Hazard for the International Moral Fund." *Cultural Dynamics*, 18(1): 33–60.
Knafo, Samuel. 2006. "The Gold Standard and the Origins of the Modern International Monetary System." *Review of International Political Economy*, 13(1): 78–102.
Knafo, Samuel. 2013. *The Making of Modern Finance: Liberal Governance and the Gold Standard*. New York: Routledge.
Knapp, G.F. [1924] 1973. *The State Theory of Money*. Clifton, NY: Augustus M. Kelley.
Koch, Alexander (ed.). 2011. *General Strike*. Berlin: KOW.
Koddenbrock, Kai. 2019. "Money and Moneyness: Thoughts of the Nature and Distributional Power of Capitalist Political ??? of cultural economy. doi.org/10.1080/17530350.2018.15456??.
Koning, J.P. 2013. "Line in the Sand." *Moneyness*, March 5. Available online: http://jpkoning.blogspot.com/2013/03/line-in-sand.html.
Koning, J.P. 2014. "To Recapitulate. . . ." *Moneyness*, Thursday, July 3. Available online: http://jpkoning.blogspot.com/2014/07/to-recapitulate.html.
Kremers, Ruben, and James Brassett. 2017. "Mobile Payments, Social Money: Everyday Politics of the Consumer Subject." *New Political Economy*, 22(6): 645–660.
Krippner, Greta R. 2005. "The Financialization of the American Economy." *Socio-Economic Review*, 3(2): 173–208.
Krippner, Greta R. 2011. *Capitalizing on Crisis: The Political Origins of the Rise of Finance*. Cambridge: Harvard University Press.
Krugman, Paul. 2012. "Asimov's Foundation Novels Grounded My Economics." *The Guardian*, December 4. Available online: www.theguardian.com/books/2012/dec/04/paul-krugman-asimov-economics.
Kumhof, Michael. 2013. "Financial Reform for a Sustainable Economy, Part 2." Presentation to Global Utmaning. Available online: www.youtube.com/watch?v=YnAtHbDptj8.
Kuroda, Akinobu. 2008a. "Concurrent but Non-Integrable Currency Circuits: Complementary Relationships Among Monies in Modern China and Other Regions." *Financial History Review*, 15(1): 17–36.
Kuroda, Akinobu. 2008b. "What Is the Complementarity Among Monies? An Introductory Note." *Financial History Review*, 15(1): 7–15.
Kusimba, Sibel, Yang Yang, and Nitesh Chawla. 2015. "Family Networks of Mobile Money in Kenya." *Information Technologies and International Development*, 11(3): 1–21.

Kusimba, Sibel, Yang Yang, and Nitesh Chawla. 2016. "Hearthholds of Mobile Money in Western Kenya." *Economic Anthropology*, 3(2): 266–279.

Kwon, Heonik. 2007. "The Dollarization of Vietnamese Ghost Money." *Journal of the Royal Anthropological Institute*, 13(1): 73–90.

La Berge, Leigh Claire. 2015. *Scandals and Abstraction: Financial Fiction of the Long 1980s*. Oxford: Oxford University Press.

La Berge, Leigh Claire. 2018. Decommodified Labor: Conceptualizing Work After the Wage. *Lateral* 7(1). Available online: http://csalateral.org/issue/7-1/decommodified-labor-work-after-wage-la-berge/.

Laidler, David. 1969. "The Definition of Money: Theoretical and Empirical Problems." *Journal of Money, Credit and Banking*, 1(3): 508–525.

Laidler, David. 1991. *The Golden Age of the Quantity Theory*. Hertfordshire: Harvester Wheatsheaf.

Laidler, David. 2003. "Monetary Policy without Money: Hamlet without the Ghost." Western University Department of Economics Research Report 2003–7. Available online: https://ir.lib.uwo.ca/cgi/viewcontent.cgi?referer=www.google.com/&httpsredir=1&article=1226&context=economicsresrpt.

Langley, Paul. 2008. *The Everyday Life of Global Finance: Saving and Borrowing in Anglo-America*. Oxford: Oxford University Press.

Lapavitsas, Costas. 2013. *Profiting Without Producing: How Finance Exploits Us All*. New York: Verso.

Larsen, Lotta Björklund. 2017. *Shaping Taxpayers: Values in Action at the Swedish Tax Agency*. New York: Berghahn.

Lauer, Josh. 2008. "Money as Mass Communication: US Paper Currency and the Iconography of Nationalism." *The Communication Review*, 11(2): 109–132.

Lave, Jean. 1993. "The Practice of Learning." In Seth Chaiklin and Jean Lave (eds.), *Understanding Practice: Perspectives on Activity and Context*. Cambridge: Cambridge University Press, 3–32.

Lavoie, Marc. 1984. "The Endogenous Flow of Credit and the Post Keynesian Theory of Money." *Journal of Economic Issues*, 18(3): 771–797.

Lazzarato, Maurizio. 2012. *The Making of the Indebted Man*. Cambridge: MIT Press.

Lee, Benjamin, and Randy Martin. 2016. *Derivatives and the Wealth of Societies*. Chicago: University of Chicago Press.

Léger, Marc James. 2012. *Brave New Avant Garde: Essays on Contemporary Art and Politics*. Alresford: Zero.

Lehrer-Graiwer, Sarah. 2014. *Lee Lozano: Dropout Piece*. London: Afterall.

Lemon, Alaina. 1998. "'Your Eyes Are Green like Dollars': Counterfeit Cash, National Substance, and Currency Apartheid in 1990s Russia." *Cultural Anthropology*, 13(1): 22–55.

Lenin, Vladimir I. [1917] 1948. *Imperialism, the Highest Stage of Capitalism: A Popular Outline*. London: Lawrence and Wishart.

Lepecq, Guillaume. 2016. *Cash Essentials: Beyond Payments*. Available online: www.cashessentials.org/docs/default-source/booklet/cashessentials-beyond-payments.pdf.

Levitt, Peggy. 2001. *The Transnational Villagers*. Berkeley: University of California Press.

Lewis, Michael. 2012. *The Big Short: Inside the Doomsday Machine*. New York: W.W. Norton.

Lindhardt, M., 2009. "More Than Just Money: The Faith Gospel and Occult Economies in Contemporary Tanzania." *Nova Religio: The Journal of Alternative and Emergent Religions*, 13(1): 41–67.

Lippard, Lucy. 1973. *Six Years: The Dematerialization of the Art Object from 1966 to 1972*. Berkeley: University of California Press.

LiPuma, Edward, and Benjamin Lee. 2004. *Financial Derivatives and the Globalization of Risk*. Durham: Duke University Press.

Lowrie, I. 2017. "What Sort of Thing is the Social? Or, Durkheim and Deleuze on Organization and Infrastructure." In S. Ellenzweig and J.H. Zammito (eds.), *The New Politics of Materialism: History, Philosophy, Science*, 154–177. London: Routledge.

Luxemburg, Rosa. 2003. *The Accumulation of Capital*. Agnes Schwarzschild (trans.). New York: Routledge.

Luxton, Meg, and Kate Bezanson (eds.). 2006. *Social Reproduction: Feminist Political Economy Challenges Neo-Liberalism*. Montreal: McGill-Queen's University Press.

Luzzi, Mariana. 2010. "Las Monedas de la Crisis: Pluralidad Monetaria en la Argentina de 2001." *Revista de Ciencias Sociales de la Universidad Nacional de Quilmes*, Segunda Época, 17: 205–221.

MacKenzie, Donald. 2006. *An Engine, Not a Camera: How Financial Models Shape Markets*. Cambridge: MIT Press.

Malik, Suhail, and Andrea Phillips. 2012. "Tainted Love: Art's Ethos and Capitalization." In Maria Lind and Olav Velthius (eds.), *Contemporary Art and Its Commercial Markets: A Report on Current Conditions and Future Scenarios*. Berlin: Sternberg, 209–240.

Mann, Ronald J. 2006. *Charging Ahead*. Cambridge: Cambridge University Press.

Marcuse, Herbert. 1978. *The Aesthetic Dimension: Towards a Critique of Marxist Aesthetics*. Boston: Beacon.

Marsh, Nicky. 2008. *Money, Speculation and Finance in Contemporary British Fiction*. London: Continuum.

Marsh, Nicky. 2014. "Debt and Credit." In Paul Crosthwaite, Peter Knight and Nicky Marsh (eds.). *Show Me the Money: The Image of Finance, 1700 to the Present*, 7–31. Manchester: Manchester University Press.

Martin, Emily. [1986] 2015. *The Meaning of Money in China and the United States*. Chicago: HAU.

Martin, Felix. 2015. *Money: The Unauthorized Biography—From Coinage to Cryptocurrencies*. New York: Vintage.

Martin, Isaac William. 2008. *The Permanent Tax Revolt: How the Property Tax Transformed American Politics*. Stanford: Stanford University Press.

Martin, Randy. 2002. *Financialization of Daily Life*. Philadelphia: Temple University Press.

Martin, Randy. 2007. *An Empire of Indifference: American War and the Financial Logic of Risk Management*. Durham: Duke University Press.

Martin, Randy. 2015a. *Knowledge LTD: Towards a Social Logic of the Derivative*. Philadelphia: Temple University Press.

Martin, Randy. 2015b. "Money after Decolonization." *South Atlantic Quarterly*, 114(2): 377–393.

Marx, K. and Engels, F., 2002. *The Communist Manifesto*. New York: Penguin.

Marx, Karl. [1867] 1992. *Capital, Volume I*. Ben Fowkes (trans.). New York: Penguin.

Marx, Karl. [1894] 1981. *Capital, Volume III*. David Fernbach (trans.). London: Penguin.

Marx, Karl. 1895. *The Class Struggles in France*. London: Martin Lawrence.

Massengill, Reed. 1999. *Becoming American Express: 150 Years of Reinvention and Customer Service*. New York: American Express Company.

Massey, Doreen. 1991. "A Global Sense of Place." *Marxism Today*, 38.

Matthews, Dylan. 2012. "Modern Monetary Theory Is an Unconventional Take on Economic Strategy." *The Washington Post*, February 18. Available online: www.washingtonpost.com/business/modern-monetary-theory-is-an-unconventional-take-on-economic-strategy/2012/02/15/gIQAR8uPMR_story.html.

Maurer, B., 2005. *Mutual Life, Limited: Islamic Banking, Alternative Currencies, Lateral Reason*. Princeton: Princeton University Press.

Maurer, Bill, and Lana Swartz (eds.). 2017. *Paid: Tales of Dongles, Checks, and Other Money Stuff*. Cambridge: MIT Press.

Maurer, Bill, Smoki Musaraj, and Ivan Small (eds.). 2018. *Money at the Margins: Global Perspectives on Technology, Financial Inclusion, and Design*. New York: Berghahn.

Maurer, Bill, Taylor C. Nelms and Lana Swartz. 2013. "'When Perhaps the Real Problem is Money Itself!' The Practical Materiality of Bitcoin." *Social Semiotics*, 23(2): 261–277.

Maurer, Bill, Taylor C. Nelms, and Stephen C. Rea. 2013. "'Bridges to Cash': Channelling Agency in Mobile Money." *Journal of the Royal Anthropological Institute*, 19(1): 52–74.

Maurer, Bill. 2006. "The Anthropology of Money." *Annual Review of Anthropology*, 35: 15–36.

Maurer, Bill. 2012. "Mobile Money: Communication, Consumption and Change in the Payments Space." *Journal of Development Studies*, 48(3): 1–16.

Maurer, Bill. 2012. "Payment: Forms and Functions of Value Transfer in Contemporary Society." *Cambridge Anthropology*, 30(2): 15–35.

Maurer, Bill. 2015. *How Would You Like to Pay? How Technology Is Changing the Future of Money*. Durham: Duke University Press.

May, Tim. 1992. "The Crypto Anarchist Manifesto." Available online: https://archive.org/details/TheCryptoAnarchistManifesto.

May, Tim. 1996. "Untraceable Digital Cash, Information Markets, and BlackNet." Available online: http://osaka.law.miami.edu/~froomkin/articles/tcmay.htm.

McCullagh, Declan. 2001. "Digging Those DigiCash Blues." *Wired* (June 14).

McKee, Yates. 2016. *Strike Art: Contemporary Art and the Post-Occupy Condition*. London/New York: Verso.

McKinnon, Ronald I. 1993. "The Rules of the Game: International Money in Historical Perspective." *Journal of Economic Literature*, 31(1): 1–44.

McLeay, Michael, Amar Radia, and Ryland Thomas. 2014. "Money Creation in the Modern Economy." *Bank of England Quarterly Bulletin*, Q1: 14–27. Available online: www.bankofengland.co.uk/quarterly-bulletin/2014/q1/money-creation-in-the-modern-economy.

McRobbie, Angela. 2001. "'Everyone is Creative': Artists as New Economy Pioneers?" *OpenDemocracy* (August 19). Available online: www.opendemocracy.net/node/652.

McRobbie, Angela. 2005. *The Uses of Cultural Studies*. London: Sage.

McRobbie, Angela. 2015. *Be Creative: Making a Living in the New Culture Industries*. Cambridge: Polity.

Meade, J.E. 1951. *The Theory of International Economic Policy*. London: Oxford University Press.

Mehrling, Perry. 2011 *The New Lombard Street: How the Fed Became the Dealer of Last Resort*. Princeton: Princeton University Press.

Mehrling, Perry. 2013. "The Inherent Hierarchy of Money." In Lance Taylor, Armon Rezai, and Thomas R. Michl (eds.), *Social Fairness and Economics: Economic Essays in the Spirit of Duncan Foley*. Milton Park: Routledge, 394–404.

Meister, Robert. 2016. "Liquidity." In Benjamin Lee and Randy Martin (eds.), *Derivatives and the Wealth of Society*. Chicago: University of Chicago Press: 143–173.

Melitz, Jacques. 1970. "The Polanyi School of Anthropology on Money: An Economist's View." *American Anthropologist*, 72(5): 1020–1040.

Meltzer, Eve. 2013. *Systems We Have Loved: Conceptual Art, Affect, and the Antihumanist Turn*. Chicago: University of Chicago Press.

Meyer, B., 1998. "'Make a Complete Break with the Past.' Memory and Post-colonial Modernity in Ghanaian Pentecostalist Discourse." *Journal of Religion in Africa*, 28 (Fasc. 3): 316–349.

Meyer, B., 1999. *Translating the Devil: Religion and Modernity among the Ewe in Ghana* (Vol. 21). Edinburgh: Edinburgh University Press.

Meyer, B., 2010. "Aesthetics of Persuasion: Global Christianity and Pentecostalism's Sensational Forms." *South Atlantic Quarterly*, 109(4): 741–763.

Mies, Maria. 1986. *Patriarchy and Accumulation on a World Scale: Women in the International Division of Labour*. London: Zed.

Mihm, Stephen. 2007. *A Nation of Counterfeiters: Capitalists, Con Men, and the Making of the United States*. Cambridge: Harvard University Press.

Minsky, Hyman P. 1957. "Central Banking and Money Market Changes." *Quarterly Journal of Economics*, 71(2): 171–187.

Minsky, Hyman P. 1986. *Stabilizing an Unstable Economy*. New Haven: Yale University Press.

Moggridge, D.E. 1989. "The Gold Standard and National Financial Policies, 1919–39." In Peter Mathias and Sidney Pollard (eds.), *The Cambridge Economic History of Europe from the Decline of the Roman Empire*. Vol. 8. Cambridge: Cambridge University Press, 250–314.

Molesworth, Helen. 2002. "Tune In, Turn On, Drop Out: The Rejection of Lee Lozano." *Art Journal*, 61(4): 64–71.

Moore, Basil. 1988. *Horizontalists and Verticalists: The Macroeconomics of Credit Money*. Cambridge: Cambridge University Press.

Morawczynski, Olga. 2009. "Exploring the Usage and Impact of 'Transformational' Mobile Financial Services: The Case of M-PESA in Kenya." *Journal of Eastern African Studies*, 3(3): 509–525.

Morduch, Jonathan, and Rachel Schneider. 2017. *The Financial Diaries: How American Families Cope in a World of Uncertainty*. Princeton: Princeton University Press.

Mosler, Warren. 2009. "Proposals for the Treasury, the Federal Reserve, the FDIC, and the Banking System." Available online: http://moslereconomics.com/wp-content/pdfs/Proposals.pdf.

Muir, Sarah. 2015. "The Currency of Failure: Money and Middle-Class Critique in Post-Crisis Buenos Aires." *Cultural Anthropology*, 30(2): 310–335.

Nardi, Bonnie and Yong Ming Kow. 2010. "Digital Imaginaries: How we Know what we (Think we) Know about Chinese Gold Farming." *First Monday* 15.6/7 (June 7, 2010). Available online

Neiburg, Federico. 2010. "Sick Currencies and Public Numbers." *Anthropological Theory*, 10(1–2): 96–102.

Neiburg, Federico. 2016. "A True Coin of Their Dreams: Imaginary Monies in Haiti." *Hau*, 6(1): 75–93.

Nelms, Taylor C., and Bill Maurer. 2014. "Materiality, Symbol, and Complexity in the Anthropology of Money." In Erik Bijleved and Henk Aarts (eds.), *The Psychological Science of Money*. New York: Springer, 37–70.

Nelms, Taylor C., Bill Maurer, Lana Swartz, and Scott Mainwaring. 2017. "Social Payments: Innovation, Trust, Bitcoin, and the Sharing Economy." *Theory, Culture & Society*, 35(3): 13–33.

Nelson, Anita. 1999. *Marx's Concept of Money: The God of Commodities*. New York: Routledge.

Nersisyan, Yeva, and Flavia Dantas. 2017. "Rethinking Liquidity Creation: Banks, Shadow Banks, and the Elasticity of Finance." *Journal of Post Keynesian Economics*, 40(3): 279–299.

Nersisyan, Yeva, and L. Randall Wray. 2016. "Modern Money Theory and the Facts of Experience." *Cambridge Journal of Economics*, 40(5): 1297–1316.

Nersisyan, Yeva, and L. Randall Wray. 2017. "Cranks and Heretics: The Importance of an Analytical Framework." *Cambridge Journal of Economics* 41(6): 1749–1760.

Nersisyan, Yeva. 2013. "Multifunctional Banking and Financial Fragility: What Should Banks Do?" Ph.D. dissertation, University of Missouri-Kansas City.

Newlyn, W.T. 1960. "The Radcliffe Report: A Socratic Scrutiny." *Banker's Magazine*, 189: 21–26.

Nocera, Joe. 2013. *A Piece of the Action: How the Middle Class Joined the Money Class*. New York: Simon and Schuster.

North, Peter. 2006. *Money and Liberation: The Micropolitics of Alternative Currency Movements*. Minneapolis: University of Minnesota Press.

Nove, Alec. 1976. *An Economic History of the USSR*. Revised edition. Harmondsworth: Penguin.

Nyquist, Curtis. 1995. A Spectrum Theory of Negotiability. *Marquette Law Review*, 78(4): 899–971.

O'Brien, Shaun. 2017. "Understanding Consumer Cash Use: Preliminary Findings from the 2016 Diary of Consumer Payment Choice." Federal Reserve Bank of San Francisco, November 28. Available online: www.frbsf.org/cash/publications/fed-notes/2017/november/understanding-consumer-cash-use-preliminary-findings-2016-diary-of-consumer-payment-choice/.

O'Dwyer, Rachel. 2018. "Cache Society: Transactional Records, Electronic Money, and Cultural Resistance," *Journal of Cultural Economy*, doi.org/10.1080/17530350.2018.1545243.

O'Rourke, Frank. 2015. *Instant Gold*. Amazon Digital: Mundania Press.

Opitz, Alfred. 2015. "The Magic Triangle: Considerations on Art, Money and S***." In Isabel Capeloa Gil and Helena Gonçalves da Silva (eds.), *The Cultural Life of Money*. Berlin: De Gruyter, 107–118.

Osborne, Peter (ed.). 2002. *Conceptual Art*. London: Phaidon.

Ould-Ahmed, Pepita. 2010. "Can a Community Currency Be Independent of the State Currency? A Case Study of the *Credito* in Argentina (1995–2008)." *Environment and Planning A*, 42(6): 1346–1364.

Ozman, A., 1909. "Where the Latter Rain First Fell: The First One to Speak in Tongues." *The Latter Rain Evangel*, 1(4):2.

Paerregaard, Karsten. 2014. *Return to Sender: The Moral Economy of Peru's Migrant Remittances*. Washington, DC: Woodrow Wilson Center Press.

Panich, Leo, and Sam Gindin. 2012. *The Making of Global Capitalism: The Political Economy of the American Empire*. New York: Verso.

Papadimitriou, Dimitri B., L. Randall Wray, and Yeva Nersisyan. 2010. "Endgame for the Euro." Levy Economics Institute Public Policy Brief No. 113. Available online: www.levyinstitute.org/publications/endgame-for-the-euro.

Papadopoulos, Georgios. 2015. "Currency and the Collective Representations of Authority, Nationality, and Value." *Journal of Cultural Economy*, 8(4): 521–534.

Parry, Jonathan, and Maurice Bloch (eds.). 1989. *Money and the Morality of Exchange*. Cambridge: Cambridge University Press.

Pasquale, Frank. 2015. *The Black Box Society: The Secret Algorithms That Control Money and Information*. Cambridge: Harvard University Press.

Pedersen, David. 2002. "The Storm We Call Dollars: Determining Value and Belief in El Salvador and the United States." *Cultural Anthropology*, 17(3): 431–459.

Pedersen, David. 2013. *American Value: Migrants, Money, and Meaning in El Salvador and the United States*. Chicago: University of Chicago Press.

Peebles, Gustav. 2011. *The Euro and Its Rivals: Currency and the Construction of a Transnational City*. Bloomington: Indiana University Press.

Peebles, Gustav. 2012. "Filth and Lucre: The Dirty Money Complex as a Taxation Regime." *Anthropological Quarterly*, 85(4): 1229–1256.

Perry, J. 1986. "Gift, the Indian Gift, and the 'Indian Gift.'" *Man* (new series), 21(3): 453–473.

Perry, J. and M. Bloch. 1989. "Introduction: Money and the Morality of Exchange." In Parry, J., and Maurice Bloch (eds.), *Money and the Morality of Exchange*. New York: Cambridge University Press.

Phillips, A.W. 1958. "The Relation between Unemployment and the Rate of Change of Money Wage Rates in the United Kingdom, 1861–1957." *Economica*, 25(100): 283–299.

Pickles, Anthony J. 2013. "Pocket Calculator: A Humdrum 'Obviator' in Papua New Guinea?" *Journal of the Royal Anthropological Institute*, 19(3): 510–526.

Pickles, Anthony. 2016. "Gambling." In *The Cambridge Encyclopedia of Anthropology*. Available online: http://doi.org/10.29164/16gambling.

Piketty, Thomas. 2014. *Capital in the Twenty-First Century*. Arthur Goldhammer (trans.). Cambridge: Harvard University Press.

Pine, Frances T. 2002. "Dealing with Money: Zlotys, Dollars and Other Currencies in the Polish Highlands." In Ruth Mandel and Caroline Humphrey (eds.), *Markets and Moralities: Ethnographies of Postsocialism*. Oxford: Berg: 77–97.

Pitluck, Aaron Z., Fabio Mattioli, and Daniel Souleles. 2018. "Finance Beyond Function: Three Causal Explanations for Financialization." *Economic Anthropology*, 5(2): 151–171.

Plant, Sadie. 1992. *The Most Radical Gesture: The Situationist International in a Postmodern Age*. New York: Routledge.

Poe, Edgar Allan. 1849. "Von Kempelen and His Discovery." *The Flag of Our Union*. April 14, 1849. Available online: http://xroads.virginia.edu/~hyper/poe/kempelen.html.

Pohl, Fredric and C.M. Kornbluth. 1981. *The Space Merchants*. New York: Ballantine.

Polanyi, Karl. [1944] 2001. *The Great Transformation*. Boston: Beacon.

Polanyi, Karl. 1957. "The Economy as Instituted Process." In Karl Polanyi, Conrad M. Arensberg, and Harry W. Pearson (eds.), *Trade and Market in Early Empires*. Glencoe: The Free Press: 243–269.

Polillo, Simone. 2011. "Money, Moral Authority, and the Politics of Creditworthiness." *American Sociological Review*, 76(3): 437–464.

Pozsar, Zoltan. 2014. "Shadow Banking: The Money View." Office of Financial Research, Treasury Department, Working Paper Series 14-04. Available online: www.financialresearch.gov/working-papers/files/OFRwp2014-04_Pozsar_ShadowBankingTheMoneyView.pdf.

Prahalad, C.K. 2006. *The Fortune at the Bottom of the Pyramid*. Upper Saddle River: Pearson Education.
Praspaliauskiene, Rima. 2016. "Enveloped Lives: Practicing Health and Care in Lithuania." *Medical Anthropology Quarterly*, 30(4): 582–598.
Pribilsky, Jason. 2012. "Consumption Dilemmas: Tracking Masculinity, Money and Transnational Fatherhood between the Ecuadorian Andes and New York." *Journal of Ethnic and Migration Studies*, 38(2): 323–343.
Pugh, Allison. 2009. *Longing and Belonging: Parents, Children, and Consumer Culture*. Berkeley: University of California Press.
Radcliffe Committee. 1959. *Report of the Committee on the Working of the Monetary System*. London: HMSO.
Rea, Stephen C., and Taylor C. Nelms. 2017. "Mobile Money: The First Decade." *IMTFI Working Paper* 2017-1. Available online: www.imtfi.uci.edu/files/docs/2017/Rea_Nelms_Mobile%20Money%20The%20First%20Decade%202017_3.pdf.
Reinhardt, B., 2014. Soaking in Tapes: The Haptic Voice of Global Pentecostal Pedagogy in Ghana. *Journal of the Royal Anthropological Institute*, 20(2): 315–336.
Rheingold, Howard. 1993. *The Virtual Community: Homestead on the Electronic Frontier*. Cambridge: MIT Press.
Ritter, Gretchen. 1997. *Goldbugs and Greenbacks: The Antimonopoly Tradition and the Politics of Finance in America*. New York: Cambridge University Press.
Rivlin, Gary. 2010. *Broke, USA: From Pawnshops to Poverty, Inc.—How the Working Poor Became Big Business*. New York: HarperCollins.
Robbins, J., 2004. "The Globalization of Pentecostal and Charismatic Christianity." *Annual Review of Anthropology*, 33: 117–143.
Robbins, Joel, and David Akin. 1999. "An Introduction to Melanesian Currencies." In David Akin and Joel Robbins (eds.), *Money and Modernity: State and Local Currencies in Melanesia*. Pittsburgh: University of Pittsburgh Press, 1–40.
Robinson, Kim Stanley. 1995. *Pacific Edge*. New York: Orb.
Robinson, Kim Stanley. 1995. *The Gold Coast*. New York: Orb.
Robinson, Kim Stanley. 1995. *Wild Shore*. New York: Orb.
Robinson, Kim Stanley. 2013. *2312*. New York: Orbit.
Rogers, Douglas. 2005. "Moonshine, Money, and the Politics of Liquidity in Rural Russia." *American Ethnologist*, 32(1): 63–81.
Rogoff, Kenneth. 2016. *The Curse of Cash*. Princeton: Princeton University Press.
Roig, Alexandre. 2016. *La Moneda Imposible: La Convertibilidad Argentina de 1991*. Buenos Aires: Fondo de Cultura Económica de Argentina.
Roitman, Janet. 2005. *Fiscal Disobedience: An Anthropology of Economic Regulation in Central Africa*. Princeton: Princeton University Press.
Rona-Tas, Akona and Alya Guseva. 2014. *Plastic Money: Constructing Markets for Credit Cards in Eight Postcommunist Countries*. Stanford: Stanford University Press.
Rösch, Ulrich. 2013. *We Are the Revolution! Rudolf Steiner, Joseph Beuys and the Threefold Social Impulse*. Forest Row: Temple Lodge Publishing.
Rosin, H., 2009. "Did Christianity Cause the Crash?" *The Atlantic*, December.
Rosler, Martha. 1997. "Money, Power, Contemporary Art." *Art Bulletin*, 79(1): 20–24.
Rosler, Martha. 2013. *Culture Class*. Berlin: Sternberg Press.
Ross, Kristin. 2002. *May '68 and Its Afterlives*. Chicago: University of Chicago Press.
Rossman, Gabriel. 2014. "Obfuscatory Relational Work and Disreputable Exchange." *Sociological Theory*, 32(1): 43–63.

Rotman, Brian. 1987. *Signifying Nothing: The Semiotics of Zero*. Basingstoke: Macmillan.
Roy, Ananya. 2010. *Poverty Capital: Microfinance and the Making of Development*. New York: Routledge.
Roy, O. 1994. *The Failure of Political Islam*. Cambridge: Harvard University Press.
Roy, O. 2006. *Globalized Islam: The Search for a New Ummah*. New York: Columbia University Press.
Roy, O. 2014. *Holy Ignorance: When Religion and Culture Part Ways*. Oxford: Oxford University Press.
Rudnyckyj, D. 2014. "Economy in Practice: Islamic Finance and the Problem of Market Reason." *American Ethnologist*, 41(1): 110–127.
Rudnyckyj, D. 2016. "Islamizing Finance: From Magical Capitalism to a Spiritual Economy." *Anthropology Today*, 32(6): 8–12.
Ruml, Beardsley. 1946a. "Taxes for Revenue are Obsolete." *American Affairs*, 8(1): 35–39.
Ruml, Beardsley. 1946b. "Tax Policies for Prosperity." *The Journal of Finance*, 1(1): 81–90.
Russell, Eric Frank. 1951. "And Then There Were None." *Astounding Science Fiction*, 47(4). Available online: www.abelard.org/e-f-russell.php.
Rutherford, Danilyn. 2001. "Intimacy and Alienation: Money and the Foreign in Biak." *Public Culture*, 13(2): 299–324.
Rutherford, Stuart. 2000. *The Poor and Their Money*. New Delhi: Oxford University Press.
Sahlins, M., 1999. "What is Anthropological Enlightenment? Some Lessons of the Twentieth Century." *Annual Review of Anthropology*, 28(1): i–xxiii.
Samarin, W.J. 1972. *Tongues of Men and Angels: The Religious Language of Pentecostalism*. New York: Macmillan.
Sandrock, John E. 2007. "The Use of Bank Note as an Instrument of Propaganda." *The Currency Collector*. Available online: www.thecurrencycollector.com/pdfs/The_Use_of_Bank_Notes_as_an_Instrument_of_Propaganda_-_Part_I.pdf.
Saunders, Frances Stonor. 2001. *The Cultural Cold War: The CIA and the World of Arts and Letters*. New York: New Press.
Schedvin, C.B. 1992. *In Reserve: Central Banking in Australia, 1945–75*. St. Leonards: Allen & Unwin.
Schuster, Caroline E. 2015. *Social Collateral: Women and Microfinance in Paraguay's Smuggling Economy*. Berkeley: University of California Press.
Schwartz, Anna J. 2008. "Money Supply." In David R. Henderson (ed.), *The Concise Encyclopedia of Economics*. 2nd edition. Library of Economics and Liberty. Available online: www.econlib.org/library/Enc/MoneySupply.html.
Schwittay, Anke. 2011. "The Financial Inclusion Assemblage: Subjects, Technics, Rationalities." *Critique of Anthropology*, 31(4): 381–401.
Scott, Brett. 2014. "Visions of a Techno-Leviathan: The Politics of the Bitcoin Blockchain." *E-International Relations*. Online.
Scott, Brett. 2016. "How Can Cryptocurrency and Blockchain Technology Play a Role in Building Social and Solidarity Finance." *United Nations Research Institute for Social Development*. Working Paper 2016-1. Online.
Scott, Brett. 2016. "The War on Cash." *The Long and Short*. Available online: https://thelongandshort.org/society/war-on-cash.
Servon, Lisa. 2017. *The Unbanking of America: How the New Middle Class Survives*. New York: Houghton Mifflin Harcourt.

Shapiro, S. and Barnard, P., 2017. *Pentecostal Modernism: Lovecraft, Los Angeles, and World-Systems Culture*. London: Bloomsbury.
Sheard, Paul. 2013. "Repeat After Me: Banks Cannot and Do Not 'Lend Out' Reserves." *Standard and Poor's Ratings Direct* (August 13). Available online: www.kreditopferhilfe.net/docs/S_and_P__Repeat_After_Me_8_14_13.pdf.
Shell, Marc. 1994. *Art and Money*. Chicago: University of Chicago Press.
Sheng, Andrew, and Ng Chow Soon. 2015. *Bringing Shadow Banking into the Light: Opportunity for Financial Reform in China*. Hong Kong: Fung Global Institute.
Sherman, Matthew. 2009. *A Short History of Financial Deregulation in the United States*. Washington, DC: Center for Economic and Policy Research. Available online: http://cepr.net/documents/publications/dereg-timeline-2009-07.pdf.
Shipton, Parker. 1989. *Bitter Money: Cultural Economy and Some African Meanings of Forbidden Commodities*. Washington, DC: American Anthropological Association.
Sholette, Gregory, and Oliver Ressler (eds.). 2013. *It's the Political Economy, Stupid: The Global Financial Crisis in Art and Theory*. London: Pluto.
Shriver, Lionel. 2016. *The Mandibles: A Family, 2029–2047*. New York: Harper.
Siegel, Katy, and Paul Mattick. 2004. *Art Works: Money*. London: Thames and Hudson.
Simmel, Georg. [1978] 2011. *The Philosophy of Money*. Tom Bottomore and David Frisby (trans.). London: Routledge.
Simmons, Matty. 1991. *The Great Credit Card Catastrophe*. New York: Barricade Books.
Singh, Supriya. 1997. *Marriage Money: The Social Shaping of Money in Marriage and Banking*. St. Leonards: Allen & Unwin.
Singh, Supriya. 2013. *Globalization and Money: A Global South Perspective*. New York: Rowman & Littlefield.
Sirkeci, Ibrahim, Jeffrey H. Cohen, and Dilip Ratha (eds.). 2012. *Migration and Remittances During the Global Financial Crisis and Beyond*. Washington, DC: World Bank.
Skidelsky, Robert. 1992. *John Maynard Keynes: The Economist as Saviour, 1920–1937*. London: Macmillan.
Skidelsky, Robert. 2000. *John Maynard Keynes: Fighting for Britain, 1937–1946*. London: Macmillan.
Small, Ivan V. 2018 *Currencies of Imagination: Channeling Money and Chasing Mobility in Vietnam*. Ithaca: Cornell University Press. Forthcoming.
Smith, Adam. [1776] 1937. *The Wealth of Nations*. New York: Modern Library.
Smith, Richard Norton. 2014. *On His Own Terms: A Life of Nelson Rockefeller*. New York: Random House.
Sneath, David. 2006. "Transacting and Enacting: Corruption, Obligation and the Use of Monies in Mongolia." *Ethnos*, 71(1): 89–112.
Spears, Dorothy. 2011. "Lee Lozano, Defiant Painter, Makes a Comeback." *New York Times* (January 5). Available online: www.nytimes.com/2011/01/09/arts/design/09lozano.html.
Springer, Simon, Kean Birch, and Julie MacLeavy (eds.). 2016. *The Handbook of Neoliberalism*. New York: Routledge.
Stakemeier, Kerstin, and Marina Vishmidt. 2016. *Reproducing Autonomy: Work, Money, Crisis and Contemporary Art*. London: Mute.
Star, Susan L. 1999. "The Ethnography of Infrastructure." *American Behavioral Scientist*, 43(3): 377–391.

Stearns, David L. 2011. *Electronic Value Exchange: Origins of the VISA Electronic Payment System*. London: Springer.
Steedman, Carolyn. 1986. *Landscape for a Good Woman: A Story of Two Lives*. London: Virago.
Stein, Herbert. 1969. *The Fiscal Revolution in America*. Chicago: University of Chicago Press.
Stephenson, Neal. 1999. *Cryptonomicon*. New York: Avon.
Stephenson, Neal. 2003. *Quicksilver*. New York: William Morrow.
Stephenson, Neal. 2004. *The Confusion*. New York: William Morrow.
Stephenson, Neal. 2004. *The System of the World*. New York: William Morrow.
Stephenson, Neal. 2011. *Reamde*. New York: William Morrow.
Steyerl, Hito. 2015. "Duty-Free Art." *E-Flux* 63 (March). Available online: www.e-flux.com/journal/duty-free-art/.
Stigum, Marcia, and Anthony Crescenzi. 2007. *Stigum's Money Market*. 4th edition. New York: McGraw-Hill.
Stix, Helmut. 2013. "Why Do People Save in Cash? Distrust, Memories of Banking Crises, Weak Institutions and Dollarization." *Journal of Banking & Finance*, 37(11): 4087–4106.
Stout, Noelle. 2016a. "#*Indebted*: Disciplining the Moral Valence of Mortgage Debt Online." *Cultural Anthropology*, 31(1): 81–105.
Stout, Noelle. 2016b. "Petitioning a Giant: Debt, Reciprocity, and Mortgage Modification in the Sacramento Valley." *American Ethnologist*, 43(1): 1–14.
Strange, Susan. 1971. *Sterling and British Policy: A Political Study of an International Currency in Decline*. Oxford: Oxford University Press.
Strassler, Karen. 2009. "The Face of Money: Currency, Crisis, and Remediation in Post-Suharto Indonesia." *Cultural Anthropology*, 24(1): 68–103.
Stross, Charles. 2005. *Accelerando*. New York: Ace.
Stross, Charles. 2007. *Halting State*. New York: Ace.
Stross, Charles. 2013. *Neptune's Brood*. New York: Ace.
Suri, Tavneet, and William Jack. 2016. "The Long-Run Poverty and Gender Impacts of Mobile Money." *Science*, 354(6317): 1288–1292.
Sutton, Horrace. 1958. "Just Write It on the Tab, Joe." *The Washington Post and Times Herald* (September 21).
Swan, T.W. 1960. "Economic Control in a Dependent Economy." *Economic Record*, 36(73): 51–66.
Swan, T.W. 1963. "Longer-Run Problems of the Balance of Payments." In H.W. Arndt and W.M. Corden (eds.), *The Australian Economy: A Volume of Readings*. Melbourne: F.W. Cheshire, 384–395.
Swartz, Lana. 2014. "Gendered Transactions: Identity and Payment at Midcentury." *Women's Studies Quarterly*, 42(1): 137–153.
Swartz, Lana. 2017. "Blockchain Dreams: Imagining Techno-Economic Alternatives After Bitcoin." In Manuel Castells (ed.), *Another Economy is Possible: Culture and Economy in a Time of Crisis*. Cambridge: Polity, 82–105.
Swartz, Lana. 2017. "Cards." In Bill Maurer and Lana Swartz (eds.), *Paid: Tales of Dongles, Checks, and Other Money Stuff*. Cambridge: MIT Press.
Swartz, Lana. 2018. "What Was Bitcoin, What Will It Be? The Techno-Economic Imaginaries of a New Money Technology." *Cultural Studies*, 32(4): 623–650.
Synan, V., 1997. *The Holiness-Pentecostal Tradition: Charismatic Movements in the Twentieth Century*. Grand Rapids, MI: Eerdmans.

Szabo, Nick. 2005. "Bit Gold." *Unenumerated*. Available online: http://unenumerated.blogspot.co.uk/2005/12/bit-gold.html.

Taussig, Michael. 1977. "The Genesis of Capitalism amongst a South American Peasantry: Devil's Labor and the Baptism of Money." *Comparative Studies in Society and History*, 19(2): 130–155.

Taylor, Erin B., and Heather A. Horst. 2013. "From Street to Satellite: Mixing Methods to Understand Mobile Money Users." *EPIC*, 88–102.

Taylor, Marcus. 2012. "The Antinomies of 'Financial Inclusion': Debt, Distress and the Workings of Indian Microfinance." *Journal of Agrarian Change*, 12(4): 601–610.

Taylor, Mark C. 2011. "Financialization of Art." *Capitalism and Society*, 6(2): Article 3.

Thai, Hung Cam. 2014. *Insufficient Funds: The Culture of Money in Low-Wage Transnational Families*. Stanford: Stanford University Press.

Thaler, Richard H. 1999. "Mental Accounting Matters." *Journal of Behavioral Decision Making*, 12(3): 183–206.

Thiel, Peter. 2009. "The Education of a Libertarian." *Cato Unbound*. Available online: www.cato-unbound.org/2009/04/13/peter-thiel/education-libertarian.

Thiel, Peter. 2014. "Could This be the New Counter-culture?" Interview with Glenn Beck. *Glenn*. Available online: www.glennbeck.com/2014/10/21/could-this-be-the-new-counter-culture/.

Thompson, Don. 2008. *The $12 Million Stuffed Shark: The Curious Economics of Contemporary Art*. New York: Palgrave Macmillan.

Thornton, Sarah. 2008. *Seven Days in the Art World*. New York: W.W. Norton.

Tiessen, Matthew. 2015. "The Appetites of App-Based Finance." *Cultural Studies*, 29(5–6): 869–886.

Tinbergen, Jan. 1966. *Economic Policy: Principles and Design*. Amsterdam: North-Holland.

Tooze, Adam J. 2014. *The Deluge: The Great War and the Remaking of Global Order, 1916–1931*. London: Allen Lane.

Tooze, Adam. 2018. *Crashed: How a Decade of Financial Crises Changed the World*. New York: Viking.

Trapp, Micah M. 2018. "'Never Had the Hand': Distribution and Inequality in the Diverse Economy of a Refugee Camp." *Economic Anthropology*, 5(1): 96–109.

Truitt, Allison. 2013. *Dreaming of Money in Ho Chi Minh City*. Seattle: University of Washington Press.

Tschoegl, Adrian. 2010. "The International Diffusion of an Innovation: The Spread of Decimal Currency." *Journal of Socio-Economics*, 39(1): 100–109.

Tucker, Carl, Jr. 1951. "Credit System Lures 40,000 Eaters-Out in 1st Year of Operation: Diners' Club Has Big Attraction." *Wall Street Journal* (March 28).

Turner, Fred. 2008. *From Counterculture to Cyberculture: Stewart Brand, the Whole Earth Network, and the Rise of Digital Utopianism*. Chicago: University of Chicago Press.

Tymoigne, Éric, and L. Randall Wray. 2013. "Modern Money Theory 101: A Reply to Critics." Levy Economics Institute Working Paper No. 778. Available online: www.levyinstitute.org/publications/modern-money-theory-101.

Tymoigne, Éric. 2014. "Modern Money Theory and Interrelations between the Treasury and the Central Bank: The Case of the United States." Levy Economics Institute Working Paper No. 788. Available online: www.levyinstitute.org/publications/modern-money-theory-and-interrelations-between-the-treasury-and-the-central-bank.

Unger, Harlow. 1968. "Floating Hotel Concept Splashes Shipping Industry." *The Washington Post, Times Herald* (March 31).

United States Congressional Budget Office. 2016. "Natural Rate of Unemployment (Long-Term)." FRED, Federal Reserve Bank of St Louis. Available online: https://fred.stlouisfed.org/series/NROU.

United States Postal Service. 2007. "The United States Postal Service: An American History 1775–2006." *Government Relations*.

Valdés, Juan Gabriel. 1995. *Pinochet's Economists: The Chicago School in Chile*. Cambridge: Cambridge University Press.

Van der Zwan, Natascha. 2014. "Making Sense of Financialization." *Socio-Economic Review*, 12(1): 99–129.

Van Lerven, Frank, Graham Hodgson, and Ben Dyson. 2015. "Would There Be Enough Credit in a Sovereign Money System?" London: Positive Money. Available online: http://positivemoney.org/publications/enough-credit-sovereign-money-system/.

Varoufakis, Yanis. 2013. *The Global Minotaur: America, Europe, and the Future of the Global Economy*. 2nd edition. London: Zed.

Varoufakis, Yanis. 2016. *And the Weak Suffer What They Must? Europe's Crisis and America's Economic Future*. New York: Nation.

Velthius, Olav and Erica Coslor. 2012. "The Financialization of Art." In Knorr Cetina and Preda (eds.), *The Oxford Handbook of the Sociology of Finance*. Oxford: Oxford University Press, 471–487.

Velthius, Olav. 2007. *Talking Prices: Symbolic Meanings of Prices on the Market for Contemporary Art*. Princeton: Princeton University Press.

Vercellone, Carlo. 2007. "From Formal Subsumption to General Intellect: Elements for a Marxist Reading of the Thesis of Cognitive Capitalism." *Historical Materialism*, 15(1): 13–36.

Verdery, Katherine. 1995. "Faith, Hope, and *Caritas* in the Land of the Pyramids: Romania, 1990–1994." *Comparative Studies in Society and History*, 37(4): 625–669.

Vigna, Paul and Michael J. Casey. 2015. *The Age of Cryptocurrency: How Bitcoin and the Blockchain Are Challenging the Global Economic Order*. New York: St. Martin's Press.

Volcker, Paul. 2008. "Remarks by Paul Volcker at a Luncheon of the Economic Club of New York. New York, April 8, 2008." Available online: http://blogs.denverpost.com/lewis/files/2008/04/volckernyeconclubspeech04-08-2008.pdf.

Wacker, G. 2003. *Heaven Below: Early Pentecostals and American Culture*. Cambridge: Harvard University Press.

Wagner, Ethan, and Thea Westreich Wagner. 2013. *Collecting Art for Love, Money and More*. London: Phaidon.

Walker, Joshua Z. 2017. "Torn Dollars and War-Wounded Francs: Money Fetishism in the Democratic Republic of Congo." *American Ethnologist*, 44(2): 288–299.

Walley, Christine J. 2013. *Exit Zero: Family and Class in Postindustrial Chicago*. Chicago: University of Chicago Press.

Walsh, Andrew. 2003. "'Hot Money' and Daring Consumption in a Northern Malagasy Sapphire-Mining Town." *American Ethnologist*, 30(2): 290–305.

Wang, Claire. 2017. "Cash Holdings: A New View on Cash." Federal Reserve Bank of San Francisco. Available online: www.frbsf.org/cash/publications/fed-notes/2017/june/cash-holdings-new-view-on-cash/.

Wark, Jayne. 2006. *Radical Gestures: Feminism and Performance Art in North America*. Montreal: McGill-Queen's University Press.
Wasik, Bill. 2017. "The Magazine's Money Issue: Tracing the Strange Connections of a Global Economy." *New York Times Magazine* (May 4). Available online: www.nytimes.com/2017/05/04/magazine/the-magazines-money-issue.html.
Watson, Thomas J., Jr. 1965. "Man and Machine—The Dynamic Alliance." *Proceedings from the National Automation Conference*, American Bankers Association, 9–14.
Weatherford, Jack. 1997. *The History of Money*. New York: Three Rivers Press.
Webb, Steven B. 1989. *Hyperinflation and Stabilisation in Weimar Germany*. Oxford: Oxford University Press.
Weeks, Kathi. 2011. *The Problem with Work: Feminism, Marxism, Antiwork Politics, and Postwork Imaginaries*. Durham: Duke University Press.
Weigele, K., 2004. *Investing in Miracles: El Shaddai and the Transformation of Popular Catholicism in the Philippines*. Honolulu: Hawaii University Press.
Weschler, Lawrence. 1999. *Boggs: A Comedy of Values*. Chicago: University of Chicago Press.
Whitfield, Esther. 2007. *Cuban Currency: The Dollar and "Special Period" Fiction*. Minneapolis: University of Minnesota Press.
Wilkis, Ariel. 2013. *Las Sospechas del Dinero: Moral y Economía en la Vida Popular*. Buenos Aires: Paidos.
Williams, Raymond. 1983. "Culture." In *Keywords: A Vocabulary of Culture and Society*. Revised edition. Oxford: Oxford University Press, 87–93.
Williams, Raymond. 2005. *Culture and Materialism: Selected Essays*. New York: Verso.
Wilson, Kristina. 2009. *The Modern Eye: Stieglitz, MoMA, and the Art of the Exhibition, 1925–1934*. New Haven: Yale University Press.
Wolf, Martin. 2014. "Strip Private Banks of Their Power to Create Money." *Financial Times* (April 24). Available online: www.ft.com/content/7f000b18-ca44-11e3-bb92-00144feabdc0.
Wolff, Janet. 1984. *The Social Production of Art*. New York: New York University Press.
Womack, Jack. 1987. *Ambient*. New York: Grove Press.
Womack, Jack. 1993. *Random Acts of Senseless Violence*. New York: Grove Press.
Woodford, Michael. 2008. "How Important is Money in the Conduct of Monetary Policy?" *Journal of Money, Credit and Banking*, 40(8): 1561–1598.
Woodruff, David. 1999. *Money Unmade: Barter and the Fate of Russian Capitalism*. Ithaca: Cornell University Press.
Wray, L. Randall (ed.). 2004. *Credit and State Theories of Money: The Contributions of A. Mitchell Innes*. Cheltenham: Edward Elgar.
Wray, L. Randall. 1990. *Money and Credit in Capitalist Economies: The Endogenous Money Approach*. Aldershot: Edward Elgar.
Wray, L. Randall. 1998. *Understanding Modern Money*. Cheltenham: Edward Elgar.
Wray, L. Randall. 2010. "What Do Banks Do? What Should Banks Do?" Levy Economics Institute Working Paper No. 612. Available online: www.levyinstitute.org/publications/what-do-banks-do-what-should-banks-do.
Wray, L. Randall. 2014. "From the State Theory of Money to Modern Money Theory: An Alternative to Economic Orthodoxy." Levy Economics Institute Working Paper No. 792. Available online: www.levyinstitute.org/publications/from-the-state-theory-of-money-to-modern-money-theory.

Wray, L. Randall. 2015. *Modern Money Theory: A Primer on Macroeconomics for Sovereign Monetary Systems*. 2nd edition. New York: Palgrave Macmillan.

Yan, Q., and J. Li. 2016. *Regulating China's Shadow Banks*. Milton Park: Routledge.

Yan, Yunxiang. *The Flow of Gifts: Reciprocity and Social Networks in a Chinese Village*. Stanford: Stanford University Press.

Yeh, Rihan. 2016. "Commensuration in a Mexican Border City: Currencies, Consumer Goods, and Languages." *Anthropological Quarterly*, 89(1): 63–92.

Yúdice, George. 2003. *The Expediency of Culture*. Durham: Duke University Press.

Zelizer, Viviana A. [1994] 1997. *The Social Meaning of Money: Pin Money, Paychecks, Poor Relief, and Other Currencies*. Princeton: Princeton University Press.

Zelizer, Viviana. 2002. "Kids and Commerce." *Childhood*, 9(4): 375–396.

Zelizer, Viviana. 2005. *The Purchase of Intimacy*. Princeton: Princeton University Press.

Zelizer, Viviana. 2011. *Economic Lives: How Culture Shapes the Economy*. Princeton: Princeton University Press.

INDEX

Italic numbers are used for illustrations.

abstraction, money as an 93
activism and art 161–4, *164*
airtime 128
alienation and money 171
Allen, A.A. 97, 98
alms-giving 121
American Express 33–8, *34–5*, 44
anonymous element of money 85, 93
anthropology of money 109–10
anti-Semitic propaganda 144
Argentina *112*, 114–15
art and money 5–6, 9–10, 23
art and representation 135–64
　theories of reproduction 138–43
　works of money-art (1973) 143–53
　works of money-art (2008) 153–64
art, commodification of 143–4, 147, 160
artistic taste 147
artistic use of money 143
Asimov, Isaac 167
Australia 67, 74, 79
Automated Clearing House (ACH) 49
automated teller machines (ATM) 47
Azusa Street, Los Angeles, California 88, *89*

balance of payments 64–5
Banco Palmas 156–7
bank liabilities 72

Bank of America 40, 44, 45
Banking School 196
banking systems, in speculative fiction 185–6
banknotes, used in art 143, *144*
banks, alternative sources of finance 76
Banks, Iain M., *Culture* series 183
barter 114–15
Basel Accord 82
Bátiz-Lazo, Bernardo 177
Belgium 55
Bellamy, Edward, *Looking Backward: 2000–1887* 177
Berman, Marshall 4
Bethel Bible School, Topeka, Kansas 86–7, *86*
Better Than Cash Alliance 130
Beuys, Joseph, *KUNST=KAPITAL* 143–6, *144*
Bishop, Claire 160
bit gold 48
Bitcoin 169, 178, 179, 180–1, *181–2*, 182–3, 184
Black-Scholes formula 153
BlackNet 48
Blanton, A. 96–7
Blinder, Alan 81
Bloch, Maurice 118
blockchain technology 183, 184

Bloomingdale, Alfred 44
bmoney 48
bond houses 75–6
Bornstein, Erica 121
Bourdieu, Pierre 147
Brand, Bob 60
Bretton Woods system 14, 62–9
Britain 60–1, 63, 75, 78–9, 119, 123
British money 106
budgeting of cash 116–17
Burdekin, Richard 71
Burkett, Paul 71

Cabaret (film) 1
capital, in fiction 166
capitalism
    alternatives to in speculative fiction 174–6
    and art 147–9, 160, 163
    and culture 95
    and financialization 153, 154–5
    and money 1, 197
    and reproduction 138–43, 157
cash, management of 115–27
cash, qualities of 132
cashless society 19, 129–32
Castoriadis, Cornelius 137
cell phone money. *See* mobile phone money
central bank independence 201–2, 203
Charga-Plate system 41
charge cards 41–4
Chaum, David 48
Chawla, Nitesh 128
checks 38–40
Chicago Plan 200
Chile 71, 154
chip-and-signature 27–8
Christophers, Brett 2
circulation of money 19–20, 139–40
class institutions 140–1
Clay, Henry 60–1
Cleaver, Harry 139
coins, defacement of 144, *145*
Coleman, S. 98
colonialism 153
Comaroff, J. 93
Comaroff, J.L. 93
commercial paper market 213–14
commodity, money as a 1, 195, 197

commodity standards. *See* gold standard
community currencies 114–15, 155–6, 169
computer games 181–2, 183
computerized banking 40–1
convict love tokens 144
Cooper, Melinda 13
creation of money 18
credit cards 45–7
credit, in speculative fiction 177
Creswell, Tim 29
crisis of care 157–8
cross-border remittance flows 113–14
Crosthwaite, Paul 166, 172
CryptoCredits 48
cryptocurrencies 180
    See also Bitcoin
culture and money 6–10
currencies. *See* hard currencies; local currencies; national currencies
currency and value in speculative fiction 168–77
currency pegs 70–1
Currency School 195
cyberpunk and money 171–2

Dai, Wei 48
Davies, William 9, 10
Dawes Plan 59
De Certeau, Michel 108
debit cards 47, 177
Debord, Guy 109
debt-free money 191, 199–200, 204
debt limits 215
decimalization 106
defacement of money 143–4, *144–5*
definitions of money
    commodity vs credit-debit relationship 194–5
    Keynes on 53
    as a liability of its issuer 202
    and monetarism 77
    and network effects 3–4
    and proliferation of financial instruments 14, 198
    and proximity to government 213
    as a social technology 169–70
    See also moneyness
deflation 59, 60
Delany, Samuel R., *The Tale of Old Venn* 171

Deleuze, Gilles 93, 95
demand deposits 202, 213
Depression 61, 73, 114, *115*, 193, 200
deregulation of money 81–2
derivatives 81, 153
devaluation of currencies 62, 65
Dick, Philip K., *Ubik* 177
DigiCash 48
digital cash 47–9
Diners' Club 41–4
dirty money 117–18
Doctorow, Cory, *Down and Out in the Magic Kingdom* 169
Dodd, Nigel 166, 190
donations of art 148

earmarking of money 116–17
economic theory and money 193
economy as speculative fiction 178
Edin, Kathryn J. 127
Edwards, Paul 28
electronic funds transfer system (EFTS) 40, 46–7
Electronic Recording Machine-Accounting (ERMA) 40, *41*, 44
endogenous money theory 198
Engels, Friedrich 120–1
England, George Allan, *The Golden Blight* 168
European Monetary Union 210–11
everyday, concept of 108–9
everyday money, instability and inventiveness of 105–34
    cashless society 129–32
    earmarking 116–17
    finance 125–7
    giving and gambling 120–3
    instability and inventiveness 105–8
    language of money 117–19
    mobile phones 49, 118, 119–20, 127–9
    multiple money 108–15
    poverty and pedagogy 123–5
    storage of money 119–20
exchange rates 59, 62, 64–5, 69–71
express companies, USA 31–2

FairCoin 180
Fargo, J.C. 36–7
Federal Reserve Board 73–4
Federal Reserve interest 209

Federal Reserve System 39–40
feminism 141–3, 151
Ferguson, James 126
Ferry, Elizabeth 169
Fforde, J.S. 78–9
finance and inventiveness 125–7
financial inclusion 129–30
financialization of money 8–9, 18, 22–3, 136–8, 153, 154
Finke, R. 94
Fisher, Irving 17, 72
Florida, Richard 157
Foley, Duncan 17
Forder, James 66
foreign money orders 35–6
fractional reserve banking 195
Fraser, Andrea 158–9
Fraser, Nancy 157
Friedman, Milton 17, 66, 67, 73, 77, 78, 200
full employment 63, 65–8

gambling 121–3
geheimagentur, *Schwartzbank* 155–8, *156*
gentrification 157
German art. *See* art and representation
Germany 58–9
Gibson, William
    Neuromancer 171–2
    The Peripheral 172, 174
gig economy 154
giving of money 120–1
Glass-Steagall Act (1933) 74
global financial crisis (GFC) 2, 21, 177, 193.
globalized capital 172, 174
gold, in speculative fiction 168–9, 179, 180, 188
gold standard 1–2, 12, 55–61, 64
Gordon, Robert J. 61, 67
Gough, Zach, *Bourdieu: A Social Currency* 158–61, *159*
government bonds 75–6, 209–10
government spending 204–5
Graeber, David 165, 170, 171
Great Depression 61, 73, 114, *115*, 193, 200
Great War 55, 57
greenbackers 199, 200, 204, 206
Grubb, Farley 206

Guattari, Félix 93, 95
Güell, Nuria and Levi Orta 161–4, *162*
Guyer, Jane 110

Haacke, Hans, *MoMA Poll* 146–9, *148*
Haigh, Thomas 177
Han, Clara 126
hard currencies 112–13
Hardt, Michael 155
Harvey, David 139, 140
Haynes, N. 98–9, 100
Hicks, John 61
hierarchy of money 72–4
hire-purchase agreements 75
history of money 10–15
hyperinflation 58–9

ideas of money 53–82
   beyond banks 74–6
   evolution of money 81–2
   exchange rates 61–71
   gold standard 55–61
   hierarchy of money 71–4
   monetarism and after 77–81
ill-gotten gains 117–18
imaginary wealth 137
imagination, money as a medium of 7–8
inflation 13, 57, 58–9, 66
infrastructures for payment 28
Ingham, Geoffrey 3, 212
Innes, A. Mitchell 193, 197, 207
instability and inventiveness of money 105–8
institutional critique 146
interbank market in federal funds 75
interest and Islam 102
International Monetary Fund 64
international money agreement 62–3, 64
international money transfer 35–7, 47
interpretation of money in speculative fiction 165–90
   currency and value 168–77
   debt and the financial crisis 185–9
   money and technology 177–85
investment in art 148–9
irregular cash flows 126
Islam 94, 100
Islamic banking 102
issues of the age, monetary reform 191–215
   1920s orthodoxy and Keynes's alternative 194–9

   debt-free money and narrow banking 199–202
   government bonds and interest on reserves 209–11
   money as debt 202–9
   private money creation 211–14
   reform since the 1920s 191–4

Jackson, Eric M. 49
James, Deborah 126
Jevons, William Stanley 56
jungle, money as a 3

Kalecki, Michal 65
Keynes, John Maynard
   aspects of money 53
   bank reserve-deposit ratio 73
   Belgian government blunder 55
   effective demand 192–3, *192*
   and the gold standard 59–60, 68
   on inflation 57
   and monetary theory 3
   neoclassical theory 196–8
   postwar monetary regime 62, *63*, 64, 74
King, Mervyn 80
Knapp, Georg Friedrich 197, 202
Kusimba, Sibel 128

La Berge, Leigh Claire 166, 172
labour standard 61–2
language of money 117–19
Latin America 61, 70
Lave, Jean 107
laying on hands 96, *97*
lending, non-bank 74–5
Lenin, Vladimir 57
letters of credit 36–7
Lewis, Michael, *The Big Short* 185
Leyshon, Andrew 2
liabilities 15, 72, 76, 198, 202
loans of art 148
local currencies 114–15, 155–6, 169
Lowrie, I. 95
Lozano, Lee, *REAL MONEY PIECE* 149–53, *151*
Luxemburg, Rosa 140

M-Pesa 127–8, *128*
Machlup, Fritz 64

Magnetic Ink Character Recognition (MICR) 39, 40
managed money 56–7, 68–71
management of money, everyday 115–27
Mann, Geoff 2
Marsh, Nicky 166
Martin, Randy 22, 153, 170
Marx, Karl 93, 139
Massey, Doreen 29
MasterCard 45
Maurer, Bill 5, 180, 182
May, Tim 48
McRobbie, Angela 161
meaning and money 8
Mehrling, Perry 82
Meister, Robert 23
Melanesia 110
Meyer, Larry 80
microfinance 129–30
Minsky, Hyman P. 75, 76, 193
mobile phone money 49, 118, 119–20, 127–9
modern age of money 2
Modern Monetary Theory (MMT) 18
modernity of money 4–5
MoMA, New York 146–7, 149
monetarism 12–13, 14–15, 77–81
monetary liquidity, categories of 19
monetary policies 55, 74, 81–2
 See also monetarism
monetary reform 191–215
 1920s orthodoxy and Keynes's alternative 194–9
 debt-free money and narrow banking 199–202
 government bonds and interest on reserves 209–11
 money as debt 202–9
 private money creation 211–14
 reform since the 1920s 191–4
money itself 53–4
money-of-account 53
money orders 33–6
money supply 72
moneyness 19–20, 22, 23, 72, 213
Morduch, Jonathan 127
mortgages 59, 81, 129, 177
movement of money 29
Mr. Robot (television series) 190
multiple money 108–15

mutilation of coins 144, *145*
mystification of money 166

narrow banking 191–2, 200–1
national currencies 30, 106–7
natural rate of unemployment 66, 67, 81
Nazis, anti-Semitic use of money 144
Negri, Antonio 155
Nelms, Taylor C. 180, 182
neoclassical theory 196–7
neoliberalism 154
neutrality of money 3, 18, 93, 196, 197, 198
Niccol, Andrew, *In Time* 169
non-bank lending 74–5
non-sovereign currencies 210–11

Occult Economies 93
online role-playing games 181–2, 183
O'Rourke, Frank, *Instant Gold* 168
Orta, Levi 161–4, *162*
Ozman, Agnes 86

paper checks 38–40
paper money 56, 195, 201, 206–7
paper money and the mail 30–8
Papua New Guinea *111*, 120
Parham, Charles Fox 87
Parry, Jonathan 118
participatory art 160–1
payment card networks 44–7
PayPal 49
Peebles, Gustav 118
Pentecostalism 87–100
philanthropic giving 120–1
Phillips, A.W. 66
Piketty, Thomas, *Capital in the Twenty-First Century* 165, 166, 190
pockets 119, 120
Poe, Edgar Allan, *Von Kempelen and His Discovery* 169
Polanyi, Karl 1, 109
political monetarism 78
politics of money 22–3
popular culture 118
popular music 1, 2
portfolios of the poor 125
Positive Money movement 199, 200
post-Keynesian economic theory 198
postal money orders 33

postal service, USA 30–3
poverty, responses to 123–7, 129
Pozsar, Zoltan 213
prayer cloths 97
price stability 65–8
private money creation 15–16, 20–1, 199–201, 212–13, 214
private shipping companies, USA 31–2
Prosperity Gospel 93, 94, 95, 96, 98, 100

quantity theory of money 56, 72, 73, 193, 195, 197

Real Bills Doctrine 196
redemption of debt 24–5, 206–9
redenomination of currencies 106–7
refugees and money 113–14
regulation of banks 74, 82
regulatory action, call for 24
Reinhardt, B. 98
religion and money 6, 11
    See also ritual and religion
remittance flows, cross-border 113–14
Rentenmark 59
reproduction and capitalism 138–43, 149
repurchase agreements 75–6
reserve-deposit ratio 73
Rheingold, Howard 47
ritual and religion 83–103
    deterritorialization of religion and money 90–100
    Pentecostalism 86–90
Roberts, Oral 96–7, 97, 98
Robinson, Kim Stanley
    The Gold Coast 175
    Pacific Edge 175–6
    2312 176–7
    The Wild Shore 174–5
Rockefeller, Nelson 146–7
role-playing games 181–2, 183
Roy, O. 94, 95
Ruml, Beardsley 205
Rural Free Delivery 33
Russell, Eric Frank, *And Then There Were None* 169

Safaricom 127
Schaefer, H. Luke 127
Schneider, Rachel 127
Schultze, Charles 78

Schwartz, Anna 2, 73
science fiction and money 9–10
    See also interpretation of money in speculative fiction
Scott, Brett 166, 178, 179
Self-Sustaining Creative Economy Award 162
sending money abroad 35–7, 47
service sector 155
Seymour, William 88
shadow banking 82, 213
Shriver, Lionel, *The Mandibles: A family, 2029–2047* 187–9
Simmel, Georg 93, 109
Simmons, Matty 43
Skidelsky, Robert 59–60
slow money 186–7
social institutions 140–1
social life, reproduction of 141–3
social sculpture 145
sociological study of money 109–10
soft currencies 113
sound money 13, 17
speaking in tongues 88, 89, 90, 91
special-purpose money 109–10
speculative fiction. *See* interpretation of money in speculative fiction
spirit money 114, *114*
stagflation and policy 65–6
Star, Susan Leigh 28
Stark, R. 94
state currency 72
state spending 24
Stearns, David L. 177
Steedman, Carolyn 123
Stephenson, Neal
    Cryptonomicon 178–9, 180
    Reamde 181–2
storage of money 119–20
stories and experiences of money 124–5
Strike Debt 163
Stross, Charles
    Accelerando 183
    Halting State 183–5
    Neptune's Brood 185–6
suffragettes, use of coins 143, *145*
Swartz, Lana 4, 180, 182, 183
Sweden 132
Switzerland 16
Szabo, Nick 48

tally sticks 207, *208*
tax havens 161–2
taxes
    role of 24, 204, 205, 206–7, 209
    in speculative fiction 178, 179, 189
teaching about money 123–4
technologies 27–51
    automated and computerized money 38–41
    Bitcoin 169, 178, 179, 180–1, *181–2*, 182–3, 184
    cards, clubs and networks 41–7
    mobile phone money 49, 118, 119–20, 127–9
    paper and the mail 30–8
    in speculative fiction 177–85
    virtual and global 47–9
theft prevention 119
theories of money 18, 56, 72–3, 193, 195–8
Thiel, Peter 49
time-travelling money 172, 174
Tinbergen, Jan 66
tithes 121
Tiv people of Nigeria 109
Tooze, Adam J. 59
toys and games 123–4, *124*
tracts in the form of paper money 83–5, *84*, 102
trade unions 60
travel expenses 43
traveler's checks 36–7
tribal systems of money 171
Troika Fiscal Disobedience Consultancy 162
Truitt, Allison 108

unemployment, natural rate of 66, 67, 81
United States of America
    approaches to money 17
    bank regulation 74
    dollar exchange rate 62, 69
    Federal Reserve interest 209
    gambling of money 122–3
    and the gold standard 57, 61, 63–4, 69
    monetarist principles in 13
    money market 75
    Pentecostalism 86–92
    post-global financial crisis measures 16
    poverty in 124, 127
    reserve-deposit ratio 73
    technologies of money 28, 30–47
    See also Great Depression; speculative fiction
urban renewal 157

value of money 14, 64
VISA 45
Volcker, Paul 13, 201–2
Volcker shock 78
Vollgeld 16
voluntary donations 120
vulnerabilities of cash 119

wage-setting 60–1, 65–8, 78–9
Wages for Housework 141, *142*
Ward, Eddie 62
Watson, Thomas J. Jr. 40
Wells Fargo Express Company 31–2, *31*
Western Union 41
Wilkis, Ariel 116
Williams, Raymond 6
Winklevoss, Cameron 183
Winklevoss, Tyler 183
Womack, Jack, *Random Acts of Senseless Violence* 187
women and money 127, 128–9, 141–3, *145*, 151
women, religious leaders 92
work, changes in 154
World War I 55, 57
World War II 74
Wu-Tang Clan 2

Yang, Yang 128

Zambia 98–9, 100
Zelizer, Viviana 116, 117